*The Callas Legacy*

# The  CALLAS Legacy

## THE COMPLETE GUIDE TO HER RECORDINGS ON COMPACT DISCS

*Fourth Edition*

# John Ardoin

*Foreword by Terrence McNally*

Amadeus Press
Reinhard G. Pauly, General Editor
Portland, Oregon

First published in North America in 1995
by Amadeus press (an imprint of Timber Press, Inc.)
The Haseltine Building
133 S.W. Second Avenue, Suite 450
Portland, Oregon 97204, U.S.A.
1-800-327-5680 (U.S.A. and Canada only)

Reprinted 1996

ISBN 0-931340-90-X

Photoset in North Wales by
Derek Doyle & Associates, Mold, Clwyd.
Printed in Great Britain by
Redwood Books Limited, Trowbridge.

FOR LARRY
*"Ah! non credea mirarti*
*sì presto estinto . . ."*

16 September 1974

# Contents

*My candle burns at both ends;*
    *It will not last the night;*
*But, ah, my foes, and oh, my friends*
    *It gives a lovely light.*

                              Edna St. Vincent Millay

# Foreword ∾

Like most people, I first heard the voice of Maria Callas on a record. It was an appropriate introduction to a singer whose career was relatively brief and whose actual performances in this country were few.

The year was 1953, the recording was *Lucia di Lammermoor* and I was a high school student in Corpus Christi, Texas, who bussed tables at the Robin Hood Cafeteria in order to buy opera records. I was fifteen, a dreamer, and I thought she was singing just for me. I still do.

Listening to Callas is not a passive experience. It is a conversation with her and, finally, ourselves. Callas speaks to us when she sings. She tells us her secrets—her pains, her joys—and we tell her ours right back. "I have felt such despair, such happiness," Callas confesses. "So have I, so have I!" we answer. It is ourselves we recognize in Violetta or Norma or Lucia when we listen to Callas sing them.

No one before her had "heard" Lucia the way she did. Nor had they been able to articulate Donizetti's music with such deep and specific feeling. Lucia became a recognizable human being. The Fountain Scene was an expression of both tragic foreboding and ecstatic first love. The Mad Scene became the cumulative threnody for that love betrayed when the forebodings had become reality. All at once it was possible to care about Lucia. She had become a human being. As she did with almost everything she sang, Callas changed our very perception of the role and its possibilities. In so doing, she not only gave us Donizetti's heroine but she also changed the face of opera. After Callas, Lucia, *Lucia di Lammermoor* and the entire bel-canto repertory would never be the same. We are still dealing with and reeling from her revolution.

To say that Callas changed the face of opera is not an overstatement. It is simply to acknowledge that she showed us the meaning in music we either took for granted or had never really heard. Callas did not have to resurrect the unfamiliar bel-canto operas she did (*Anna Bolena, Il Pirata, Poliuto, Il Turco in Italia*) to make her impact on the performing history of opera. She had already done so with this first recorded *Lucia*. She raised the ante for what it means to be a great opera singer. Mechanical singers, lazy singers, cautious singers must have hated her. Just when you thought it was safe to get by with another of your chirping Lucias, flaccid Normas, or pedestrian Violettas, along came this great singing shark devouring every note in the score, striking sparks of drama, making the old seem brand new again, and generally chasing other singers out of "their" repertory.

Callas sees and hears in the great Romantic repertory of Bellini, Donizetti, and Verdi what other singers are deaf and blind to: the *poetry* of the music. They sing notes, Callas sings meaning. They sing in phrases, she phrases in paragraphs. They strive to produce generically pretty sounds, she makes specific noises. Listening to Callas sing Lucia on that first recording was a revelation. I was hearing my most intimate feelings expressed in song. No singer had ever spoken to me so clearly. No wonder I thought she was singing just for me. It was love at first listen.

But to a fifteen-year-old in South Texas, she was necessarily a voice without a face. She was the Queen of La Scala in Milan, I was a busboy at the Robin Hood Cafeteria on South Staples and never, surely, our twain would meet. The records would have to suffice. And so I loved her as a blind man must come to love someone: with all my other senses engaged. Her voice *was* the face, and I came to know and love almost every feature of it through her many recordings. It is still the best way to know Callas. And now it is the only way. To truly "see" Maria Callas, you only have to put on one of her recordings. Fortunately, it's all there: the unforgettable sound of the voice itself, the scrupulous musicianship, the intensity of the feelings, and the flashes of genius that still astonish but can never be duplicated.

Callas' physical beauty was no doubt a part of her allure in the theater and her stature as a legend in our collective memory. It has been preserved in photographs and the handful of video tapes of her in actual performance that have come down to us. You owe it to yourself to see them. Her recorded legacy, happily, is vast, and it is there that her immortal beauty, her art, has been preserved for the rest of human history.

Without her recordings, I wonder if Maria Callas would exist as forcefully in our hearts and imaginations as she does today. Indeed, some twenty-five years after her last stage performance in 1965, and almost fifteen years after her death in 1977, Callas remains more vivid than most sopranos singing today. Who was it we heard singing *Traviata* at the Metropolitan last month anyway? Callas' Violetta (I heard two performances at the old Met in 1958), on the other hand, was simply unforgettable. I am, I confess, one of the lucky ones: I saw Callas. The busboy at Ray High School made it to Columbia College in New York. It was her debut as Norma at the old Met on October 29, 1956. I waited in line three days for a place in standing room. It was an unforgettable experience of my youth and I would not trade it for anything, but I realize now I "saw" her just as clearly on that first recording of *Lucia* in 1953 as I did when she actually stood on that great stage and sang "Casta diva." As I said, to see Callas you only have to listen to her records. We see her with our hearts and minds. Our eyes and ears are only the conduits to that place deep within us where we experience her.

Thus, John Ardoin's excellent book is almost a photo album of Callas' career from the 1949 *Turandot* fragments at the Colón in Buenos Aires to the last concert appearances with Di Stefano in 1974. Live performances are discussed as well as are the studio recordings for EMI. It is note-complete and indispensable. It is also well-written and fair-minded. My devotion to Callas is idolatrous; Ardoin's more level-headed. The right man wrote this book. I would have had you run out and buy absolutely everything. John Ardoin will steer you to the best of her many recordings, both studio and pirated.

Callas' first recording of *Tosca* for EMI in 1953 has always been on everyone's list of all-time great operatic recordings. I will not dissent from that consensus, but it would not be a desert island disc of mine. That collection would have to start with either the first EMI *Norma* or the performance from Covent Garden, November 18, 1952, or the one from La Scala,

December 7, 1955. I said "either"; the truth is I find all three essential and that's without discussing the *second* EMI *Norma* or the final *Norma* from the Paris Opéra in 1965. As for *Lucia*, there is not only that first EMI recording but the fabled "Berlin" *Lucia* of September 29, 1955. The EMI recordings of *La Sonnambula* and *I Puritani* would also have to come along with me. Callas singing Bellini is close to bliss. Of the Verdi performances, I could not be without the studio *Il Trovatore* or *Un Ballo in Maschera*. The one Puccini performance I would take along would be *La Bohème*, an opera she never sang in the theater but made very much her own in the studio. And then there are the recital albums. I would insist on the "Puccini Heroines" and "Coloratura/Lyric" albums, but I would not really be happy unless I could have all the Verdi recital albums, too. The fact is I want them all and don't be surprised if you do, too. (The happy truth is I *have* them all and I hope I never end up on a desert island.)

When I named a play of mine *The Lisbon Traviata*, the tape of that performance had not yet surfaced. The title was thus meant to represent the mythic, the unobtainable. Since I completed the play, EMI has released the performance and it is readily available. I wonder if I wrote a play called *The Chicago Trovatore*, *The Venice Walküre*, or *The Genoa Tristan*—equally legendary performances of which tapes are rumored to exist—would EMI oblige us again? If I thought they would, I would begin all three plays today. Like all opera lovers, I hope many more such tapes will surface and this is not the last installment of Mr. Ardoin's estimable survey.

But Callas' art, fortunately, is inexhaustible, even if her recordings are not. She has given us a lifetime's work to be grateful for, learn from, and wonder at. The proof is tangible. It is in these pages. It is on her recordings. We are in her debt forever. Opera has new possibilities thanks to her. It is up to us to embrace them. After Callas, there is no turning back.

Terrence McNally
February 28, 1991

# *Preface* ⌒

Sound recordings have preserved styles of musical performance and the art of individual musicians since the final decade of the nineteenth century. Despite the vast importance of this legacy, it remained limited (in all but a few cases) to studio performances until the 1930's, when radio was widely accepted as a means of communicating music.

Enterprising collectors soon began taking down broadcast performances on acetate discs. This was an extremely expensive process, however, and only a small percentage of live prewar operatic and concert broadcasts were preserved in sound. A major breakthrough came after World War II, with the popularization of tape as a recording medium and the eventual low cost of tape equipment. A further means of expanding the memory-bank of sound came in the 1960's, when transistor tape recorders reached a sophistication and compactness that allowed enthusiasts to record artists from their seats in the concert hall or opera house.

One of the first musicians of this century whose achievements have been captured in every form of modern recording was the soprano Maria Callas. The years from 1949 (her first commercial discs) to 1974 (her final tour) have yielded in sound thirty-four of her forty-seven roles complete, plus excerpts from an additional seven and a host of other material. As many of her roles were recorded in performances ranging over a span of years, a close examination of her growth as an artist is possible.

Such an examination is the aim of this book. The wealth of material available, plus the fascinating variety of Callas' performances, made such a book not only feasible but necessary. The fact that a study of Callas the musician (and this is her primary glory) has such a wide range of sources is in itself a measure of her influence, and of a creative personality that I believe to have been unique.

As the spectre of Callas continues to cast its long shadow over the musical landscape in the years following her death, and to reveal posthumously through recordings new musical horizons and directions to a generation of artists and admirers which was unable to experience her on stage, so the importance of her legacy—every scrap in whatever sound and from whatever period—has grown apace. It is indicative of her stature that her hold on our imagination has intensified rather than lessened since her death, and there is every reason to assume what remains of her art on disc will be of equal if not increased concern and instruction to future generations.

With the coming of the Compact Disc, Callas was the first modern artist to have her entire commercial output transferred to the new medium, and as of this writing, the majority of her noncommercial and broadcast material has also appeared on CD. In 1977, Walter Legge, who produced the main body of Callas' commercial recordings, said, "I maintained that I was making tapes which would sell as records for twenty or thirty years or more and sound better when the originals were subjected to better transferring and played on reproducing apparatus of the future." These were prophetic words indeed, and they have special meaning when it comes to Callas' legacy in sound.

On Compact Discs her voice emerges with greater fullness, presence, and range. Comparing the LP edition with the CD equivalent of Callas' EMI recordings of, for example, *Aida* and *Rigoletto*, with their boxed-in, constricted sound, is a potent reminder of how much compression and compromise was involved in the production stages between the studio performance and the pressing of the LPs.

Hearing Callas on CD brings one as close as is humanly possible to owning copies of the master tapes. It also allows one to experience whole acts without interruption, which in turn brings greater focus to Callas' dramatic insights and increases the impact of her performances. The noncommercial recordings benefit perhaps even more from the CD format because of the generally poor quality of vinyl used for the LP pressings of this broadcast and transistor material.

Some might wish to attach the tag "discography" to this book; I hope not. A discography is a listing of recordings, an end in itself. Here the recordings have only been a means of examining the development of an art. Naturally this book details, as well as explores, the legacy Callas has left for us today and for those who will come under her influence tomorrow; but these details are no more than roadsigns along the main route.

To create as complete a picture as possible, I have dealt with every scrap of recorded sound by Callas that I have been able to unearth, including recorded interviews, a list of which is given at the end. In the Compact Disc edition of *The Callas Legacy*, however, I have not attempted to include every record number, as I did in the LP editions of this book. In the case of the EMI commercial material, only the current catalogue number is provided. In the case of the noncommercial items, either the only available version is listed, or the set that is preferred in terms of transfer and sound. If no number is provided, the material has not yet appeared on CD.

As to quotes from librettos, those which only pinpoint the location of a musical passage are not translated. However, where the sense of a scene or aria is required, a translation is provided. In such instances, it was sometimes necessary to paraphrase, for often the quote is given out of context, and I have wished to convey more of a dramatic situation than a literal translation would allow. Furthermore, once cuts and variants have been noted in the discussion of a role, it can be presumed that they prevail in later performances unless altered too slightly to warrant comment.

There are certain facts relative to Callas' career that unfortunately remain confused and uncertain; surprisingly enough, this is true of several recording dates. My decisions in regard to dates and other pertinent data are as in the chronology included in my *Callas* (Holt, Rinehart and Winston, New York, 1974; Thames and Hudson, London, 1974), and in Arthur Germond's performance annals in Henry Wisneski's *Maria Callas: The Art Behind the Legend* (Doubleday, New York, 1975).

As in the third edition of *The Callas Legacy*, I have corrected lingering mistakes and added new live performances and commercial discs that were issued since 1991. I am also extremely grateful to Ray Dellinger for helping me to set the Callas record straight for a fourth time.

John Ardoin
Dallas, 1995

# *1949* ~

PUCCINI: *Turandot:* "In questa reggia" to end of Act II; Act III excerpt. With Mario del Monaco (Calaf), Helena Arizmendi (Liù), Juan Zanin (Timur), Virgilio Tavini (Emperor Altoum). Tullio Serafin conducting. Performance of 20 May 1949, Teatro Colón, Buenos Aires. [Eklipse 44.]

BELLINI: *Norma:* "Oh! rimembranza." With Fedora Barbieri (Adalgisa), Tullio Serafin conducting. Performance of 17 June 1949, Teatro Colón, Buenos Aires. [Eklipse 33.]

The first significant recordings of Callas' voice are her first commercial recordings, made for the Italian firm of Cetra in Turin in 1949. There is every reason, however, to believe that earlier broadcast material exists and will eventually surface: for example, *Turandot* from Teatro la Fenice in January 1948; *Tristan und Isolde* from Genoa in March 1948; and the radio concert in Turin that preceded the Cetra sessions.

It has also been alleged that during the period when Callas was coached by Louise Caselotti in New York (1946–47) she made a number of 78-rpm discs for study purposes. These discs were supposedly turned over to a lawyer when Caselotti's husband, Edward Bagarozy, brought suit in 1955 against Callas over a contractual difference.

Then there is the question of the "Nina Foresti" recording of "Un bel dì" from *Madama Butterfly* on the Major Bowes Amateur Hour broadcast on 7 April 1935. It is known that Callas appeared on one of the earliest Bowes programs before she left to study in Greece in 1937. The transcription discs of the Amateur Hour program have been preserved, and tape transfers were placed at my disposal. However, in the period when it might have been possible for Callas to have been a contestant, there was not a singer named Mary Ann Callas (as she was called at school) or even Anna Maria Kalogeropoulos (as she was, in part, christened). I presumed she had appeared under a false name, one invented perhaps to prevent her father's knowing, for he disapproved of his wife's domineering ambitions for their younger daughter.

I listened to all female contestants between the years 1935 (when the program began) and 1937, performing anything that could be considered remotely serious. The one possibility was a soprano named "Nina Foresti," who sang "Un bel dì" as her audition piece. [Eklipse 33.] There was good reason to suspect the name, for Miss Foresti's letter to the Bowes staff and her subsequent formal application were submitted under the name of "Anita Duval." It was only at the time of the audition that Miss Duval became Miss Foresti.

The tape of the Foresti audition (given a "D" rating by the Bowes staff with the note, "Faint possibility for future") revealed a singing voice weak and quite unlike anything known to be by Callas. The speaking voice, however, in quick banter with Bowes before singing, bears an astonishing resemblance. Also, during their chat, the girl states that her father is a "druggist" (as was George Callas), who had lost his business (as had Callas' father five years before). This, together with statements in the letter and application which fit details in Callas' life at this time—she would have been eleven, but her mother has written she passed for sixteen—made me believe that if a recording existed of Callas on the Bowes show, this was it. To complicate matters, Callas steadfastly denied ever singing under any name but her own. However, in his book *Diva: Life and Death of Maria Callas*, her cousin Stephen Linakis confirms that Foresti, Duval, and Callas were one and the same person, a fact later admitted by Callas to her friend Nadia Stancioff.

The earliest example of her voice, apart from the Amateur Hour appearance, is to be found in two excerpts from the 1949 season in Buenos Aires. In this period, it was a voice obviously of a good size; Callas still considered herself a dramatic soprano at this point in her career, one whose repertoire centered on Turandot, Aida, the *Forza* Leonora, Norma, Abigaille, and Kundry. Her performances as Elvira in *I puritani* earlier in 1949, undertaken while also singing the *Walküre* Brünnhilde, at the urging of conductor

Tullio Serafin, pointed the direction in which her career would travel; but further performances of *Puritani* and her first appearances as Lucia di Lammermoor were over a year in the future.

It was also a voice that ranged just short of three octaves in public performance, from an F-sharp below the staff heard in *I vespri siciliani* to an E above the staff heard in Rossini's *Armida*. It was not a voice beautiful in a classic sense; there was a good deal of metal in its upper register and the lower and middle ranges often sounded heavily veiled, bottled or as though she were muzzled. It was, at times, a sound not unlike George Bernard Shaw's famous description of a cello: "A bee buzzing in a stone jug." It was a voice with physiological flaws, and no amount of discipline could produce from it a consistency of sound. Even in her early years, her top could turn unruly and waver out of control. Yet it was a voice that was uniquely armed to convey emotion, and with Callas one was rarely able to separate her voice from what she expressed with it.

Apart from the tantalizing glimpses of the young Callas in superb vocal form, the excerpts from Buenos Aires serve as evidence that this significant season was, at least in part, broadcast. It contained the final *Turandots* of Callas' career and her second series of appearances as *Norma* (the role was still less than a year old in her repertory). In addition to these two dramatic parts, she also appeared as Aida, although nothing from these performances has as yet come to light.

When the extended scene from Act II of *Turandot* was first made public by the French label Rodolphe, there were some who believed the recording was a hoax—a composite made from the commercial recordings of the opera by Callas on Angel and del Monaco on London, and doctored with static, applause, and other extraneous noise to simulate a live broadcast. Although the sound of the performance does seem artificial in places (as though a record had been redubbed to make it sound more tinny and hollow), a close comparison of the two commercial sets with the Buenos Aires extract shows too many variations in matters of phrasing, accent, length of high notes, and matters of ensemble to doubt its authenticity.

Callas' singing here is much rawer and lacks the subtleties found in her solo version of "In questa reggia" and in the complete recording of the opera. Instead, one hears the same sort of forthright, vivid singing and the gleaming vocal steel present in the Act III excerpt, which has been accepted as truly from Buenos Aires. Also, in the Buenos Aires scene from Act II, del Monaco goes for the top C at "No, no Principessa altera!" which he does not attempt in the London set.

More telling, however, is the only spot where Turandot and Calaf sing together: "Gli enigmí sono tre, la morte é una" (Turandot's text for this moment). In Callas' commercial version with Eugenio Fernandi as Calaf, the ensemble is in perfect unison. On del Monaco's set with Inge Borkh as Turandot, she leaves the C a fraction before he does, where in the Buenos Aires performance *he* leaves the C before Callas does. In short, rather than a fake, this is a major addition to the Callas legacy.

The *Turandot* fragments from Act III last only a matter of minutes, but they stop one's breath with the excitement and brilliance of Callas' attacks, her wealth of temperament, and the magnificent way in which her voice rides the progressively ascending final phrases of the duet with Calaf. There is more substance to the *Norma* excerpts both temporally and interpretatively, with Callas lightening her voice in this section in a way we will not encounter again until the London performances three years later.

Part of the pleasure of this extended excerpt is Callas vis-à-vis the vibrant Adalgisa of Fedora Barbieri, who would be her exciting colleague in the Cetra recording of *La gioconda,* and again share honors in *Norma* at the time of Callas' debut at the Metropolitan Opera. The colors of Barbieri's voice and the way in which they illuminate Adalgisa's phrases make her, at this time in her career, a worthy foil for Callas' art, and a more stirring opponent than Ebe Stignani, with whom Callas recorded the score initially for EMI, or Giulietta Simionato, who appeared in the 1950 Mexico City *Norma.*

BELLINI: *I puritani:* "Qui la voce"; *Norma*: "Casta diva." WAGNER: *Tristan und Isolde:* "Liebestod." Orchestra of RAI, Turin, Arturo Basile conducting. [Recorded 8-10 Nov. 1949 for Cetra, reissued as Fonit Cetra 5.]

At the RAI concert of March 1949, the basis of the Cetra sessions, Callas set a pattern she would follow in future concerts: two dramatic arias paired with two florid arias. The idea behind this was one of sound showmanship. She was establishing at the outset of her career a preeminence founded on an astonishing ability to fuse agility and power. She sang the "Liebestod" from *Tristan,* "O patria mia" from *Aida,* "Qui la voce" from *I puritani* and "Casta diva" from *Norma.* Of these, all but the *Aida* aria were recorded later the same year.

Of the three Cetra 78s, the *Puritani* aria is the prize. In few other arias has Callas so precisely distilled the essence of melancholy, and few other performances of it linger so urgently in the memory. This haunting effect was produced by a lavish supply of vocal color and an authoritative rhythmic freedom. The cavatina lies largely in the middle range, and the covered and reedlike quality of Callas' voice—Chicago critic Claudia Cassidy graphically termed it "part-oboe, part-clarinet"—ideally expressed the dreamy, dazed state of Elvira's mind. On the words "voce" and later "sospir," Callas uses what has been aptly termed her "little-girl sound," a straightforward placement that will be encountered many times in the course of her career and that could be, as it is here, infinitely touching and fragile, as though seemingly imperiled. This entire scene is, furthermore, a concentrated study in rubato. Callas' ability to achieve her potent dramatic ends by bending phrases without breaking them is based on a give-and-take process with word meanings and stresses. Because it grows from the text and because she colors with inordinately good taste, there is always the sound of naturalness, with no hint of the challenges met and solved. Throughout, Callas scrupulously follows the phrasing asked for by the score and takes particular care with two-note patterns. This attention to phrasing produces magical results, particularly in the downward diatonic scales in the first part of the cabaletta and later the downward chromatics, written by Bellini and shaped by Callas as single phrases.

There are few examples in singing where so absolute a command of voice is wedded with such equality to such agility and justness of dramatic statement. The wonder of the feat is doubled, coming from a woman of twenty-five. Though Callas

5

begins at "O rendetemi la speme," she takes the cuts used in concert performances and also abbreviates the cabaletta, ending with an interpolated firm, full-throated E-flat in alt (a note foreign to all dramatic sopranos and most lyrics).

Only two of the nearly ninety *Normas* Callas was eventually to sing were behind her when she recorded "Casta diva" for Cetra. She begins with the aria itself (in the Pasta key of F major, a key becoming to her timbre and approach) shorn of its recitative; the chorus is omitted. The cavatina seems more sculpted than sung, with its melismatic passages smooth as polished stone. Though Callas later refined the cabaletta further, she rarely achieved as prepossessing a version of the cavatina. Already present in her singing here and in the *Puritani* disc is a prodigious attention to detail, whether dynamics or ornaments, such as the acciaccature of the *Norma* aria. At the cavatina's conclusion, following a featherweight descending chromatic scale, Callas chooses a nonprinted ending, rising slowly to F at the top of the staff. Intermediate recitatives are cut, and Callas plunges immediately into the cabaletta. It is sung rather too outwardly to place us within the character's mind as the text dictates, and she has only begun to sort out the proportions within and between its phrases so as to make the music flow with naturalness. One verse only is taken, the coda is abbreviated, and the section is capped with an added high C approached curiously from the lower G. Basile also eliminates the concluding march.

Callas' performance of the "Liebestod" is more a resignation to death than a transfiguration through it. This memento of her Isolde (sung in Italian) is a very human statement with a great weight of sadness brought to bear on the music. Callas' deep use of legato throughout is the predominate vocal feature, with Wagner's long, stretching lines coated in dark tone. She carefully observes the many rests sprinkled throughout, which are like sighs and are so important in establishing the atmosphere of the scene. The final impression is of one gigantic phrase embracing the music in a feeling of earthiness. Basile's contributions are fairly routine. This squareness is felt more in the Bellini arias because *Norma* and *Puritani* have a greater need of transparency and elasticity of expression, qualities Callas seems almost to beg for from Basile, usually in vain.

VERDI: *Nabucco*. With Gino Bechi (Nabucco), Amalia Pini (Fenena), Gino Sinimberghi (Ismaele), Luciano Neroni (Zaccaria), Iginio Ricco (High Priest), Luciano della Pergola (Abdallo), Silvana Tenti (Anna). Vittorio Gui conducting. Performance of 20 December 1949, Teatro San Carlo, Naples. [Legendary Recordings 1005.]

Callas closed 1949 with her only stage appearances in *Nabucco,* although the second-act aria, "Anch'io dischiuso," was to become one of her favorite concert items. That no further performances took place is not only odd but lamentable, for she is magnificent in every way in the Amazonian role of Abigaille. This set provides the earliest documentation of a complete role sung by Callas in actual performance.

At her entrance, in this Neapolitan *Nabucco,* Callas takes hold of the music with great fierceness, unleashing on the word "Prode," which begins on a low B, a chest voice that her first Cetra discs do not even hint at. The effect is electrifying, especially when followed by two extended runs, the second covering two octaves and thrown out with brilliant abandon (note particularly how she uses the turn at the end of the second to spring to the finish). With the trio, it becomes clear that Callas in live performance is quite a different creature from Callas quoting arias out of context. Her juxtaposition to other characters in dramatic conflict is a rousing stimulus for her, and she uses words as much as notes as her weapons for attack and defense.

Callas' deepest responses are often triggered when the composer calls for emotions traditionally basic to the female psyche. Scratch the warrior in *Nabucco* or the priestess in *Norma* and just under the surface is a vulnerable woman. In the trio from the first act of *Nabucco,* for example, there are two important matched phrases. The first—"Io t'amavo" ("I loved you")—is sung sotto voce, as Verdi asks, and with a caress to the tone that seems to say "Io t'amo ancora" ("I still love you"). The parallel phrase, however, is all bite—"Una furia . . . è quest'amore" ("This love is a fury"). Here Verdi has marked an accent on the first syllable of "furia"; Callas follows suit and leaves no doubt of what the composer had in mind.

Her extraordinary ability to encapsulate an emotion with her voice was often best defined by her colleagues' inability to do the same in a similar situation. You need only hear the mindless response in the trio of Gino Sinimberghi, who has the same matched phrases and with even a greater variety of stresses, to appreciate what Callas achieved earlier. The instances are rare when other singers are encountered in a Callas performance who respond to music with the same critical attention to dynamics, note values, the direction of phrases, and the romance of words.

The first-act trio and, later, the second-act aria also demonstrate the excellent vocal state of Callas in this period, even to the purity and ease of her top Cs. This primal note for a soprano often lay out of balance with the rest of Callas' voice even in her salad days. With no difficulty she could handle C-sharp or B, but C itself was frequently a fearsome hurdle. It could always be touched, but sustaining it, especially at forte, was physically and mentally more a matter of will than technique.

Another prominent feature of the *Nabucco* is Callas' security in singing widely spaced leaps such as the octave-and-a-half jump in the first-act finale and the two-octave drop in the recitative of Abigaille's aria. More important, however, than merely singing such intervals is the eminent musical sense she makes of them in both instances.

The centerpiece of the role of Abigaille is "Anch'io dischiuso." Here we find Verdi combining two styles of Italian opera. The recitative is entirely his own, but the aria places him deeply in Donizetti's debt. This set piece is extremely complex not only in the sheer number of notes to be sung, but in the myriad elements of stress and color demanded. But the true challenge lies in what is being expressed, for the aria is as intricate dramatically as it is musically. Only a personality capable of great emotional responses could bring this scene fully to life, only an Isolde voice with a *Puritani* agility could make sense of its vocal lines. Callas did so in her first contact with *Nabucco,* and in a manner that still stands unrivaled. She not only calibrated the aria's notes with mastery, but she illuminated its words.

It is easier, however, to appreciate Callas' command of Verdi's long, *cantabile* lines than it is to understand her uncanny pacing of his recitatives. When it came to recitatives, Callas had an inborn architectural sense that told her just which word in a musical sentence to emphasize and even which syllable within that word to bring out.

After the lightning bolts of recitative that precede "Anch'io dischiuso," all is tranquil in the aria. Callas makes its melismas almost float, thanks in part to the sense of lift that results from her close adherence to Verdi's phrasing. After a lovely pianissimo C, she takes an unwritten, upward ending for the cavatina, much like the one she employed at the conclusion of "Casta diva." Following the exchange with the High Priest, Callas, with weighted tone, produces the *declamato* marked in the score, slowing down the drive of the preceding *allegro mosso*. The cabaletta is studded with real, urgent trills; especially effective in sheer kinetic power is a chain of them rising an octave to top C. She weeds out, as was her training and inclination, the second verse of the cabaletta and pushes headlong to an added C to conclude the aria.

The finale of the second act belongs largely to others, but Callas as Abigaille returns in Act III and makes its duet "Donna, chi sei?" the act's focal point. Emotionally and vocally this scene is more a duel than a duet, a mighty confrontation between Abigaille and Nabucco. Callas' voice here is all exultation, all triumph. You hear in nearly every phrase the unmasked pleasure of Abigaille's victory and revenge over Nabucco. Callas tops it all with a tremendous ringing E-flat in alt, which Gino Bechi follows with a top A-flat. Though Bechi drags his feet in the first part of the duet, being especially careless with phrase endings, he does rise to the occasion in the *stretta*, where his cries of "Deh! perdona" are just the right foil for Callas' lashing "Invan, invano."

Abigaille's penitent appearance in the final act is a brief but affecting duet for voice and cello. What she says—"Chi mi toglie al ferreo pondo del mio delitto?" ("Who will relieve me of the iron burden of my crime?")—is admittedly melodramatic, but not in the way Callas expresses it. She believes, and we are made to believe by the honesty of her rapport with the text and the music.

# *1950* ∽

BELLINI: *Norma*. With Kurt Baum (Pollione), Giulietta Simionato (Adalgisa), Nicola Moscona (Oroveso), Concho de los Santos (Clotilde), Carlos Sagarminaga (Flavio). Guido Picco conducting. Performance of 23 May 1950, Palacio de las Bellas Artes, Mexico City. [Melodram 26018.]

In May 1950, Callas made her debut in Mexico City as Norma, and in retrospect these Latin-American performances and those that followed in the same year and the next two are of vital importance in tracing her growth as an artist. From this period come her earliest complete Norma, Aida, Tosca, Violetta, and Elvira on disc, as well as her first Leonora in *Il trovatore*, Lucia di Lammermoor, and Gilda.

Despite personal preferences for Callas in one role or another, it is as Bellini's Norma that she is most likely to be remembered. She sang the part more often than any other in her repertoire of forty-seven roles, and it was the vehicle of her English (Covent Garden, 1952), American (Chicago, 1954), and Metropolitan Opera (1956) debuts.

Long before Callas' entry upon the international scene, Norma had been reduced to a staid, classic figure, one at times more Gluckian than Bellinian. Sopranos before Callas who infused the part with dramatic substance (Gina Cigna, for example) often lacked the schooling to do full justice to the role's elaborate vocal lines. Others, who could command the intricacies of Norma's music, did so with a coolness that left much of the character unrealized. Callas returned a heroic stance to the part without sacrificing musical values; we can well believe that her balance between drama and agility came the closest in modern terms to those qualities of Giuditta Pasta which had led Bellini to craft Norma expressly for that unique artist.

Callas is not in her best vocal form at the outset of the Mexico City performance. During Norma's first scene her voice is thick and often unresponsive, which leads to some unduly aggressive singing as though she were struggling to make her voice move, to draw back the dark veil that often covered it in this period. However, in the recitatives, Callas not only observes but leans strongly into *appoggiature* to lend a properly heroic mood. She also interpolates the traditional upper A-flat—a rather unsteady one—on the words "Io mieto."

With the aria itself, Callas takes the pressure from her voice. "Casta diva," however, lacks mystery and atmosphere as well as the flow of line heard on the Cetra disc. Again, the cabaletta is more sung than probed. The second act brings Callas together for the first time with the Adalgisa of Giulietta Simionato, a pairing that would be repeated in London, Chicago, Milan, and Paris. The Paris performances would be their final appearance together, fifteen years after Mexico, just a few months before Simionato's retirement and during Callas' final portrayals of Norma.

In this first collaboration neither singer gives a subtle account of the second-act duet (actually Scene 7 of Act I; modern practice has broken Bellini's two-act opera into four acts). There are a few peculiarities in "Ah! si fa core" which should be noted, however. Towards its end, Callas drops out after a long held G on the word "vivrai," leaving Simionato to tackle alone the scales that follow. Callas then joins her for the cadenza in thirds at the end, but in the final set, which rises to top C for Norma and A for Adalgisa, Simionato loses her place and after dissonant intervals of a second winds up to my surprise (and no doubt hers) with Callas on the C. Order is restored in the polonaise "Oh! non tremare," which Callas sings with enormous gusto. Standard cuts mar a good deal of the trio with Pollione and the finale of the scene, but Callas brings the section to a point with a brilliant added top D.

The third act finds Callas at last into her vocal stride. This scene, where Norma contemplates the murder of her children, always drew a special response from her, particularly the long D-minor phrase beginning "Teneri, teneri figli." Though this phrase will evolve into an expression of infinite sorrow by the time of the Paris *Normas*, it is (though hefty in sound) already

11

very touching. In the duet "Deh! con te" (sung down a tone), Callas achieves some wonderful word colorations and in several spots spins out notes with remarkable control. Simionato's singing continues to be straightforward in the main, and again she strays from pitch when paired with Callas in thirds. Nothing out of the ordinary distinguishes their performance of "Mira, o Norma"; it is transposed to E-flat major, and Simionato finishes with Callas on a top B-flat.

By the last act, Callas' voice seems to be responding to her every wish. Though she deepens the shades of word colors throughout this act in later performances, she never achieves as easy and beautiful an effect on the quasi-cadenza rising to high C just before Clotilde's entrance. Callas' finest moment in this performance comes in the duet "In mia man," where she brings into play the same sense of triumph as was heard in the third-act *Nabucco* duet. There is no doubt that Callas was born with an instinct to enjoy the upper hand in a dramatic situation. The knowledge that she has the fate of the man who betrayed Norma in her grasp leads her to some extraordinary vocal effects, particularly the section "Si, sovr'essi alzai la punta" ("Yes, I raised the dagger over them"), referring to Norma's attempted murder of Pollione's children. Then, when Norma warns him she will soon commit the "fearful excess," Callas employs one of those hollow, open sounds on the word "eccesso," which she reserved for moments of the greatest dramatic tension. This sound becomes even more meaningful when contrasted seconds later with the phrase "E d'esser madre mi poss'io dimenticar" ("I must forget I am a mother"). She saturates the line with the most pitiable sounds, as though telling us that Norma, while vowing anew to murder her children, will be incapable of the act once more. In thus preparing us for Norma's ultimate act of mercy and her death with Pollione at the opera's end, Callas has worked a minor theatrical miracle.

One other moment of exaltation over Pollione comes with Callas' knifelike attack on "Solo! tutti," followed by a flash of notes in "Romani a cento a cento, fian mietuti, fian distrutti" ("Romans by the hundreds will be cut down, will be destroyed"). When she vows that Adalgisa, too, will be punished, Callas makes full use of the opportunity Bellini has provided for drama through a chain of rising trills on "Adalgisa fia punita." In the giant twin-finale (such a structural feature of the opera and among the most deeply felt pages in the repertoire), conductor Guido Picco shows little sympathy for what Callas is attempting to shape during this crucial moment of Norma's sacrifice. In many instances earlier in the performance, Callas was able to work round his unyielding leadership; here it proves impossible. Picco is so bent on pushing the music forward that Callas is helplessly pulled along by his baton. Also by this point the ensemble has begun to disintegrate in other ways as well (this and the other Mexico City recordings leave the inescapable impression that questions of rehearsal were given minimal consideration). The chorus and orchestra are inattentive, inaccurate and ragged, and Kurt Baum and Nicola Moscona sound bored. Baum leaves out a phrase, while Moscona makes a false entry he does not bother to correct. All these transgressions combine to rob the finale of its power.

VERDI: *Aida.* With Kurt Baum (Radames), Giulietta Simionato (Amneris), Robert Weede (Amonasro), Ignacio Ruffino (The King), Nicola Moscona (Ramfis), Carlos Sagarminaga (Messenger), Rosa Rodriguez (Priestess). Guido Picco conducting. Performances of 30 May and 3 June (excerpts only) 1950, Palacio de las Bellas Artes, Mexico City. [30 May on Melodram 26009; 3 June in Eklipse 44.]

A week after the *Norma* broadcast, we find the Bellini cast (with the addition of baritone Robert Weede) performing *Aida,* which Callas had first sung two years earlier in Turin. In between *Norma* and *Aida* in Mexico had come a repeat of *Norma,* and the month-long season was still to bring two further *Aidas,* two *Toscas* and three *Trovatores.* It was a busy time for Callas, who was singing an average of one performance every three days. But as the performances prove, she went from strength to strength as the season progressed.

As Aida, she rivets one from the outset by the sharpness of her rhythm. Her first phrases come across as gasps of fear, establishing with immediacy the personal drama that torments Aida. These feelings, however, are largely kept in check until "Ritorna

13

vincitor." There, they burst out in a mighty flood of fury and hatred as Callas echoes Amneris' cry for victory with a venomous, chilling slash of sound. In Callas' voice, the varied phrases of "Ritorna vincitor" show, each in a different way, the emotions of a torn, besieged heart. It is no accident on the part of Verdi or Callas that the aria builds to its ending; there is found the true plight of Aida. This coda, "Numi pietà," is more than a supplication; it is Aida so in conflict that she resigns her fate to a force greater than any human one. Callas lavishes such a wealth of stress and color on this prayer that her handling of the first part of the aria seems almost skimpy in comparison. "Numi pietà" is filled with that concentrated legato, so prominent a feature of Callas' singing, which so drenched a line with feeling. She sings the concluding phrases in a free vein, placing *fermate* on the A-flat of "tremendo," on the A-flat and G of "Ah, pietà" and on the B-flat of the final "soffrir!" She further weights the section emotionally by adding an *allargando,* which grows from the *poco stringendo* section just before.

The dramatic sparring between Callas and Simionato which began in Act I grows to a full confrontation in the first scene of Act II. Here Simionato's singing is as alive as it was immobile in *Norma,* making her a stirring adversary for Callas. Simionato begins the Amneris-Aida duet with elaborate sweetness, while agitation and darkness color Callas' responses. Gradually, Simionato's voice takes on edge and power, and eventually dominates. For the first time we encounter Callas in dramatic circumstances where she cannot claim the upper hand, and it lessens to a perceptible degree the tension of her performance. However, as if in compensation, she gives an even fuller voicing of the second appearance of "Numi pietà," making it heavier and more forward, affording a contrast to its appearance in "Ritorna vincitor" and underlining Aida's desperate state.

Though Aida's part in the second scene of Act II is not of pivotal dramatic importance, an extraordinary feat by Callas demands attention. Instead of the written ending for Aida in the Triumphal Scene, Callas soars upward an octave and sustains a full-voiced E-flat in alt virtually through the end of the orchestral postlude. Supposedly this addition was suggested by the then manager of the Mexico City season, Antonio Caraza-Campos.

He owned a score of *Aida* that had belonged to Angela Peralta, a nineteenth-century singer who had first sung Aida in Mexico and who had included the interpolated E-flat. Callas told Caraza-Campos that if he wanted to hear her E-flat he would have to engage her for *Puritani*; this he did in 1952. In the meanwhile, Callas had a disagreement with Baum during the dress rehearsal of *Aida,* and following the first act on opening night, Moscona—who had known Callas since her student days in Greece—came to her dressing room complaining of the manner in which Baum was holding on to high notes. Callas decided then and there to add the E-flat which had been urged upon her, provided Simionato and Weede would agree to its inclusion. Both did, and obviously Baum was given as big a jolt as the audience when the moment arrived. He declared furiously that he would never sing again with Callas (unfortunately, his threat was in vain). The added note is, of course, pure circus and why not? It fits well with the scope and pageantry of the scene and is thrilling in sheer visceral excitement.

With Act III and Aida's "O patria mia," we come up against a problem within Callas' art which has to be dealt with. This arose in a score such as *Aida* where there exists a "vocal" aria as opposed to a "dramatic" one. For example, "O patria mia," unlike "Ritorna vincitor," deals with a single thought. There is little chance for emotional contrasts though an excellent opportunity to make beautiful phrases for their own sake. This was never a part of Callas' makeup, though it came naturally to such a famous Aida as Zinka Milanov, whose primary reaction to music was more vocal than dramatic. Milanov usually produced an exquisite "O patria mia" and an uneven "Ritorna vincitor." With Callas, the opposite was true. Where Aida's first aria brimmed with vitality and urgency, the second sounds comparatively uninvolved once past the recitative with its "Io tremo" ("I tremble"), a sentiment Callas was never at a loss to voice. But the idea of lamenting for five minutes over the "green hills, the perfumed shores of home" did not appeal to Callas' finer theatrical sensibilities. "O patria mia" also demonstrates the sort of approach to top C that gave Callas trouble in the palmy Mexican days when she was so vocally secure and had E-flats to burn. Grabbing a C out of the air, as in Norma's "Oh! non tremare," was one

15

thing; building to it in the course of a long phrase and then sustaining it was something else. The C in "O patria mia" was one note that would never come right. This is not so important in itself, but given Callas' tepid handling of the aria, it becomes more a matter of concern.

Once past this trouble spot, however, everything is righted in the strong duet Verdi fashioned for Aida and Amonasro. In fact, Callas is so eager to plunge into this more rewarding scene that she does so several bars early while the orchestra is playing the final phrases of her aria. She expresses surprise a second time at seeing Amonasro, and the duet is propulsively launched. Like the father-daughter contretemps in *Nabucco*, this duet is a stormy one, with rage one moment, a plea the next. Here, and in the duet with Radames that follows, we hear again that unique legato Callas used when she wished to underline a particular thought. It is as though she is singing through the very middle of notes, stitching them together tightly into a single phrase. Meanwhile, Baum indulges in some vocal fencing, holding notes overtime as though to reassure the audience of his presence and perhaps as revenge for Callas' second-act E-flat.

Sanity is restored with Callas' insinuating singing of "Fuggiam gli ardori inospiti" and later "Là tra foreste vergini." In the *stretta* of the duet, "Sì fuggiam," Callas manages to dig her spurs deep enough into Picco to get a heated response after Baum's sluggish first statement. Her voice grabs Picco and Baum and pulls them along, creating a stirring climax at "Nella terra avventurata de'miei padri." The intensity she begins here carries over into the trio until the end, where Baum forgets to ask, "Chi ci ascolta?" and Weede has to volunteer, "D'Aida il padre e degli Etiopi il Re." This, to say the least, takes the edge off the drama. Baum also elects not to sing his lines after Amneris' re-entry, no doubt to hold himself in readiness for the act's final sentence, "Io resto a te," with its string of top A's so dear to a tenor.

There is not much theatrical substance for Callas in the Tomb Scene, though she does find a graceful solution for "O terra addio." Oddly enough, where one would have expected her to illuminate—the awkward phrase "Vedi? di morte l'angelo," a first cousin to Gioconda's "Vo' farmi, vo' farmi più gaia"—Callas produces disappointing results by bearing down too hard on the passage. However, the performance of *Aida* on 3 June has also been preserved in part, and there this phrase *is* lovingly managed. This repeat performance exists with large sections missing (the Nile duets in particular), but in what survives—"Ritorna vincitor," "Fu la sorte," "O patria mia," and the Tomb Scene—there is no perceptible alteration in Callas' dramatic course.

PUCCINI: *Tosca.* With Mario Filippeschi (Mario), Robert Weede (Scarpia), Gilberto Cerda (Angelotti), Francisco Alonso (Sciarrone), Carlos Sagarminaga (Spoletta), Concho de los Santos (Shepherd). Umberto Mugnai conducting. Performance of 8 June 1950, Palacio de las Bellas Artes, Mexico City. [Melodram 36032.]

Although Callas frequently expressed her disdain for the role of Tosca as well as for the music of Puccini, the role nevertheless played a significant part in her career. It was her first major part with the Athens Royal Opera (she was only eighteen at the time), and it was as Tosca that she made her final operatic appearance (5 July 1965, at Covent Garden). Also, the most telling film extant of Callas in live performance is Act II of Tosca from Covent Garden in 1964.

As she had not sung the Puccini heroine since Athens, the part was almost new to her. Her performance in Mexico is almost neon in its coloration, and the only advantage gained from her oversinging here is the frame of reference it provides for the refinements she later brought to the role, when her Tosca became more Milanese than Roman.

Callas begins the first act in thick voice and sounds more the grand prima donna than the doubting, impulsive, feminine creature which her Tosca later became. Phrases lack an easy and natural balance and flow, while a close-knit ensemble between Callas and conductor Umberto Mugnai is more the exception than the rule. Compounding the musical uncertainty of the duet is Filippeschi's crude, inexact singing. Nor is the later scene in Act I with Scarpia more finely drawn. There are surface indications of a strong instinct at work, but one that is still searching for its proper outlet.

Again, Callas remains on the surface of the drama with Scarpia in Act II, despite her deep-chested utterances of such moments as "L'anima mi torturate!" By the time we reach Scarpia's "Già, mi dicon venal" it is uncomfortably apparent that a bigger problem dogs this performance. Mugnai brings little of the give-and-take between pit and stage so necessary in *Tosca* to make the most of Puccini's fluctuating shades of tempo. Without this, all hope of momentum and tenseness is lost. By "Vissi d'arte" the scene is deep in a musical mire. Callas does not help matters by her overelaborate singing of the aria, a moment best treated as an extended aside in order not to rob the murder scene of a sense of inevitability.

In the last act, Callas makes a dashing entrance only to have "Amaro sol per te" made commonplace by Filippeschi's broad vocalism. She lets loose a final volley of drama following the execution of Mario, but it is not enough to redeem this provincial performance.

VERDI: *Il trovatore.* With Kurt Baum (Manrico), Giulietta Simionato (Azucena), Leonard Warren (Count di Luna), Nicola Moscona (Ferrando), Carlos Sagarminaga (Ruiz), Ana Maria Feuss (Inez). Guido Picco conducting. Performances of 20 June and 27 June (excerpts only) 1950, Palacio de las Bellas Artes, Mexico City. [20 June on Melodram 26017; 27 June on Eklipse 14.]

This most interesting of the 1950 Mexico City performances has an equally interesting footnote. When Callas was engaged for the first Leonora of her career, she went to her mentor, conductor Tullio Serafin, for help on the role. To her surprise, he refused, saying that he had no intention of laying the groundwork for another conductor's performances. Thus, Callas was left on her own to prepare one of the most exacting roles in the Verdian canon. (This will have a particular significance when we come to the Naples *Trovatore* of January 1951, Callas' first performance of the opera with Serafin.)

When Serafin refused to help with *Trovatore*, Callas plunged into the score in the only way she knew how—"like a sponge," absorbing every note and expression mark (she also indulged in a few unorthodox interpolations). In doing so, she managed to

18

restore a sense of the real bel-canto nature of this Verdi heroine, a nature that had been glossed over by years of heavier sopranos singing the part imprecisely.

Of all of Verdi's ladies, Leonora is among the most melancholy. If for no other reason, this made her ripe for Callas' highly personal mode of expression. Leonora's first recitative has within it the sort of contrasts that always lent Callas dramatic impetus, and how aptly dreamlike she makes the phrase "Come d'aurato sogno." Underneath the rich layer of legato.Callas applies to the aria "Tacea la notte placida" is an all-prevailing air of mystery, despite an odd cut of half-a-dozen bars in the second verse. Her one miscalculation here is following the D-flat at the end of the cavatina with a C which acts as a springboard to an E-flat in alt. Unlike the E-flat in *Aida,* the effect is jarring in its intrusion upon a well-established mood. Also, by leaving the seventh of Verdi's E-flat major chord, she dilutes the tension generated by this dissonance. Callas further substitutes an arpeggio for the scale written in the concluding cadenza, though she finishes it as written.

In the cabaletta—rather half of it, as the second verse is cut— Callas recoups any loss her E-flat cost her. The wealth of detail her voice unearths here is breathtaking. It is as if an old painting, familiar but dim, has been cleaned to its original tints. The solid bel-canto schooling she received from Elvira de Hidalgo pays off handsomely, for not only does she sing all the notes of the cabaletta, with real trills, *staccati,* and all rests in place, but she colors and plays with the notes, reminding us what a florid part Leonora is when sung correctly. At the end of the cabaletta, Inez' lines are cut, and Callas unfortunately decides to go for yet another E-flat, and a not too stable one at that.

This *Trovatore* and its repeat three days later were the only times Callas sang with Leonard Warren, and the first-act trio is full of the vocal blood-and-thunder that permeated this mighty encounter. At its conclusion, Callas sails to an added D-flat, a note on which she is joined by Baum, who attempts to out-sustain her and loses. There is a touching sadness to Callas' singing of the beautiful but short phrase beginning "Degg'io volgermi" in the second scene of act two. But her real contribution to this scene is the way she molds the short eighth notes of the

19

finale ("E deggio e posso crederlo?"). These three-note patterns are a model of how to color through phrasing, as is the gentle way Callas handles the *acciaccature* Verdi adds later to Leonora's already complex line. Why, or how, it became the custom for the tenor to join in Leonora's question "Sei tu dal ciel disceso?" I cannot say. But a quick translation ("Are you from heaven descended?") reveals it as inappropriate for Manrico, quite apart from the manner in which it upsets the musical balance at that moment.

"Tradition" (in its destructive sense) has also spoiled, to a much greater extent, another section of *Trovatore*. In the fourth act's first scene, the expressive cabaletta "Tu vedrai che amore in terra," to Leonora's "D'amor sull'ali rosee," was always cut to my knowledge until Callas' recording of the opera at La Scala for EMI in 1956. What is at stake here is the loss not merely of a superb stretch of music, but of the uniqueness of Verdi's approach to form during this transitional period of his writing. Taken on their own, "D'amor sull'ali rosee" and "Tu vedrai che amore in terra" add up to the standard cavatina-cabaletta design that was the backbone of aria structure from Rossini to middle Verdi. "Tu vedrai," of course, is more a reflective than a virtuoso cabaletta, but so is "Quel sangue versato" to Elisabetta's "Vivi, ingrato" in the final scene of Donizetti's *Roberto Devereux*, for example. And, of course, the more deeply one studies Verdi, the stronger the link with Donizetti is found to be.

The unusual feature of Leonora's fourth-act scene is that Verdi separates her cavatina and cabaletta not by recitative or even a recitative-like scene, but by a brooding monument of ensemble— the "Miserere." This structure grew entirely from his imagination and not from a prescribed form, and all sense of the wonder of his achievement is lost by cutting the cabaletta. Lamentably, the practice is still the norm, and this Mexico City performance, too, jumps from the "Miserere" to the Leonora-di Luna duet.

In "D'amor sull'ali rosee," Callas again spins a mood of night and shadows, though in a heavier way than will be the case later. Towards the aria's end, she eschews the alternatives given in modern scores, which allow a soprano to duck first a top C and then a D-flat. Very few singers elect to bypass the C, but Callas is one of the handful who include the written D-flat. After second thoughts on the matter, she will later disagree with Verdi and forego the D-flat. The problem with this particular note is the wide leap which approaches it. This skip of over an octave places too great an emphasis on the note and causes it to stand apart from the arching melodic lines which precede it.

As the juxtaposition of "D'amor sull'ali rosee" with the "Miserere" helps to define Verdi's strength as a man of the theater, so does Callas' singing of both define some of the properties of her art. The ability is given to few (only Leontyne Price comes to mind) to go with equal ease from the ethereal heights of "D'amor" to the morbid depths of the "Miserere." For the "Miserere," Callas produces her darkest, most foreboding sounds. Notable too are the two-note phrases on "Palpiti al cor," which become just that—"a throbbing of the heart."

The heavy-laden mood of the ensemble carries over into the Leonora-di Luna encounter. Only a singer who has met the challenges of *Norma* could master the phrases "Mira, di acerbe lagrime," with its dramatic weight, and "Vivrà! contende il giubilo," with its cascades of notes. Callas not only produces every note in time and in tune, but she shades and molds these notes, making careful distinction between legato and staccato—and all in a bravura tempo. Not even Callas will prove a match for herself here in later *Trovatores*. She caps the duet with a top C (this interpolation fits nicely into the framework of the scene), which Warren waits out like a gentleman before joining Callas on the written F.

After Leonora's entrance in the prison scene, we again have some excessively competitive singing from Baum. But once his bluster is spent, Callas has a chance to restore musical sense with her poignant singing of the rising line "Prima che d'altri vivere."

There are also excerpts from the performance of 27 June. By this time, Warren had left the cast. Mexico City's extremely high altitude was not comfortable for him, and he was replaced by Ivan Petroff (the Bulgarian baritone, not the Russian bass of the same name) for the final *Trovatore*. The sections recorded were "Tacea la notte," the trio-finale of Act I, the Leonora-di Luna duet from Act IV, and the opera's finale. Callas' singing remains largely consistent with the first performance with a few minor changes. In the aria she goes for the first E-flat interpolation and

21

barely makes it. This close call must have been behind her decision to omit the second E-flat, missing here. However, in the trio she again takes a concluding D-flat and Baum once again joins her on it. This time, however, he manages to last longer. Finally, the rapid sections of the last-act duet are not so well articulated by Callas, and Petroff makes a colorless di Luna after the force of Warren's singing the week before.

**VERDI:** *Aida.* With Ebe Stignani (Amneris), Mirto Picchi (Radames), Raffaele de Falchi (Amonasro), Augusto Romani (Ramfis), Anna Marcangeli (Priestess). Vincenzo Bellezza conducting. Performance 2 October 1950, Teatro dell'Opera, Rome. [Melodram 26109.]

This recording begins towards the end of "O patria mia" and continues to the conclusion of the act. It was recorded in the wings for the late baritone Raffaele de Falchi, who joins Callas as Amonasro. The sound is remarkable, the performance vivid.

Coming just four months after her initial Mexico City *Aida*, the role is still cast in a heroic mold by Callas. She and her colleagues are working on an immense vocal and dramatic scale in the Nile Scene and presumably in the remainder of the performance, which was not recorded.

Callas ascends to a rock-solid C in her aria, making the ascent into a single phrase beginning with the lower E-flat. Again the highpoint is the father-daughter encounter in spite of de Falchi's melodramatic outcries. With Callas, however, the drama is true, as she moves from almost audible tears in "Padre! a costoro, schiava non sono" to a silky sensuality later with Radames at "Fuggiam gli ardori inospiti."

**WAGNER:** *Parsifal.* With Africo Baldelli (Parsifal), Boris Christoff (Gurnemanz), Rolando Panerai (Amfortas), Dimitri Lopatto (Titurel), Giuseppe Modesti (Klingsor), Aldo Bertocci and Mario Frosini (Knights), and Lina Pagliughi, Renata Broilo, Anna Maria Canali, Liliana Rossi, Silvana Tenti, and Miti Truccato Pace (Flower Maidens). Vittorio Gui conducting. Concert performance of 20 November (Act I) and 21 November (Acts II and III) 1950, RAI, Rome. [Melodram 36041.]

After her return from Mexico and performances in Rome of *Aida* and Rossini's *Il turco in Italia,* Callas closed 1950 with her final performance of Kundry in *Parsifal,* a role she performed only four times on stage, also in Rome. This RAI performance is the only complete documentation of Callas in one of her three Wagnerian roles. While Kundry was not a major part in Callas' repertoire, she still brings some special qualities to the music of this fascinating character. In large measure, this might well be attributed to the silky, languid vocal line possible when Kundry is performed in Italian, as here. It has been suggested that *Parsifal* in Italian sounds like good Montemezzi; while this is certainly an oversimplification of a complex matter, it is true that *Parsifal* in translation does become a work of a different complexion.

As the part of Kundry is negligible in Acts I and III, it is Act II which most concerns us, and in a recorded performance it is Kundry the temptress who predominates in the second act. Of course the seductive Kundry takes her all-important quality of contrast from the woeful Kundry of the Klingsor scene, and at the outset of the act Callas does draw a dark curtain of tone over the character's lines. This gives a new perspective to the lilt of her voice when it is next encountered calling Parsifal's name after the Flower Maiden scene. Incidentally, a curious footnote to this performance is the appearance of Lina Pagliughi as the first Flower Maiden; I seriously doubt whether there is a precedent for a performance of *Parsifal* which includes two famous Lucias.

As the scene with Parsifal and Kundry builds in intensity, so does Callas' performance, and she makes a remarkable moment of the crazed "Den ich verlachte, lachte, lachte," with its descending eighth notes, each sharply etched, even though the singing of Africo Baldelli as Parsifal remains monochromatic and undramatic throughout. The act peaks with Callas taking three alternative top notes (an A rising to B-flat and then to B) suggested in the Peters score, and she underlines the collapse of Klingsor's castle with a piercing scream. While one should not read too much into Callas' Kundry, the vibrance and urgency she brings to the part, and particularly her sensual singing of "Ich sah das

Kind," do not allow these records to be regarded merely as curiosities; there is genuine drama here where frequently there is only posturing. Many cuts are taken in this concert performance, but they are of minor concern in Act II and are restricted principally to Parsifal's music. Considering Baldelli, there is no sense of loss.

# 1951 〜

VERDI: *Il trovatore.* With Giacomo Lauri-Volpi (Manrico), Cloe Elmo (Azucena), Paolo Silveri (Count di Luna), Italo Tajo (Ferrando), Teresa de Rosa (Inez), Luciano della Pergola (Ruiz), Gerardo Gaudioso (Gypsy), Gianni Avolanti (Messenger). Tullio Serafin conducting. Performance of 27 January 1951, Teatro San Carlo, Naples. [Melodram 26001.]

The performances of *Trovatore* in Mexico City are best heard as preparation for the three Naples performances the following January when Callas first sang Leonora under Serafin's direction. By considering these two series of performances together, we can approach an understanding of the artistic relationship which existed between the soprano and her longtime friend.

They had met in 1947 when he conducted her Italian debut at the Verona Arena as Gioconda, and it was Serafin's influence in the theaters of the day that provided most of Callas' early Italian engagements. There is little doubt that Serafin exercised a strong hand on Callas' growth as an artist (as he had on Rosa Ponselle's twenty years earlier). Under his tutelage and with him in the pit, Callas prepared and sang for the first time many of her principal roles—Norma, Elvira in *I puritani*, Violetta, and Aida. Though Serafin did not share honors with Callas in opera houses during the high-water period of her career (principally because he was feuding with La Scala's management), he did conduct most of the recordings she made under La Scala's auspices. Their artistic relationship lasted until Callas' second recording of *Norma* for EMI in 1960.

A close comparison of the Mexico and Naples *Trovatores* indicates that Serafin reinforced and refined what Callas felt intuitively. Had she been deprived of his counsel, she might not have made her way as quickly as she did professionally and musically, but neither would she have been less of an artist. The Mexico City *Trovatore* without Serafin's help is an uncommon achievement. In comparison, the Naples *Trovatore* amounts to a sorting out, a shifting of emphases (particularly on stresses within recitatives) and an added buoyancy of phrase which comes when a master-singer and a master-conductor are united in a single viewpoint.

Serafin shapes "Tacea la notte" for Callas more largely than was the case in Mexico; the crescendo he makes, for example, at the end of the first verse (the line rising to B-flat) is enormous. The effect is repeated at the end of the second verse and is backed up by Callas' taking an interpolated ending which rises scalewise and forte to A-flat. The cadenza has again been altered and, oddly enough, it is more at variance with Verdi's harmony than the cadenza Callas used in Mexico. Here and at the end of the cabaletta, either Serafin or Callas has wisely done away with the E-flats in alt, although the cabaletta's conclusion takes yet another turn. In place of the written E-flat trill, Callas drops out six beats then comes in on an E-flat, moves to B-flat (which is held a moment) and resolves the line to the written A-flat.

While the recitative for "D'amor sull'ali rosee" seems less free here than in Mexico, the aria is sung in a far suppler manner, with Serafin's support affording a greater lift to phrases. Indeed, throughout, there is a wealth of orchestral detail without a loss of overall line. With Serafin you saw at a glance both leaves and forest. At the end of "D'amor," Callas again takes the written D-flat, and the aria's cadenza is superbly colored and balanced. The "Miserere" is surprisingly subdued, and the Leonora-di Luna duet also lacks tension on the whole, despite some powerful dramatics from Callas, who again tops "Mira di acerbe" with a high C. Of importance is the more eloquent handling of the opera's final scene by Callas. She has found a quite touching and paler color for the phrase "Prima che d'altri," and with Serafin's sympathetic support it becomes hauntingly implanted in one's memory.

She is partnered in this performance by the veteran tenor Giacomo Lauri-Volpi, nearly at the end of a career begun thirty-two years earlier. Like Serafin, he was an early and ardent champion of Callas.

VERDI: *Un ballo in maschera:* "Ma dall'arido stelo." PROCH:
"Deh torna, mio ben." THOMAS: *Mignon:* "Je suis Titania."
Manno Wolf-Ferrari conducting. Concert of 12 March 1951, RAI,
Turin. [Proch in Legato 172; *Ballo* and *Mignon* LP only.]

These arias represent only part of a concert. Callas also sang
"Leise, leise" from Weber's *Der Freischütz.* Neither the *Ballo*
nor *Mignon* aria seems to have been preserved intact. *Mignon* is
sung in Italian; later Callas would record it in French, as well as
a number of other arias not generally associated with her career.
At the time these records were issued, many expressed surprise
at the repertoire without knowing that Callas had learned much
of this material with de Hidalgo. In fact, the amount of music
she absorbed while a student is both amazing and unpredictable—
songs of Schubert and Brahms, the Bach Passions, the Rossini and
Pergolesi *Stabat Maters.* The only nonoperatic performance she
gave outside Greece, however, was of Stradella's oratorio *San
Giovanni Battista* in Perugia in 1949. She long wanted to sing
the Verdi *Requiem* and was announced for it in London in 1953
and again in Dallas in 1969, but neither performance materialized.
   It was also in Athens that she first came into contact with
Verdi's *Ballo,* having performed the third act as part of a student
program in May 1940. Amelia's second-act aria is filled with the
sort of diverse emotions that always brought out the most expressive side of Callas. Tumbling out with almost manic rapidity are
fright, sadness, apprehension, terror, and supplication. Verdi has
helped a singer read between the lines of Antonio Somma's text
with such directions as *con dolore, con spavento, con voce soffo-
cata* and *con passione.* In short, this is a scene to be lived as much
as sung. It requires the sort of commitment of which Callas was
the mistress.
   From the outset she lends an air of impending tragedy by her
vivid word tints and accents. The recitative bristles with unrest,
finding release only in "Ebben! quando la sorte mia, il mio dover
tal è . . . s'adempia, e sia" ("All right, if this is my destiny, let
it be"). But this resignation to fate gives way in the aria first to
fright (short notes and rests are delivered like gasps of breath)
and then to virtual hysteria. For the conclusion after a short
cadenza, Callas substitutes an upward ending. The aria begins
right on the recitative; the orchestral introduction is missing.

Proch's variations on "Deh! torna, mio ben" are yet another remnant from Callas' study with de Hidalgo in Greece. Callas long retained an affection for this once popular coloratura showpiece and wanted to record it, but Serafin objected to its admittedly slight musical value. Callas tosses off its high-lying difficulties, trills, scales, *staccati,* and arpeggios with extraordinary freedom and abandon while maintaining a musical shape to the whole not heard in other recordings of this music. The piece is capped by an exultant high E-flat, which even she did not quite manage to equal in the years that immediately followed. Incidentally, those who own de Hidalgo's Fonotipia recording of the Proch will find many interesting parallels between teacher and student, a coincidence that does not arise in other arias they recorded in common.

Only some forty percent of the *Mignon* aria has survived. This is a real loss, for Callas is in marvelous form and brings to what is normally little more than a showpiece an unusual wealth of expression. There is enormous freedom to her singing, especially the elaborate passagework following "Plus vive que l'oiseau, plus prompte que l'éclair!" She sings this section very lightly and with great care, creating rounded phrases. In the cadenza, Callas takes trouble to make a difference between the alternating legato and staccato fanfare figures that precede the octave leaps. The octaves are all in tune (no small thing) and crowned by an excellent E-flat in alt.

**VERDI:** *I vespri siciliani.* With Giorgio Kokolios-Bardi (Arrigo), Enzo Mascherini (Monforte), Boris Christoff (Procida) Bruno Carmassi (Bethune), Mario Frosini (Vaudemont), Mafalda Masini (Ninetta), Gino Sarri (Danieli), Aldo de Paoli (Tebaldo), Lido Pettini (Roberto), Benno Ristori (Manfredo). Erich Kleiber conducting. Performance of 26 May 1951, Teatro Comunale, Florence. [Legendary Recordings 1008.]

Though this *Vespri siciliani* marked Callas' debut at Florence's annual May Festival, it was her third engagement in the city. Her association with Florence grew to be a special one, with six out of eight of her contracts there for roles she was performing for the first and, in two instances, the only time in her career: Norma, Violetta, Elena, Euridice (the stage premiere of Haydn's *Orfeo ed Euridice*), Rossini's Armida, and Medea.

Ironically Elena in *Vespri* was sung more often by Callas than other Verdian parts with which she is more closely associated, such as Lady Macbeth, Abigaille, or Amelia. Despite a number of similarities in the vocal writing between Elena and the *Trovatore* Leonora, Elena is a figure who looks more forward to the two Amelias than backward to Leonora. Callas sets her before us from the first as a strong-willed woman, and it is a pity her singing of the first-act aria "Deh! tu calma" is not better known; it is a rich effort in creating theater through voice. Even before the aria and its eerie recitative, Callas prepares us for the unusual by the extraordinary way she delivers the line "Sì canterò."

Verdi instructs that this be sung *con calma,* and calm it is on the surface when Callas utters it. Yet there lurks beneath these four syllables an unspoken thought which says, "Yes, I will sing, but you will not like the song." Instead of the pleasantry a detachment of French soldiers expects—"Ascolti il pianto del marinar"—("Hear the sailor's weeping")—Elena sounds a call to arms, urging her fellow Sicilians to rise against their invaders. The emphasis Callas gives the words "Il vostro fato è in vostra man" ("Your fate is in your hand") is chilling and further set off by the quiet beginning she makes of the ensuing allegro ("Su coraggio"), as though sung under her breath. The allegro builds to a brilliant peak, with Callas delivering a full-voiced top B. I only regret that it has been trimmed in half, but it does little good to bemoan cuts here or elsewhere in this *Vespri*. The opera was tailor-made for the outsized tastes of the Paris public of the 1850s, with swollen choruses and a monster ballet. An uncut *Vespri* would run some four hours, so it is inevitable that much music must go in a modern performance.

Elena's aria is followed by a visionary piece of writing, the quartet "D'ira fremo all'aspetto." In this harmonically difficult section, one continually marvels at Callas' sure sense of pitch. Not only are Elena's odd intervals sung with complete accuracy, but they are shaped with an authority which makes them seem entirely natural. Act II brings the first of two large duets for tenor and soprano. The music of the first is not the best Verdi,

29

and Callas is forced to make her way unaided by the tenor Giorgio Kokolios-Bardi, a crude artist—she was plagued by bad luck with tenors in the early years of her career (Sinimberghi, Baum, Filippeschi, Baldelli, et al.). She nevertheless manages a touching moment midway in the duet with the phrase "Presso alla tomba ch'apresi." This line and later the rising one on "Tu dall'eccelse" hark back to music for Leonora, and Callas achieves the same sort of plaintive mood that had characterized her melancholy singing of *Trovatore*.

This quality is even more effectively brought to bear in the fourth-act duet (the part of Elena is of little consequence in Act III, especially given the cuts in this production). The *Gran duetto* forms the heart of the act, and its similarity of structure to the fourth-act duet in Meyerbeer's *Les Huguenots* is too strong to have been accidental. After all, Verdi no doubt wanted to make good with his first Paris commission, and the popular Meyerbeer work might well have served him as a model. Again it is the polarity of emotions that stirs Callas to extraordinarily expressive heights. As Elena reviles Arrigo for his supposed betrayal of her and her people, there is bite and venom in Callas' voice, later replaced by a sad resignation in her forgiveness of Arrigo and the realization that a void has replaced their former love. This shift in mood is summed up in the core of the duet, a long-spun cantilena beginning "Arrigo, ah parli a un cor." Callas sings this with great elasticity of phrase and rich tone. This section, as well as the entire duet, exploits a soprano's lower register (down to F-sharp below middle C). The lowest perimeter comes at the end of a two-and-a-half octave chromatic scale, where, unfortunately, Callas misjudges her breath and the bottom of the phrase fails to sound. But she quickly regains her composure in the final moments (sung down an octave), making a particularly effective moment of a low trill.

In the final section of the duet, Kokolios-Bardi bruises an attractive melody in B-flat built round a triplet figure, but the theme is illuminated when Callas follows with the same line. Another quite original quartet, this time with chorus, ends the act, but it becomes more of a duet as Callas and Boris Christoff eclipse the routine efforts of Kokolios-Bardi and Enzo Mascherini.

Elena's best-known moment, the so-called Bolero (termed by Verdi a "Siciliana"), opens the last act. Kleiber begins the aria briskly, but Callas enters at a slower tempo to lend the aria the *con grazia* marked in the score. This set piece has nothing to do with the drama and is actually out of character for Elena as we have known her up until this point. It is, frankly, a virtuoso piece. Callas keeps it light, with a marvelous spring to phrases. Her rhythmic singing of the coda is a special feature of the whole, which fulfills itself first as music and then as a display of vocal prowess. The trill from F-sharp to top C, for example, is notable for the deftness and roundness of Callas' phrasing. She makes a misjudgment at the very end of the "Bolero" when she reaches for an E in alt and splits the note in two. She manages to regain the tone, but the climax has been breached. The trio-finale is weak stuff (even with a grand top C from Callas), and this *Vespri* ends limply.

VERDI: *Aida.* With Mario del Monaco (Radames), Oralia Dominguez (Amneris), Giuseppe Taddei (Amonasro), Ignacio Ruffino (King), Roberto Silva (Ramfis), Carlos Sagarminaga (Messenger), Rosa Rodriguez (Priestess). Oliviero de Fabritiis conducting. Performance of 3 July 1951, Palacio de las Bellas Artes, Mexico City. [Melodram 26015.]

Callas' second season in Mexico consisted of only two roles— a repeat of *Aida* and the addition of *La traviata*. It was in most respects a happier engagement than the year before, given the presence of Oliviero de Fabritiis as conductor and overall stronger casting. Though Callas sang only two *Aidas* between her two years in Mexico, the role was obviously developing in her mind from a series of highlights to an integrated whole. In "Ritorna vincitor," for example, where "Numi pietà" had been the principal feature of the 1950 performance, we now have more of an entity, with a telling solution found for "L'insana parola" and, later, "I sacri nomi di padre d'amante." "Numi pietà" is still rightly the focus of the aria, but now all before leads logically to it.

Callas is also in brighter voice in 1951, and while the flame of her singing burns no less intensely, it has taken on a further glow and steadiness, and she now includes the blue center of the flame as well as its red edge. She is helped immeasurably by de Fabritiis, whose view of the score provides an expansive sound and approach in sympathy with Callas' musical ideas. She again includes the top E-flat at the conclusion of the "Triumphal Scene" (Baum is no longer the excuse; she obviously enjoys the effect of the note), and if anything it is more rousing and epic than the year before.

Even "O patria mia" has more profile to it, though there are phrases which are still inconclusive. The duets which follow are stirringly realized in both theatrical and vocal sense by Callas, but Taddei and del Monaco both tend to oversing. Despite del Monaco's lack of subtlety, there is, at least, the clarion compensation of his voice, a heroic sound of amazing brilliance and concentration. His larger-than-life approach makes a certain impact in the Nile Scene (and later in the Judgment Scene with Oralia Dominguez, singing her first Amneris), but it is quite out of place in the Tomb Scene. Here del Monaco bawls his farewell to earth with a persistence which, like a fever, overtakes Callas as well.

**VERDI:** *La traviata.* With Cesare Valletti (Alfredo), Giuseppe Taddei (Germont), Luz Maria Faran (Flora), Gilberto Cerda (Douphol), Ignacio Ruffino (Dr. Grenvil), Carlos Sagarminaga (Gastone), Cristina Giron (Annina), Francisco Alonso (D'Obigny). Oliviero de Fabritiis conducting. Performance of 17 July 1951, Palacio de las Bellas Artes, Mexico City. [Melodram 26019.]

If any singer and any role were fated to come together, it was Callas and Violetta. Her portrayal was only six months old at this performance, having been created in Florence the January before. The role was tailor-made for her awareness as an artist and her sensibilities as a woman, and the records show Callas' identity with the part and her understanding of and response to its myriad emotional inflections were ingrained from the start. Though she gradually moved from the exterior emotionalism of this *Traviata* to a more inner expression of intense, personal sorrow, Act I in Mexico is remarkably developed. This initial act, too, will change and deepen, but it is in the later acts that Callas will eventually most movingly blend the resources of her voice, intellect, and heart into one expressive and unique whole.

The strength of her first act in Mexico lies in her power to suggest the impending death of Violetta. In greeting the guests, and later in byplay with Gastone and Douphol before the "Brindisi," Callas implants an unmistakable air of sickness by pallid vocal colors and limp phrasing. The "Brindisi" itself is not sung with the usual bounce and brio, but rather with *portamenti* where one normally encounters *staccati*; phrases sigh, warning us that Violetta's energies are at a premium. In the dialogue with Alfredo before "Un dì felice" questions such as "E lo potrei?" and "Che dite?" are almost half-sung, half-spoken, stressing the effort involved in Violetta's maintaining a pretense of well-being.

Like *Trovatore*, *Traviata* is a work in transit, a mixing of an older style of writing with what was to become a new style of Italian opera in Verdi's hands. In "Un dì felice" and later in "Sempre libera," the principal examples of the "old" style, Callas transforms what is anachronistic by the lilt, shapeliness, and purpose of her phrasing. Furthermore, in "Ah, se ciò è ver, fuggitemi . . . amar non so" ("If what you say is true, leave . . . I cannot love"), Callas uses Verdi's flurry on "Amar non so" not for vocal brilliance, but as a reflection of the unrest felt by Violetta at Alfredo's declaration of love. Yet her very softness of tone here seems to say that Violetta wants his love while being afraid of it. In her voice this becomes a moment of penetrating femininity and vulnerability rather than a difficult hurdle to be leaped. Later, the arpeggios of "Dimenticarmi, allor" ("Forget me then") are given an unusual dramatic function through an echo effect Callas makes on the second of the two, both taken within a single breath. These phrases, as shaped by Callas, impart a reflective dimension to the character, add warmth, and act as a culmination of the duet.

In the final scene of Act I, the brace of arias for Violetta, Callas works with a wide range of expression. In the recitative and first half of "Ah! fors'è lui," she brings a hesitation to her singing, lingering over notes (such as the A-flat of "tumulti,"

33

which is left by way of a wide *portamento*), reinforcing Violetta's uneasiness about the evening's events. Resolution comes in the F-major section, "A quell'amor ch'è palpito," sung with a rapture which is in total contrast to all that has gone before. It is the first really healthy moment in her portrayal. The second verse of the aria is cut (as it must be if one is to hold to character), the cadenza at the conclusion is extended, and an upward ending is taken.

With Violetta's vow to abandon love, Verdi's music takes a brilliant flashing turn; Callas' characterization follows suit, as though Violetta's physical strength is now equal to her new strength of purpose. The cabaletta which follows, "Sempre libera," holds understandable terror for sopranos less well-schooled than Callas, for it calls for the sort of agility and technical command that results only from a careful bel-canto upbringing. This section has been the downfall of a number of Violettas and has led critics to speak of sopranos as either first-act or second-and-fourth-act Violettas. Usually, a singer comfortable in Act I will lack the body of sound needed to make the fullest of the later acts. The converse is just as certain. With Callas, however, there is no need for such qualifications. Her "Sempre libera" is as vocally complete as her "Gran Dio! Morir sì giovine" in Act IV (or, reckoning by Verdi's original design, Act III). Callas further sings "Sempre libera" with infectious abandon, never losing her grip on the direction and dramatic function of phrases. Every note is astonishingly in place and molded with breathtaking finish. Scales are resolute, flexible, and impart an aura of joy and life. Finally, the many top Cs of "Sempre libera" present no perils (though one of them seems sustained more by Callas' teeth, so to speak, than her breath) and are dispatched with enormous gusto. Callas drops out for four-and-a-half bars at the aria's end, then rejoins the orchestra, rising to an ecstatic, interpolated E-flat in alt.

Following the opening aria for Alfredo in Act II, de Fabritiis jumps to Violetta's entrance, another example of the sort of cut that drains vitality from Verdi's musical structure and makes a character less of a personage. Act II contains the heart of the role of Violetta; here she sacrifices her happiness for Alfredo's future. This sacrifice, when coupled with Verdi's humane music,

results in a moving dramatic unity. What keeps Callas from clos-
ing the dramatic circle of the act at this time is a much too lavish
use of voice. Her flood of sound is out of proportion to the
character and many of the sentiments of the text. Her linking of
tone to tone (as in "Dite alla giovine") is uneven as yet, and the
phrases that contain the hurt of "Così alla misera" and "Morrò,
la mia memoria" are only beginning to take shape. Already well
on its way, however, is the dignified understatement she makes
of "Amami, Alfredo," which grows from within rather than from
the surface. One element of this Mexico *Traviata* which will
unfortunately not be totally recaptured is the sympathetic Germont of Giuseppe Taddei. It ranks with the finest performances
of the role, a few lapses in intonation notwithstanding.

Act III is in better shape, from Callas' coloring of the rising
phrase "Ah perchè venni, incauta" to the pleading sounds she
finds for the later scene with Alfredo. Most impressive of all is
her wan singing of the finale, "Alfredo, Alfredo, di questo core."
In Callas' voice it becomes a great arch of sadness expressed in
the most pitiable tones. In the final act we come up against an
enigma in the art of Callas—her inability to bring as consistent
a veracity to spoken lines as she imparts to sung passages. In the
spoken recitative to "Addio del passato" and in the final pages
of the score where Violetta believes she is recovering, Callas
becomes unexpectedly mannered, with words receiving odd stress
at odd moments ("Il barone fu ferito" and "Egli a voi tornerà").
The same problem will crop up later in the first act of *Macbeth*.
I have no easy answer to the question of why there was frequently no music in Callas' speaking. Perhaps minus the support
lent by tone and a prescribed pacing for words she felt ill-at-ease
or unduly exposed. The singing of "Addio del passato," however, all but makes up for this lack through its concentration of
mood. Again, phrases are broadly drawn as in "Ah! fors'è lui."
On the word "ridenti," for example, at the end of the first
phrase of "Addio del passato," Callas makes a wide *portamento*
to an E, places a *fermata* on it, and then leaves it by means of
another *portamento*. She never quite achieves the true *fil de voce*
Verdi requires at the aria's end, for the sort of disembodied *pianissimo* tone so prominent in the singing of Montserrat Caballé
was never a part of Callas' vocal makeup. She could sing softly,

35

very softly, but she could not command those half-lit sounds which seem to have a life of their own. Such sounds were almost foreign to Callas' approach to music, where all was subjugated to a whole and nothing was a feature in itself.

One of the most beautiful moments in the last act of this performance is Callas' first statement in "Parigi, o cara." It is of the greatest simplicity. The balance of the act, however, is again upset by the same generosity of sound which had worked against her in the second act, although there are moving single words and phrases scattered throughout her singing. Like Callas' Violetta, Cesare Valletti's Alfredo is a performance in the making, but even given its incomplete aspects, he is an Alfredo worthy of such a Violetta.

PUCCINI: *Tosca*. With Gianni Poggi (Mario), Paolo Silveri (Scarpia), Gino del Signore (Spoletta), Giulio Neri (Angelotti), Guilherme Damiano (Sacristan), Anna Maria Canali (Shepherd). Antonino Votto conducting. Performance of 24 September 1951, Teatro Municipal, Rio de Janeiro. [Melodram 36032.]

This recording contains about 75 percent of Tosca's music and is a souvenir of Callas' only appearances in South America outside of the Buenos Aires season of 1949. São Paulo heard her as Norma and Violetta, and these roles plus Tosca constituted her Rio appearances. If the Mexico Tosca of 1950 could be characterized as Roman in temperament, this Rio performance is Neapolitan. Her singing throughout—and this is more a vocal Tosca than anything else—is overripe, old-fashioned, and at times dangerously close to being vulgar. She is in thick voice, and her heavily weighted middle register tends to pull down her top and make her upper register tremulous.

The duet in the first act is more exaggerated than in Mexico. Callas responds to Poggi's Mario coyly, and despite bits of apt expression during the scene (Ah! quegli occhi," for one), a strong character does not emerge. Her singing sounds as if she were proceeding note by note instead of phrase by phrase, as there are odd stresses within vocal lines which break phrases into smaller expressive units. Also, *parlando* passages ("Tu fino a stassera stai fermo al lavoro") are stilted and without the natural gait normally a feature of Callas' recitative. Votto, whose pacing of Act I was expansive enough, begins to drag the performance down during Act II. It unravels, as was the case in Mexico, losing motion and intensity. Surprisingly, with all that has gone before, Callas begins "Vissi d'arte" eloquently, but it, too, shortly bogs down, and the final B-flat sounds forced and constricted. The murder scene is a stream of hysterics and in part inconclusive as Act II is cut short, ending with Callas' cries of "Muori!"

Act III is neutral in impact, though Callas does manage a roaring top C in "Io quella lama," and seems so pleased with the note she lingers too long on it. Votto finally decides to move things along and jumps Callas before she can finish "Là, muori! Ecco un artista!" We are left without an inkling of what Callas' Tosca could and would be.

# *1952* ∽

VERDI: *Macbeth:* "Vieni! t'affretta!" DONIZETTI: *Lucia di
Lammermoor:* "Ardon gl'incensi." VERDI: *Nabucco:* "Anch'io
dischiuso." DELIBES: *Lakmé:* "Où va la jeune Indoue." Oliviero
de Fabritiis conducting. Concert of 18 February 1952, RAI,
Turin. [Fonit Cetra 5.]

This concert, which included tenor Nicolai Filacuridi, is of
prime importance not only for the extraordinary singing during
its course, but because it contains Callas' first thoughts on *Macbeth* and *Lucia di Lammermoor.* The recitative to the *Macbeth*
aria is omitted, and Callas begins with the cavatina itself. The
tempo is several degrees slower than Verdi's *andantino,* but she
holds the music remarkably together, imparting a fuller measure
of the *grandioso* marked by Verdi than would be possible at a
more active tempo. Callas had a penchant for broad tempos, or
to use her own words, she effected "attitudes" within tempos,
be it a slow attitude in a fast speed or a fast attitude within a
slow speed. By her reckoning, she is striking, in the *Macbeth*
aria, a slow attitude within a slow speed. The important thing,
however, is that she brings the whole to fruition. Her performance might not be correct within the context of a staged *Macbeth,* but there is no denying its power in this concert setting.
  The cavatina is sung incisively and with lively contrasts drawn
in rhythmic values. The aria finishes on a dashing cadenza
upward to a fine top C, one of the few shafts of light in a
performance veiled in sullen, dark tone. There is a cut taken,
removing the small part of a servant, and de Fabritiis whips up
a rousing allegro for what recitative is retained before the cabaletta. Verdi has marked the cabaletta *allegro maestoso,* and de
Fabritiis gives us 40 percent *allegro* and 60 percent *maestoso.*

Within his framework, Callas makes a majestic statement of the music, with a sense of ever moving forward and upward. The cabaletta's second verse is cut, and the percentages of tempo are reversed by de Fabritiis in the coda, which concludes with Callas spiraling to a ringing high B.

The *Lucia* excerpt is another matter entirely. It is prodigious in its finish and understanding. The wonder of her performance is increased when one remembers that she had yet to sing the part on stage. It becomes self-evident not only that Callas was born with a rare feeling for the drama of *Lucia*, but also that it made a special appeal to her musical sensibilities. She sings this highly complex scene (or rather, two-thirds of it, as "Spargi d'amaro pianto" is omitted) with what is at once enormous freedom and enormous exactitude—a dramatic and rhythmic motion all her own, which is maintained unerringly throughout.

What Donizetti has fashioned in this famous, self-contained stretch of music is endlessly fascinating. He took the standard aria structure and opened and filled it in a unique manner. However, as with Leonora's Act IV scene in *Trovatore*, the uniqueness of the Mad Scene is disguised by a slashing cut of ninety-two bars, still the practice during Callas' years as Lucia. The scene breaks into four sections—recitative (actually, recitatives interspersed with small islands of concentrated ariettas), cavatina, scena (the ninety-two bars which not only confirm Lucia's madness, but place it in context with Enrico's remorse, a matter of vital dramatic importance), and cabaletta. Callas begins the first section in a hushed, disquieted fashion, as though Lucia's thoughts were being recalled from a deep recess of her mind. Again, tempos are of liberal dimensions, and Callas' singing is of a softness that is immediately in contrast to the heroics of the *Macbeth* excerpt. Until now her voice in live performance has never seemed more pliable an instrument of expression. Certain lines are more underplayed or undersung than will later be the case, but this only doubles the fascination of her Lucia, for these lighter stresses work as potently as do the later, darker ones.

Throughout the scene Callas adds many variants to the score—an *acciaccatura*, a turn, an extra trill, and *fermate*. Her use of the latter is particularly telling in combination with scale passages within the scene. With Callas, there was always a magical lift in a rising scale passage, for she usually capped scales with a *fermata* of a precise length, giving the line a crown and making the whole more shapely. She sings "Ardon gl'incensi" as a deep *larghetto,* yet her voice remains agile throughout and seems to float, or rather be buoyed up by the music. The heart of the cavatina beats in two phrases that Callas made entirely her own—"Alfin son tua," a moment of deep eloquence and release in her voice, and "Del ciel clemente," which defines the very spirit of rubato, that give-and-take that is a principal coloration of bel-canto singing. Just before the cadenza with flute (the linchpin of the scene), Callas introduces the only variant she would discard in later performances—the final group of sixteenth notes on "sarà" are taken up a sixth so that the phrase rises to C instead of F. The cadenza Callas employs is a fairly traditional one and remained a part of her Lucia until the second EMI recording of the work, where it was drastically modified. The cadenza can be found in the first of Luigi Ricci's indispensable two-volume set of variants and cadenzas published by Ricordi, *the* handbook of bel-canto ornamentation.

In the *Lucia* performances that exist, Callas rarely enjoyed a total success in this cadenza in the sense of achieving notes in balanced proportion; there are always at least one or two not in focus with the rest (the danger spot was usually the series of repeated staccato B-flats). Also, Callas' voice was never an entirely satisfying sound by itself without the texture and overtones of an orchestra highlighting and intermingling with it. While her timbre could be admired and valued on its own for richness and darkness of color, its beauty was heightened when set in the contrasting metal of an orchestra. Yet Callas brought a new, far-reaching dimension to the *Lucia* cadenza. With her, the momentum of the drama did not stop to wait out an irrelevant vocal display. Rather it continued to flow; Callas made the cadenza the apogee of what had gone before and used it to give meaning to what would follow.

Callas' voice has frequently been criticized as not one, but many. I would say admiringly that she had at least a dozen, or rather the ability to retool her sound to fit the character she was enacting at the moment. A striking example of this comes next, as she sets aside the dazed, maiden voice of Lucia for the stentorian, warrior sounds of Abigaille. The *Nabucco* aria remains essentially the same as when we encountered it in the 'Naples performance. What had been true for Callas then, continued so. The only difference is that here the cabaletta has been shorn.

This RAI concert closes on a curious note with the "Bell Song" from *Lakmé* sung in Italian (yet another souvenir from the days spent with de Hidalgo). While this performance is stronger in every sense than the later commercial recording for EMI, and while Callas fills its pages with a seemingly improvisatory quality, this aria was not the most congenial for her. It requires the sort of mindless dash and sparkle with which Callas had little sympathy. She lavishes more introspection and legato on the piece than is good for it, and it sounds earthbound. Callas takes the traditional variants and goes one better than most sopranos by including all the scale passages before the final bell imitation. She also manages a good top E at its conclusion, offsetting the memory of an acrid E-flat in the Lucia scene.

**ROSSINI:** *Armida.* With Francisco Albanese (Rinaldo), Alessandro Ziliani (Goffredo), Antonio Salvarezza (Eustazio), Mario Filippeschi (Gernando and Ubaldo), Gianni Raimondi (Carlo), Mario Frosini (Idraotte), Marco Stefanoni (Astarotte). Tullio Serafin conducting. Performance of 26 April 1952, Teatro Comunale, Florence. [Melodram 26024.]

The 1952 Maggio Musicale was devoted to Rossini in celebration of his one hundred and sixtieth birthday, and at Serafin's urging, Callas learned her only Rossini *opera seria* role. In fact, she conquered the fiendish title role of Armida in only five days. This was pushing even her remarkable memory too far; at the dress rehearsal (by tradition, the performance reviewed in Italy), she stepped from the elaborate litter in which Armida makes her first entrance, only to draw a blank, unable to remember her first line. She took the lapse in her stride, however, asked for her words and made her entrance again. The first performance, in contrast, finds her in absolute control, singing the part as though it were as practiced as Norma. Even with five leading tenors (a factor more than any that makes *Armida* a rarity in opera houses), this performance is a one-woman show. Ziliani, Albanese, and Filippeschi not only alter their lines to slough off Rossini's demands, but turn the more demanding challenges over to Callas.

Her entrance leads directly into an unusual quartet for soprano, two tenors, and bass. Its highly episodic nature (four contrasting sections) is fairly typical of the set pieces in *Armida*, one of Rossini's least unified operas. Callas wings through the music's perilous roulades, again with those slight pauses at the top of scales which gave such a comely shape to her singing. She even compounds the music's difficulties by a cadenza rising to C-sharp at the end of Armida's first statements (cuts are not too rampant, considering the repetitiveness of the musical ideas; there are only a dozen or so bars lost in this section, for example). An interesting footnote is supplied by the andante section of the quartet, a quote (it is too exact to have been accidental) of Giuseppe Giordani's familiar "Caro mio ben."

The duet of the first act, "Amor! possente nome," is of a lovely cast and allows Callas to put Rossini's flourishes to lyrical use. But the effect is endangered by Albanese's lack of vocal elegance. Though Filippeschi has no more flexibility to his singing than Albanese, at least he does not have to skirt his top C's in the first-act finale, and he alone of the quintet of tenors provides a glimmer of vocal excitement. Callas creates a particularly lovely moment in the finale with the phrase "Deh! se cara" and brings the whole to a rousing finish with a strong high C.

Act II contains another graceful duet for Rinaldo and Armida set against a plaintive cello solo. However, grace again proves not a part of Albanese's makeup, and the effect of the whole is marred despite Callas' lovely efforts. The role of Armida comes to a head with one of the most florid of all Rossini arias, a set of variations beginning "D'amor al dolce impero." Callas sings them at her bravura best, linking long strands of melismas into single phrases, some of which range over two octaves in length. Again she amplifies the music's difficulties with a downward arpeggio, a final cadenza, and three interpolated top D's. Serafin removes two dozen bars of mainly choral music, and unfortunately a large section of music in Act III is missing as is the second act finale following the ballet.

Armida dominates the opera's finale with an involved scene beginning "Se al mio crudel," in which her voice is by turn fiery ("Barbara tigre ircana") and melting ("Dove son io?"); the latter musical sentence is the deepest and most expressive length of music given Armida by Rossini. The whole is brought to a brilliant finish with a tremendous E-flat in alt from Callas.

BELLINI: *I puritani.* With Giuseppe di Stefano (Arturo), Piero Campolonghi (Riccardo), Roberto Silva (Giorgio), Ignacio Ruffino (Gualtiero), Tanis Lugo (Bruno), Rosa Rimoch (Enrichetta). Guido Picco conducting. Performance of 29 May 1952, Palacio de las Bellas Artes, Mexico City. [Melodram 26027.]

Though closely identified with *Puritani* through her masterful recording for EMI, Callas in fact sang nearly as many Isoldes as Elviras. With the exception of the recording and two performances of the opera still to come in Chicago in 1955, her time in the role had run its course by this Mexico City appearance. Despite her involved singing of "Qui la voce," Callas is less striking in *Puritani* than, for example, in *Lucia*, for Elvira holds only a limited potential for theater. Still, Callas reaffirmed the musical side of the part in more protean form than had been heard earlier in this century, when Elvira was the plaything of lighter, high-pivoting voices. This makes the chaotic Mexico performance all the more regrettable, for it gives us but a small frame of reference by which to understand what she later achieves in the EMI set.

The cast in Mexico, apart from Callas and Giuseppe di Stefano, is woefully inadequate, and Picco is less attuned to the necessities of this score than with *Norma* in 1950. The orchestral playing and choral singing are weak, and ensembles are frequently a shambles. Callas is first heard in the offstage prayer of the first scene, but makes her first real contribution in the polonaise of Scene 3. In between comes the duet with Roberto Silva, whose woolly, imprecise singing is almost matched by Callas' thick-voiced beginning. Attempts to lighten her sound seem to preoccupy her more than the music for the moment, though she does manage a flashing added top D at the end of the scene (cuts, not incidentally, are everywhere, with one hundred and thirty-eight bars removed from the duet alone).

By the polonaise, Callas' voice is more responsive and lighter, and there are innumerable and lovely details in her singing. Picco takes a further forty-two bars out of the polonaise, and all other parts but Enrichetta drop out; what is in effect a quartet becomes virtually a solo. Callas' voice becomes a radiant mirror of Elvira's happiness through the lustrous string of chromatics on the words "il vel" and a shining, upward scale to top D, exchanged for the last set of written downward arpeggios. The finale of the act contains Elvira's most eloquent music apart from "Qui la voce." It is prefaced by a series of mournful phrases for Elvira that permit the tension to wind down to the finale. But the effect is negated by Picco, who pushes Callas so forcefully that her singing of "Vieni al tempio" loses its potency, having been poorly prepared. Before the second rising climax of "Vieni al tempio," Callas interjects a languid turn and doubles the orchestral line, soaring from three top C's to a mighty D. The cadenza at the end of the finale's first section is sung heavily and half of it is exchanged for a sustained high C. The remainder of the finale is trimmed by half. As the chorus finishes, Callas sails above it on an E-flat in alt, but sings this tonic note on a nontonic chord with unsettling results.

Picco is more cooperative during "Qui la voce," supplying a spacious setting for Callas' singing. But here the aria is more studied than spontaneous, and it is by no means as finished as the Cetra recording, with its greater subtleties of rhythm and color. Just before the cavatina's end, she exchanges an upper B-flat for a G, a change that can be heard on many old recordings of the aria and that adds further lift to the line; it will be abandoned, however, for the EMI set. The bridge between the cavatina and the cabaletta is omitted, a fairly standard practice but one that removes the lines for Giorgio and Riccardo. Again Callas weeds out the cabaletta's second verse, goes for a concluding E-flat and just narrowly escapes losing hold of it.

The third-act duet between Elvira and Arturo is the first full stretch of singing between Callas and di Stefano in this performance. In so many ways, the lyricism of di Stefano was a handsome match for Callas, for his voice was just bright enough to mingle with her darker sound to create a .many-faceted blend. However, their singing here is rather routine, and "Vieni fra queste braccia" is taken down a semitone. The coup de grâce comes in the extensive cuts Picco elects to take in the finale, which robs the ending of shape and scope. Particularly strange is the reduction of "Credeasi, misera!" to alternating solos for Arturo and Elvira, adding sixteen solo bars to Callas' part.

VERDI: *La traviata.* With Giuseppe di Stefano (Alfredo), Piero Campolonghi (Germont), Cristina Trevi (Flora), Ignacio Ruffino (Dr. Grenvil), Gilberto Cerda (Douphol), Edna Patoni (Annina), Francisco Tortolero (Gastone), Alberto Herrera (D'Obigny). Umberto Mugnai conducting. Performance of 3 June 1952, Palacio de las Bellas Artes, Mexico City. [Melodram 26021.]

This performance of *Traviata* is in most respects a step backward from the previous year. Even the first act lacks the air of sickness which so successfully permeated the 1951 performance. The failure is due not only to the competitive atmosphere of the singing, but also to the routine backing offered by Mugnai, which produces outlines rather than substance, with ensembles deplorably inexact. Typical of the vocal sparring of this *Traviata* are the inclusion of a top E-flat by Callas in the third-act ensemble, and di Stefano's singing of a gruff high C during his offstage serenade in Act I. Ironically, considering the other uncertainties of the performance, Callas' exchanges in Act II with Campolonghi (a square singer) have perceptibly deepened in several instances, as has "Prendi, quest'è l'immagine" in the last act.

DONIZETTI: *Lucia di Lammermoor.* With Giuseppe di Stefano (Edgardo), Piero Campolonghi (Enrico), Roberto Silva (Raimondo), Carlo del Monte (Arturo), Anna Maria Feuss (Alisa), Francisco Tortolero (Normanno). Guido Picco conducting. Performances of 10 June and 14 June (excerpt only) 1952, Palacio de las Bellas Artes, Mexico City [10 June Myto 91340; 14 June Eklipse 33.]

Of all the roles that remained active in Callas' repertoire, it was Lucia with which there was the strongest initial identification and with which Callas wrought her greatest revolution in the operatic theater. After decades during which the role had been mishandled by light-voiced, self-indulgent sopranos, Callas returned an epic sense of its tragic stature by her penetrating psycho- and musico-analysis of the character. In her voice and care, Lucia emerged as at once credible and with a previously unsuspected human dimension.

If this seems in part contradicted by unformed moments in this, her first performance of the role, it is probably due to new, difficult stage business combined with an unimaginative, unresponsive conductor. But if compared with the RAI Mad Scene under de Fabritiis five months earlier and the EMI recording with Serafin eight months later, the Mexico Lucia is more properly seen as a dress rehearsal for what soon became one of the towering operatic experiences of its time.

Callas begins the recitative in the second scene of the opera rather heavily. While her voice remains dark in the cavatina, "Regnava nel silenzio," her initial forcefulness gradually melts into the deep legato with which she draws the aria. It was such sombre colors, plus the low notes of the part sung as written instead of transposed up an octave, that lent Callas' Lucia such a new aura. The cavatina remains shrouded throughout, brightening only with the series of trills that precede its cadenza, a set of scales combined with an arpeggio. The cabaletta that follows, "Quando rapito in estasi," is less fully formed than the cavatina at this time. Notes tend to protrude from what are otherwise shapely lines, and the final D is rather lame. Scale passages, however, are exquisitely arched. In the second verse, in accordance with custom, Callas initiates a few simple and generally scalewise embellishments to vary the basic melodic material. It was part of her taste and outlook to keep such additives to a minimum, always organic and suitable harmonically. Only occasionally did she misjudge an embellishment, and then she was quick to abandon it. She was extremely self-critical in this matter and guilty of none of the extremes which so many who have followed her have committed in the name of "authenticity."

Callas' voice lightens in the duet that follows, as though she had put the forebodings of "Regnava nel silenzio" to rest. There are many lovely moments in this section (together with a bit too

46

much bombast from di Stefano), from the flowing ardor of "Deh! ti placa" to the silky strand made of "Verrano a te." Unfortunately, Callas does not get too far with the latter, as Picco refuses to follow her. She and di Stefano turn the tables on him a short while later by jumping a bar, and the end of the duet threatens to become a free-for-all. There are cuts made during the duet, but it is a fairly thankless task to attempt to keep track of them or of those in other operas in the early nineteenth-century repertoire. While cuts frequently serve bel-canto drama by tightening its action and eliminating redundancies, they also often emasculate or misshape an aria or scene.

In the second act, Callas is once more stymied by the wooden singing of Campolonghi. Still there is enormous dignity to her molding of "Il pallor funesto," and no amount of commonplace vocalism from a baritone could detract from the pathos expressed by Callas in the poignant *larghetto* "Soffriva nel pianto." It is, and would always be, a moment to lock in memory. The *vivace* of the Enrico-Lucia duet is a rough race to the finish, Callas to a top D and Campolonghi to a G. As was the case in stage performances until the production of *Lucia* by Sarah Caldwell in 1968 for Beverly Sills, the ensuing scene between Lucia and Raimondo is omitted. For the sextet, Callas manages to create great arches of sound (she also takes its final D-flat up an octave) despite a tempo that is destructively too fast. From the sextet to the end of the act, the whole is unbalanced and raw. The end of the scene, however, is excitingly capped by a tremendous top D added by Callas.

The Mad Scene is less finely drawn than in the Rome concert. Lines are tighter, there is too much bite to some phrases, and the outburst at "Ohimè, sorge il tremendo fantasma" is sung with too great an emphasis. Throughout, there are also minute adjustments in embellishments, with hasty, blurred moments in several of the cadenzas ("Edgardo! Oh! me felice," particularly). The E-flat that closes the cavatina is short, weak, and misses being a D by a hair. In "Spargi d'amaro pianto" Callas recaptures the insinuating character that was such a feature of the Rome performance, both verses of the cabaletta are heard, and her embellishments are planned and executed in the same chaste spirit as those for "Quando rapito." The unforgettable exception is a two octave sweep on the word "velo" in the second verse. Seconds later, Callas miscalculates the effect she wants at the end of "Io pregherò per te," where the vocal line rises an octave. She begins securely enough, but on releasing the B-flat to move to high C-flat, too great a pressure is applied and the tone turns harsh and pushed. Twenty-four bars of the coda are removed, and a final E-flat is sustained longer than the first but is no more pleasant.

Luckily, the Mad Scene from the second broadcast of 14 June has surfaced, and in it, the majority of the problems heard the first night (particularly Callas' recalcitrant top) were resolved. The E-flats are now brilliant and come easily, and musically the scene is filled with more of the finish and play of light and shadows which distinguished the Rome performance but was curiously missing the night of the Mexico City premiere.

VERDI: *Rigoletto.* With Giuseppe di Stefano (Duke), Piero Campolonghi (Rigoletto), Ignacio Ruffino (Sparafucile), Maria Teresa Garcia (Maddalena), Gilberto Cerda (Monterone), Carlos Sagarminaga (Borsa), Alberto Herrera (Marullo), Anna Maria Feuss (Giovanna), Edna Patoni (Countess Ceprano), Francisco Alonso (Count Ceprano). Umberto Mugnai conducting. Performance of 17 June 1952, Palacio de las Bellas Artes, Mexico City. [Melodram 26023.]

It is a shame that Gilda did not remain an active part of Callas' repertoire, for she could have forced the musical world to rethink the part as completely as she made it reconsider Lucia. In place of the giddy performances usually given of Gilda, Callas creates an innocent of whom circumstance makes a woman. She fashions the part from the outset as an ingenue, not a soubrette, using to remarkable effect her "little girl" sound, a brightening of her timbre with a forward placement for vowels and little of the covered mixture of vowels and consonants found in her singing of heavier roles. When we encounter Gilda first in Act II (or Scene 2 of Act I reckoning by Verdi's original design), it is as an eager child-woman, curious about the world from which she has been sheltered. There is a shyness in Callas' singing that makes Gilda's questions and responses to Rigoletto sound eminently vulnerable. Gilda's reaction to Rigoletto's "Deh non parlare al misero," for example, takes on a new meaning after years of impersonal handling by less dramatically attuned sopranos. In particular, the agitated phrases "Oh quanto dolor!" (much like those for Violetta in "Un dì felice") become more than a chain of exacting notes; they become a reflection of Gilda's restlessness and make her submission to the Duke more credible.

Callas' singing here would have been even stronger had she not been trapped between the melodramatics of Campolonghi and the rigid conducting of Mugnai. The scene is begun at a very taut clip, with no internal relation between sections. An overall binding rhythm is essential (despite various tempo fluctuations) for the scene to function as an entity. Mugnai, unfortunately, lacks Callas' understanding of flexing rhythm to impart expression, and her unerring sense of measuring the impulse of music over a broad time span. Nor are the vocal intrusions of the prompter welcome; his insistence turns this string of duets into a series of trios.

The first of several mindless cuts occurs towards the end of "Deh non parlare" and more are to come. Also, in the linking music "Ah! veglia o donna," Callas goes a little too far in striking a virginal sound, and she comes precariously close to whining. But this is the only such miscalculation in the performance. Campolonghi barely manages two phrases of "Ah! veglia" before Mugnai slashes thirty-one bars, going straight to "Alcun v'è fuori" and upsetting the musical balance. With the return of "Ah! veglia," Callas strengthens the case for a substantial-voiced Gilda. Instead of the pecking that normally serves for "O quanto affetto!" there is instead a sweetness of phrase that suggests Gilda lost in reverie. The same mood permeates her singing in the duet with the Duke. At "Ah! de' miei vergini sogni" Callas takes the rising line lovingly to a delicate and sustained B-flat. This mood, however, is broken by di Stefano rushing the beat and Mugnai trailing after him. The tenor also falls prey to a distressing habit of holding top notes more with his jaw, so to speak, than supported on his breath. He was ever erratic in this regard. While high notes could be free and open, they could as easily be flat and constricted. This was a problem shared with others who built careers on a natural, beautiful sound which received skimpy training. At the end of "E il sol dell'anima," the center of the cadenza for the Duke and Gilda is removed—wisely, I think, for it is too purely vocal a device to work hand-in-hand with the drama. The cabaletta to the duet is badly cut, and both singers rush ahead of the conductor to scale the D-flat interpolation at the conclusion.

With "Caro nome" comes the reassurance that this aria can be more than a bird-call. With Callas, it is Gilda lost in a romantic cloud, musing over her first awakening to love. In the recitative, Callas establishes what will be an important feature of this scene, her special way with dotted-note figures. She leans strongly into the long note and uses the shorter note to move forward and connect to the next similar figure. The aria itself is sung with the sort of freedom found in the Rome *Lucia* excerpt, yet with the same strictures as well; in other words, freedom based on discipline. Though light in quality, Callas' voice coats the music with legato, and phrase is linked to phrase by luxuriant *portamenti* which reinforce the aria's dreamy quality. Her trills are magically measured and aptly convey the flurry of emotions within Gilda, as does her handling of the chain of two-note phrases in the second half of the aria. No note is slurred or lost. Callas alters the end of the cadenza to rise by a series of staccati to an E in alt and finishes on a long-held B. In the aria's coda, the reprise of "Caro nome" is more weighted than initially and in place of the written sustained trill, Callas unwisely rises by thirds, trilling upward over the stave to a secure but unpoetic E.

Act III is the turning point in her performance, the metamorphosis of Gilda into a woman. The opportunity for this dramatic change was always in the score, but Callas was the first to seize the possibility so fully. Her beginning in the act is shaky, however, for the omnipresent prompter is suddenly nowhere to be heard, and Callas forgets the words to the first phrase of "Tutte le feste." Her composure quickly returns, and from the second phrase onward the aria emerges with an expressive depth of Bellinian character. Callas uses her fullest voice in the aria's final page for a dashing conclusion. Yet we are not quite finished with the adolescent Gilda. She emerges again in the duet "Piangi, fanciulla" when the drama again focuses on father and daughter. Cal-

50

las elicits a full measure of tenderness from the phrase "Padre, in voi parla un angiol." Later, two-note phrases like quick catch-breaths (set to the same words) become moving supplications, and matchless in Callas' voice are the three musical sentences on "angiol." These sweep up in turn to B-flat, A-flat, and G-flat, with the summit notes held slightly, then left by a *diminuendo*. So affecting is Callas' realization of this moment that one is left waiting in vain for other singers to touch and move in the same manner. The climax of the scene, "Sì vendetta," is partially knocked out of focus by Campolonghi's wrongheaded dramatics. Callas, on the other hand, stays brilliantly on course. She is all-passion, all-woman here, and her voice thrusts excitingly forward. The ingenue has been changed by tragedy into the heroine with an unbridled strength of purpose. Callas is in such secure voice throughout this *Rigoletto* that the radiant E-flat added to the finale comes as no surprise but seems a natural consequence of the drama.

The quartet of the last act is troublesome, for di Stefano is continually under pitch in the ensemble's many B-flats (just before, he had twice ended "La donna è mobile"—for he had been forced to encore the aria—a semitone flat). Big streams of sound from Callas continue to emphasize the new Gilda, and the two-note leaps midway and onward in the quartet are glistening to their finish. This famous set piece ends with Callas on the traditional top D-flat, but with her trio of colleagues far off pitch. When Gilda returns later in the act, we are treated to a remarkable juxtaposition of the two principal dramatic elements which make up her portrayal. Outside Sparafucile's inn, her voice is dark and apprehensive (especially powerful is the series of low Bs on "Qual notte d'orrore"). Yet when she knocks on the door of the inn, it is with the voice of the girlish Gilda, thin and frightened ("Pietà d'un mendico"). Her voice then rages with the storm of the trio, but is pulled down by the inaccurate singing of the Sparafucile and Maddelena, and gradually the scene degenerates into a shambles. Callas is able to make a full realization of Gilda's death, however. Her first lines ("Chi mi chiama" and "Ah! padre mio") are pathetically void of life, and this ebbing of strength becomes more pronounced with "V'ho ingannato," especially the line "Ora muoio per lui" ("Now I die for him").

Here the tragedy of Gilda is summed up. So fragile is the coloring of her voice here and in "Lassù in cielo," and so elastic is the phrasing, that Callas takes us beyond singing, beyond theater to a plane of realism all too rarely encountered in opera.

PUCCINI: *Tosca.* With Giuseppe di Stefano (Mario), Piero Campolonghi (Scarpia), Gilberto Cerda (Angelotti), Francisco Alonso (Sacristan and Sciarrone), Carlos Sagarminaga (Spoletta), Luz Maria Faran (Shepherd). Guido Picco conducting. Performance of 1 July 1952, Palacio de las Bellas Artes, Mexico City. [Melodram 26028.]

This set marks Callas' first substantial effort at making Tosca a fully formed character. While her singing is in part still too overt, there is more control and gradation of color and emphasis. Perhaps this was due to her continuing excellent vocal condition and a minimum of the thickness of sound heard in previous *Toscas*. There is a new rapture to phrases, once past Tosca's initial suspicions; and at the point where she speaks of how the scent of the flowers of her villa "inebria il cor," her tone well insinuates what the evening ahead is to hold. Balancing such feminine touches are convincing flashes of temperament. Both stances supply different views of the complex female force that is Tosca. Callas gives us a key to Tosca's character when Mario embraces her, and she pulls away saying "Mi hai tutta spettinata" ("Look how you've mussed me"). The tinge of coyness in Callas' reproof betrays just how much Tosca is preening under her lover's attention while protesting against it. The dark side of the character is later strengthened in the first-act scene with Scarpia. There is bite and poison in Callas' voice as she is made to doubt Mario, but the hushed sound at "Dio mi perdona" shows how vulnerable Tosca is.

The theatricality of the second act is also further developed, partly because Picco has at last a musical situation sympathetic to him. He keeps the action alive and alert, while Callas makes dramatic point after point. Even "Vissi d'arte" functions better within the whole; less voice is used and she fusses little with the aria's sprawling lines. While there are adjustments still to be made, the grand line of the second act is now well plotted. The final-act duet is held up while di Stefano is forced to encore "E lucevan le stelle," but his dual singing of the aria is worth the delay. The duet itself is stirring, and Callas admirably handles the execution scene until "Presto su! Mario!" when she lets Tosca's realization of Mario's death come too suddenly, and the climax turns to frenzy. But this too will shortly be remedied.

PONCHIELLI: *La gioconda.* With Fedora Barbieri (Laura), Maria Amadini (La cieca), Gianni Poggi (Enzo), Paolo Silveri (Barnaba), Giulio Neri (Alvise), Piero Poldi (Zuane), Armando Benzi (Isepo). With the orchestra and chorus of RAI, Turin, Antonino Votto conducting. [Recorded September 1952 for Cetra, reissued as Fonit Cetra 9.]

Despite the obvious satisfaction the role of Gioconda gave Callas, and the great satisfaction her performances on disc give a listener, the role did not pay all that great a part in her career, beyond launching her in Italy and introducing her to Serafin. The Cetra set also introduced Callas' voice to America and was made following her second series of *Gioconda*s at the Verona Arena; her final performances on stage in the role came at La Scala the following December and January. The wonder of this recording is that it came a scant three months after the Mexico *Rigoletto.* One would never have dreamed that the voice that so perfectly conveyed the rapture and innocence of Gilda also housed the raging, tiger-like emotions of Gioconda.

*Gioconda* is a sturdy platform for full-blooded singing and demands a quintet of powerful principals. Here we are given only a duo—Callas and Fedora Barbieri. The men, in varying degrees, are inadequate to the vocal sparring needed to bring *Gioconda* to life. Dramatically, the figures who people *Gioconda* are straightforward, even cardboard. What conflict there is under the surface of the story is in Gioconda herself. But it is of the most obvious sort. Even her death means little; coming after Laura and Enzo have escaped, it lacks impetus. Callas' performance springs from the conflicting emotions of Gioconda, and through them, she leaves a major document in word-illumination. Mother-love is one of these emotions, and when it dominates a scene, Callas' singing is filled with repose and assurance. But when the emotion Gioconda feels for Enzo is threatened, the animal springs forth and is colored dark and vicious by Callas.

In the main, the first act establishes the stance of each principal. With Gioconda it is her filial devotion and her unrequited love for Enzo. The former comes into play in the opening and close of the act (and how drenched with feeling is Callas' singing against the concluding chorus), and the latter peaks in the magical moment "Enzo adorato." With Callas, however, this moment is less than magical, for "Ah! come t'amo" is more earthbound than ethereal (Milanov was the mistress of this phrase). The second act, however, brings Callas firmly into her own, first in the scene with Laura and then the one with Enzo. The Gioconda-Laura duet beginning "E un anatema" is one of the most high-voltage performances to be heard on disc. The hatred expressed by Callas' voice is frightening, and she underlines it with her searing chest voice, a seemingly bottomless sound of contralto opulence. Here, Ponchielli gives us the key to both Gioconda and Laura. While Laura loves Enzo "come il sogno celeste" ("like a celestial dream"), Gioconda loves him "siccome il leone" ("like a lion"). The range of "Ed io l'amo siccome il leone" in Callas' voice defines the possibilities of the human throat to convey passion at its most possessed. The scene burns with white heat, and Barbieri literally rises to the occasion on a final B-flat with Callas. Following the duet, Callas' voice is tamed by the discovery that Laura had saved the life of Gioconda's mother in Act I. The anguish of having her rival slip from her, or losing the upper hand, is made real through Callas' deeply etched singing of "Oh! madre mia! quanto mi costi." Exaltation soon floods her voice again, however, in the scene with Enzo (dully sung by Gianni Poggi). Unfortunately that unrestrained pleasure Callas took in a moment of triumph is stemmed by Votto's cutting for forty-two bars after the return of the chorus, a section that contains a crucial passage for Gioconda.

An edge remains in Callas' voice in the first scene of Act III when she comes to the rescue of Laura a second time. What is admirable here is the way the drama is kept alive by Callas and at the same time an exactness of pitch and rhythm is maintained against the offstage barcarolle. Another burst of self-pity comes at the end of the scene when Gioconda again calls on her mother. Especially effective is the fresh attack made on the climactic B-flat of the phrase, followed by a *diminuendo* which gives the line a fresh lift. The final scene of the act adds little to the drama of Gioconda, but vocally we find Callas soaring above all in the finale with marvelous ease, making what is a commonplace bit of ensemble sound somehow better.

The last act is exclusively Gioconda's with the other principals acting as props for her personal drama. In the mighty outburst, "Suicidio," Callas makes its words live as no other. The sharpness of her attack and the strength and clear direction of phrases give the whole a powerful, stark quality. Balancing the more violent emotions is a penetrating introspection, such as the hollow hush with which "ultima croce del mio cammin" ends. Then, too, there is the softness of "E un dì leggiadre volavan l'ore" and the fervor of "Domando al ciel." This latter section does not quite crest as it should, for the top B is wiry; but the potency of the drama is the thing in this aria, not individual notes. It is high drama when Callas brings her low voice into active play on "dentro l'avel," driving her chest tones deeply one into the other.

In many ways the scene that immediately follows "Suicidio" is as compelling as the aria itself. Here Gioconda, like Norma, must settle the fate of one she wishes dead. But there is little sense of nobility in Gioconda's allowing Laura to live, for too much self-pity is intermingled with clemency. Though one cannot muster total sympathy for Gioconda's plight, it is not difficult to respond to the vigor of Callas' cries of "Ah! Enzo! pietà!" The next section, "Ridarti il sol," is thin musically, but Callas keeps the drama alive by the concentration of her singing, and her voice later flashes out at Enzo with the sort of cutting scorn that so transfigured her Norma, as it would her Medea. With Laura's awakening, all bite is absent from Callas' singing and in its place comes a half-voiced resignation. Memorable in this section is "A te questo rosario," in which Callas' voice has rarely been more beautiful in tone or her singing finished in line. In the final scene, Callas transforms the flippant "Vo' farmi più gaia" from an irrelevancy into an expression of unsuspected veracity. She finishes the opera with a final return to the fiery side of Gioconda, committing suicide—"Volesti il mio corpo, demon maledetto"—with a gripping lunge to an A-flat on the last syllables of "maledetto.

**BELLINI:** *Norma.* With Mirto Picchi (Pollione), Ebe Stignani (Adalgisa), Giacomo Vaghi (Oroveso), Joan Sutherland (Clotilde), Paul Asciak (Flavio). Vittorio Gui conducting. Performance of 18 November 1952, Royal Opera House, Covent Garden, London. [Legato 130.]

This performance captures Callas' Norma before one of her most loyal and understanding publics. It also contains a singer at the outset of her career who was to become the most prominent figure in the bel-canto repertoire after Callas—Joan Sutherland. Later, Sutherland would also appear as the Priestess in *Aida* with Callas.

The revival of *Norma* at Covent Garden is justly celebrated, for Callas was in top vocal form apart from the opening scene. Nerves always exacted a toll in Act I, especially in the cavatina. Callas tended to become tense and rush the repeated A's of "Casta diva," and then sharpen the B-flat which caps the phrase. This problem is evident during her London debut, and the first verse of the aria, despite some exquisite shaping of the *fioriture*, does not flow with the evenness of the second. However, the recitative before it is extraordinary in its ring of importance. Callas seems to weigh and then to savor the color and intent of each word. There is still some unevenness in the pacing of the cabaletta, and she jumps the final high C half a beat early.

Callas' voice and her grasp of the part, however, unite to wondrous effect in the second act. There is a spring to phrases and numerous limpid colorations. Her Adalgisa is the veteran mezzo-soprano Ebe Stignani, who had sung opposite Gina Cigna in the first complete recording of *Norma* in 1937. She was nearing the end of her career here, and while she lacks as wide a range of coloration as Callas, Adalgisa is, after all, a much less complex figure. Stignani, on the other hand, brings a superb concentration of voice, impetus, and style to her role, which compensates in many ways for many things (including the substitution of an A for a high C in the second-act duet). Also, the brightness of her timbre mixes wonderfully well with Callas' darker, more covered quality. The polonaise after the brace of duets is brilliantly etched by Callas, and she sprints easily to its two high C's. Her voice continues to flash in the trio and to stab out at Pollione in the finale. She once more goes for a D in alt at the end of the act, and it proves a chance well taken.

In so many instances in this performance, Gui provides Callas with most understanding help. There are few aspects to his conducting which seem open to question; the whole is unforced and he is in admirable sympathy with his singers. Nowhere is this more evident than in the third act where Callas continues to deepen her most personal response to the act's opening scene. The duets (both sung down a tone) are splendid in shape, and for the first time we experience from Callas the sense of bitter-sweetness which so transfigured Norma's "Ah! perchè, perchè" in "Mira, o Norma," especially in context with Stignani's stentorian opening statement. Their voices again mingle beautifully, and they are exemplary in phrasing and accuracy. The scene is brought to a thundering head as Stignani sails (with Callas) to a final high B-flat of magnificent proportions.

In the recitatives of the fourth act there is a return to the weighty prominence with which Callas sang those of the first act. Her measured stride is broken only with the words "Che ascolto?" The disquiet of her utterance tells us, in advance of the chorus, that it is Pollione who has been captured. From "In mia man" through the finale, Norma's lines, sentiments, and attitudes are refined since the Mexico City performance two years earlier. This time Callas, with Gui's aid, has an opportunity to enter fully into the pathos of the finales. She employs more tone than is needed, but even while generous it is never less than richly expressive. Mirto Picchi is a welcome improvement over Baum and will be even more valued when Filippeschi is encountered in the first EMI recording.

**VERDI:** *Macbeth.* With Enzo Mascherini (Macbeth), Italo Tajo (Banquo), Gino Penno (Macduff), Luciano della Pergola (Malcolm), Angela Vercelli (Lady-in-waiting), Attilio Barbesi (Servant), Mario

Tommasini (Murderer), Ivo Vinco (Herald), Dario Caselli (Doctor). Victor de Sabata conducting. Performance of 7 December 1952, Teatro alla Scala, Milan. [EMI 64946.]

This first of Callas' many extant broadcasts from La Scala is also the first of her only series of stage appearances as Verdi's darkest heroine. Lady Macbeth was her fourth role with the company (if guest appearances as Aida in 1950 are discounted). Preceding *Macbeth* had been *I vespri siciliani* (her official Scala debut), *Norma* and her only Mozartean role, Constanze in *Die Entführung aus dem Serail*.

Callas fills Lady Macbeth's music with prodigious potency and atmosphere. Her voice creates scenery and action for the mind's theater, and the inflections and tints here are luminous even for her. She continues in the firm, true voice that was such a feature of the Covent Garden *Norma*, from a shining top of bronze, rather than steel, down evenly to easy, imposing low notes. Her performance is seconded at every point but one (and that, alas, a major one) by a giant of twentieth-century conducting, Victor de Sabata, a master all too sparsely represented on records. He presents the opera almost as a brooding, massive symphonic poem, and happily absent are many of the disfiguring cuts that too frequently mar the work. There are excisions, to be sure, but in every case they are intelligent and strengthen the drama.

It is ironic that a performance that will unfold so profoundly from Callas begins in a mannered way with her leaden reading of Macbeth's communiqué. Her speaking here is more artificial than in the Mexico *Traviata*, with stilted emphasis given certain words such as "sir" and "serto." Her use of the spoken word seems doubly false when contrasted with the supercharged singing of the first aria's recitative, "Ambizioso spirto." Callas dashes propulsively through the recitative, making it climax on an ascent to, and a dazzling descent from, a top C. De Sabata's tempo for "Vieni! t'affretta!" is as right as de Fabritiis' pace (at the February Rome concert) was questionable. With de Sabata lines move, yet provide ample room for detail. In the cabaletta, de Sabata's emphasis is on *allegro* rather than *maestoso*, and this shift in stress is beneficial to Callas' performance. With his sympathetic pacing, she unfurls striking new colors for "sangue" and the phrase "Tu, notte, ne avvolgi"; both become high points within the whole.

"Vieni! t'affretta!" is the first of four arias which form the backbone of the role of Lady Macbeth. It is traditional in form, finds a parallel in Abigaille's "Anch'io dischiuso," and again places Verdi in Donizetti's debt. The second aria, "La luce langue" from the second act, is free and mixes *arioso* stretches with punctuating recitative. Then there is the almost square "Brindisi," which Verdi makes function in anything but square terms, and finally the unearthly Sleepwalking Scene. If Verdi used conventional terms in "Vieni! t'affretta!" as an exposition of Lady Macbeth's strength, the Sleepwalking Scene is unconventional in structure so as to show the disintegration of that strength. The wonder of Callas' performances is the way she recognized, either consciously or unconsciously, the function of these set pieces in deepening the character and adjusted her voice accordingly.

In her first scene with Macbeth, sung with a curious mixture of persuasion and carelessness by Enzo Mascherini, Callas establishes her dominance over Macbeth and seals Duncan's fate with her insinuating delivery of "E non intendi?" She expands the character of Lady Macbeth in the duet following the king's arrival by taking us behind the Lady's forceful outer mask to her fears: "Ch'ei fosse di letarga uscito pria del colpo mortal" ("What if he should have awakened before the fatal blow"), a question uttered in hushed tones. Her voice rises only when Macbeth needs the courage of his wife's will: "Sei vano, o Macbetto," sung with open vibratoless sounds each time the line dips down to F. After the Lady has replaced the dagger in the murder chamber, Callas' voice is filled with determination, and the sharpness of attack made on "Vien!" in the last section of the scene leaves no doubt as to who is the drama's catalyst. "Vien!" is given an even more potent meaning at the end of the duet when it is repeated four times; on each repeat Callas drains more tone and pitch from her voice, as if Lady Macbeth is losing patience with her husband's vacillations. Most of the *a cappella* ensemble of the first-act finale was lost in transmission, but the rest of the act finds Callas vocally dominant, still the principal force behind the action. She reinforces this with a vigorous interpolated D-flat at the very end of the scene.

The first part of Act II, after a brief exchange with Macbeth, belongs to Lady Macbeth and to Callas. De Sabata provides a concentrated air of mystery and evil for the aria "La luce langue," with all manner of night creatures creeping out of the orchestra pit. Callas begins with a thread of voice as though the aria were emanating from the privacy of her inner thoughts. The division Callas makes throughout the opera between Lady Macbeth's private and public thoughts is a factor that helps to lift her characterization to its persuasive heights. Such a contrast comes into play in the middle of "La luce langue," when Lady Macbeth whispers to herself "Nuovo delitto!" ("Another crime") and then answers the question out loud: "E necessario!" This is followed by a minor master-stroke on Verdi's part—"Ai trapassati regnar non cale," an eight-bar chorale put to sinister use by Callas. The final section of the aria is mettlesome in its resolve, and Callas gives a full voicing to the imminent triumph of Lady Macbeth's plot. This brief scene is a marvel in its distillation of form, for within a tight musical space are condensed the basic ingredients of recitative, cavatina, and cabaletta, all in an entirely personal manner. That "La luce langue" should exist side by side with the more conventional "Vieni! t'affretta!" defines more accurately than words Verdi's need to bend form to a unique theatrical vision.

Another penetrating example of his individuality comes in the final scene of Act II, Lady Macbeth's "Drinking Song." The use Verdi makes of a forthright, martial tune foreshadows the striking use to which he will put a similar idea forty years later in the "Brindisi" of *Otello*. The *Macbeth* "Brindisi" is presented first in sharp design, and Callas sings it with appropriate incisiveness and her usual care for detail. However, during Macbeth's asides with Banquo's assassin, it becomes an accompanying figure, thin in texture and progressively more ambiguous in harmony. In the course of the first statement, de Sabata sagely eliminates the second verse, leaving it somewhat fragmented so that its return will hit with greater verisimilitude. When the aria reappears after Macbeth's first hallucination, Callas pointedly sings it in a heavier, more covered manner, as though trying by force of her will to gloss over Macbeth's outburst and command a reversion to gaiety at the banquet. When she addresses Macbeth between the two sections of the aria ("Voi siete demente!") it is with a cool calmness that turns to bite and disdain in the finale as though she no longer cared what the onlookers might think ("Spirto imbelle!").

De Sabata elects to end the finale of Act III with the duet between Macbeth and his Lady rather than with the witches' scene. While this duet is not strong in terms of Lady Macbeth's drama, it does restate one final time the joint resolve of husband and wife. Especially resolute are her cries of "Menzogna!"—a chilling refusal to accept Macbeth's predicted downfall.

It is in Lady Macbeth's final scene that I must differ with de Sabata. There is no obvious reason why so complete a man of the theater should have wanted a tempo for the Sleepwalking Scene that is so dramatically divisive. It is too nervous in motion and too lightly articulated by the strings to bolster the terror within Lady Macbeth. By constructing the scene in several opposing moods, Verdi makes it clear that the Lady's conscience-stricken state is causing a constant shifting of the mind. Callas attempts to draw the necessary shroud of mental uncertainty over the scene by striking a slow "attitude" within the confines imposed by de Sabata, and actually manages to work out the music's dramatic necessities in a number of important places: "Una, due," "Non osi entrar?" and "Di sangue umano." But equally prime moments are negated by the undertow of de Sabata's conducting, particularly in the crucial final quarter of the scene: "A letto, a letto," "Batte alcuno!" Callas does achieve a true *fil di voce* on the aria's last phrase, which ascends to D-flat in alt, and there is finally a hint of the eerie in the postlude to the aria. But a totality has not been achieved. For this we must wait for the EMI studio recording of the scene; there a proper dramatic liaison was forged.

# *1953* ∽

MOZART: *Don Giovanni:* "Non mi dir." With the orchestra of the Maggio Musicale Fiorentino, Tullio Serafin conducting. [Recorded in Florence, January 1953, for EMI, reissued as 54437.]

It was not until 1985 that this test recording for EMI was first made public in France as part of an anthology of Mozart operatic recordings. This version of the aria, minus the recitative, is quicker in pacing and attitude than the commercial version made with Nicola Rescigno in 1963. Although Callas is more stable vocally a decade earlier, her phrasing is less magical and the mood of the aria is not as spellbinding. This first "Non mi dir" is more like a sketch than a finished drawing.

DONIZETTI: *Lucia di Lammermoor.* With Giuseppe di Stefano (Edgardo), Tito Gobbi (Enrico), Raffaele Arie (Raimondo), Valiano Natali (Arturo), Anna Maria Canali (Alisa), Gino Sarri (Normanno). With the orchestra and chorus of the Maggio Musicale Fiorentino, Tullio Serafin conducting. [Recorded in Florence, February 1953, for EMI, reissued as 69980.]

There are a number of significant nonmusical aspects to this recording of *Lucia di Lammermoor* by Callas. It marked her formal debut on the EMI label and her first performance of *Lucia* with Serafin. It was also her first collaboration on disc with Tito Gobbi (one of the few singers whose intelligence proved consistently a match for Callas') and Giuseppe di Stefano.

Walter Legge, then artist and repertory director of EMI's Columbia label, had been influential in spiriting Callas from the provincial Cetra label into the international combine that is EMI. It is significant that she made the switch at a crucial moment in the record industry—it was heading full steam into the era of the long-playing record and growing up in terms of promotion and packaging.

Callas not only added vitally to the emergence of the LP as a fully developed artistic medium (as did Tebaldi on the Decca-London label), but was a major contributor to its fortunes. Largely due to Legge's faith and initial commitment, she produced from two to four major operatic sets a year in her prime years of 1953-1960. Virtually all her records from this period were made under Legge's supervision as recording director. Apart from the Cetra *Traviata* and the 1957 recording of *Medea* for Ricordi, Callas' commercial sets beginning with *Lucia* were under EMI's aegis until 1972, when she entered Philips' recording studios in London for a duet album with di Stefano.

Though nearly forty years have passed since this *Lucia* was recorded, and though numerous other versions have followed (including a second by Callas), it remains the most satisfying performance of the work on commercial discs and is now a glory of the CD era as well. The word "perfect" is too facile and imprecise a description of Callas' performance; yet it is the word that springs first to mind because of her unerring vocal poise and the splendid balance maintained throughout between the opera's musical and theatrical elements. With Serafin's noble support, the trials and probings of the Mexico *Lucia* find a proper direction. Though Callas will turn her responses more inward in the 1959 remake, it will hold no greater truths nor delve deeper than here. With one mind, Callas and Serafin create an emotional canvas of grave and compelling splendor.

Her voice is lighter at the outset than in Mexico (darker colors and their import are saved for the Mad Scene), and a newfound suavity for "Quando rapito" (largely thanks to Serafin's agreeable walking tempo) makes for a greater unity between the two halves of the scene. Throughout one is never aware of single notes or groups of notes; the impression is rather of a seamless flow of expression. Two of the loveliest streams of sound come in the first-act duet—the soft gait of "Deh! ti placa" (touching in Mexico but infinitely moving here) and "Verrano a te." Despite a pronounced tightness in his top voice and a nonchalant way with rhythm, di Stefano's Edgardo is wonderfully virile and intensifies the feminine character of Callas' Lucia. Furthermore, Gobbi's presence ensures uncommon strength for the second-act duet and provides a marvelous foil for the poignancy of Callas' singing there.

The zenith of the recording is the Mad Scene. It is singularly rich in tempo and ripe in meaning. Its principal qualities are essentially those that distinguished her first singing of this music in Rome, yet to a heightened degree. The opening pages are couched in that dazed, somnolent sound Callas often employed in setting an atmosphere (it can be heard in *Puritani* and more so in *Sonnambula*). Again, she sings through the center of notes, fusing them together with her molten legato. This time the section "Ohimè, sorge il tremendo fantasma" is brought significantly into line with the whole as Callas implies its terror rather than stating it emphatically. The slow buildup of tension in the first half of the scene finds a release in the phrase "Alfin son tua," sung with agonizing beauty and as virtually a summation of the fantasy within Lucia's mind. Apart from a pair of notes just left of center, the cadenza is breathtaking in its sweep, and Serafin strikes a wonderfully "vocal" tempo for the cabaletta, one that allows Callas ideal freedom of movement.

VERDI: *Il trovatore*. With Ebe Stignani (Azucena), Gino Penno (Manrico), Carlo Tagliabue (di Luna), Giuseppe Modesti (Ferrando), Ebe Ticozzi (Inez), Mariano Caruso (Ruiz), Carlo Forti (Gypsy), Angelo Mercuriali (Messenger). Antonino Votto conducting. Performance of 23 February 1953, Teatro alla Scala, Milan. [Myto 90213.]

For Callas, the distinguishing quality of this *Trovatore* is her handling of Leonora's two arias. In each, lines are slimmer, more elegant, and more contained. This concentration of approach produces Callas' most suave performance of either to date. In "Tacea la notte" we find the cadenza at the cavatina's end once more altered, but for the first time the cabaletta is concluded as written. The recitatives to "D'amor sull'ali rosee" are uneven, but the aria itself is a marvel of long-lined color, chastely applied. Verdi's written D-flat is now gone, and the aria concludes more in the mood in which it began. The "Miserere" fails in its effectiveness because of Votto's over-driving, clipped tempo, and once more the cabaletta is cut. However, in this performance we do hear Callas in the duettino before "Di quella pira." Of her colleagues, only Stignani commands attention; Penno almost makes one recall Baum wistfully.

BELLINI: *I puritani.* With Giuseppe di Stefano (Arturo), Rolando Panerai (Riccardo), Nicola Rossi-Lemeni (Giorgio), Carlo Forti (Gualtiero), Angelo Mercuriali (Bruno), Aurora Cattelani (Enrichetta). With the orchestra and chorus of Teatro alla Scala, Tullio Serafin conducting. [Recorded in Milan, 24-30 March 1953, for EMI, reissued as 47308.]

Though recorded over a month after *Lucia,* this *Puritani* reached America two months earlier. It was not only the first recording of the opera, but it was the first operatic set issued on EMI's then fledgling Angel label. It was also the first in a series of remarkable albums built around the combination of Callas with the musical forces of La Scala. That her Elvira here rises phoenix-like out of the ruins of the Mexico City *Puritani* is due to a further artistic fusion with Serafin (this was their first *Puritani* together since the startling Venice performances of 1949, which Callas sang immediately following four *Walküre* Brünnhildes). Just as Serafin provided her with an opportunity to add strength and profile to her Lucia, so he does with her Elvira. He also restores a good deal of music often thought expendable, in particular large hunks of the first-act duet between Elvira and Giorgio; given the noble cantabile of Nicola Rossi-Lemeni's performance, this duet adds up to far more of an expressive unit within the whole than was possible in Mexico.

Yet this duet, the *polacca,* and the finale of the act again remind one of how little dramatic flesh there is on Elvira's bones. Of course, there are innumerable opportunities for expression and color (and Callas seizes each), but there is little opportunity to apply these to a bigger dramatic end, as is possible in *Lucia.* In

*Puritani* each set piece dictates its expressive needs on an individual basis; the overall emphasis remains, as a result, more vocal than anything else. Callas, however, manages to reflect a variety of emotional states while still giving pure vocal pleasure (from the exquisite chromatic scales of the *polacca* through the stretching phrases of "Vieni al tempio"), and this forms comment enough on what she has fashioned within this limited role. The only uncomfortable moment in the course of the recording is her doubling of the orchestral line (rising to high D) towards the end of "Vieni al tempio." Here her voice turns rebellious and wry. On the other hand, it remains rock-solid in "Qui la voce" (capped by a superb E-flat) and is brighter and more forward in placement than in the Cetra recording. My continued affection for the earlier version amounts to a personal preference for her darker tints rather than a value judgment, for both versions are prodigiously molded and infinitely touching. The episodic duet in Act III for Elvira and Arturo is vouchsafed uncommon unity by Serafin, and while di Stefano is more musically courteous than in Mexico, his voice is still dry and tight above the stave ("Vieni fra queste braccia" is again taken down a semitone). Serafin, unlike Picco in Mexico City, gives us all of "Credeasi, misera!" Again Callas poaches eight bars of di Stefano's music in the second verse, "Ella è tremante." She adapts words from earlier in the ensemble ("Se fui si barbara") for this bit of lagniappe of Elvira's.

CHERUBINI: *Medea.* With Carlos Guichandut (Jason), Gabriella Tucci (Glauce), Mario Petri (Creon), Fedora Barbieri (Neris), Mario Frosini (Captain), Liliana Poli and Maria Andreassi (Handmaidens). Vittorio Gui conducting. Performance of 7 May 1953, Maggio Musicale Fiorentino. [Hunt 516.]

As *Medea* had not been performed in Italy since 1909, this Maggio Musicale resurrection by Callas and Vittorio Gui meant that both were virtually re-creating the opera from scratch. Gui takes a broader, more weighted approach to the score than would later Leonard Bernstein or Thomas Schippers at La Scala, or Nicola Rescigno in Dallas and London, all of whom tended to go for the jugular. Gui is closest in his view of the score to Tullio Serafin, who recorded the part with Callas but never performed it in the theater.

Gui's way makes a sense of its own, given the thick girth of Callas' voice in 1953 and the heroics she lavishes on this dark drama. Important, too, is Gui's edition, which preserves more of the opera's music than the later, tighter and more swiftly moving versions by Bernstein and Rescigno. This is the only time, for example, where Callas sings Medea's last-act *scena* in its entirety. There are other sections of the score as well that can be heard with Callas' voice only in this recording. A full appraisal of Callas' portrayal must wait, however, for her Scala performances with Bernstein.

VERDI: *Aida.* With Kurt Baum (Radames), Jess Walters (Amonasro), Giulietta Simionato (Amneris), Giulio Neri (Ramfis), Michael Langdon (King), Hector Thomas (Messenger), Joan Sutherland (Priestess). Sir John Barbirolli conducting. Performance of 10 June 1953, Royal Opera House, Covent Garden, London. [Legato 187.]

For a long while it was thought that only Act III of this London *Aida* was broadcast, but a tape of the entire opera surfaced in 1994. With the exception of Jess Walters as Amonasro and Giulio Neri as Ramfis, the principals are the same as those in the 1950 broadcast of the opera from Mexico City. The major difference in these two performances, however, is the vivid, alive and polished playing of the Covent Garden orchestra under Sir John Barbirolli. Having an "Aida" by Sir John is almost of equal importance to discovering an unknown Callas performance.

While there are no rocketing top E-flats launched by Callas in the Triumphal Scene, she is generally in secure, exciting voice throughout the performance. Words are thrillingly underlined, top notes are wonderfully free, and though "O patria mia" is still more of an exterior statement than not, it is nonetheless an imposing one. Simionato is a vocal and dramatic match for Callas and sometimes she even threatens to eclipse her in Act II. Baum, however, is in unstable voice and has recurrent pitch problems.

MASCAGNI: *Cavalleria rusticana.* With Giuseppe di Stefano (Turiddu), Rolando Panerai (Alfio), Anna Maria Canali (Lola), Ebe Ticozzi (Mama Lucia). With the orchestra and chorus of Teatro alla Scala, Tullio Serafin conducting. [Recorded in Milan, 3-4 August 1953, for EMI, reissued as 49781.]

This set is Callas' only performance of *Cavalleria* outside student and apprentice days in Athens. Santuzza was her very first role, and while there are no special opportunities for musical or dramatic depth (Santuzza is of a single, though powerful, dimension), we would have missed much in the overall picture of Callas' art without this recording. Her singing here is as much a model for verismo as it is elsewhere for bel canto. For there is taste and intelligence without a loss of earthiness or passion.

Callas colors Santuzza's first lines with a sadness that turns quickly to anguish; only after the Easter service is this Santuzza's composure restored. "Voi lo sapete" is begun very simply, in a conversational way, and apart from the aria's two big outbursts ("l'amai" and "io piango") the whole is kept in check and unencumbered by an undue weight of expression. Later, Santuzza's responses in the duet with Turiddu (superbly sung by di Stefano) are icy, but melt with "Battimi, insultami," where the softness of her expression betrays how strong Santuzza's love remains even when abandoned. Bitterness enters Callas' voice during Lola's interruption "Gli dicevo che oggi è Pasqua," but again warmth returns and suffuses "No, no Turiddu, rimani ancora." Because it contains the strongest elements of contrast (pity-betrayal-remorse), Callas' finest moment comes in the duet with Alfio. Particularly moving is her molding of the impassioned phrase "Turiddu mi tolse." Of Callas' EMI sessions prior to Paris, this is the only set not recorded under the guidance of Legge.

PUCCINI: *Tosca.* With Giuseppe di Stefano (Mario), Tito Gobbi

(Scarpia), Franco Calabrese (Angelotti), Melchiorre Luise (Sacristan), Angelo Mercuriali (Spoletta), Dario Caselli (Sciarrone), Alvaro Cordova (Shepherd). With the orchestra and chorus of Teatro alla Scala, Victor de Sabata conducting. [Recorded in Milan, 10-21 August 1953, for EMI, reissued as 47175.]

In the special world of opera on disc, there are a handful of sets that by general consent are ideal. One is Beecham's recording of *Die Zauberflöte*, another is Solti's *Das Rheingold*. In this elite company belongs de Sabata's *Tosca*. It is a complete theatrical experience, and within the architectural mastery of de Sabata's performance, Callas paints the Tosca that previously she has only sketched. All the dramatic ingredients—jealousy, passion, fury—are balanced, and colored with a plentitude of expression. Though she is supreme in realizing the role's full-blooded emotions with realism and taste, it is the small brush strokes of detail that make the portrait so finished.

Where as Gilda she unfolded the woman in the child, here we have childish aspects within a proud woman. Her voice is dark but not unduly covered, full but not thick; through it, words glow and live. It is the 1952 Mexico performance polished and made compelling. As Tosca, Callas is fearful of her love in the scenes with Mario and protective of that love when in conflict with Scarpia. The charm of di Stefano makes the first as real as the lust of Gobbi makes the latter credible.

This was Callas' first Tosca to the Scarpia of Gobbi, a brief but celebrated operatic association. Though they had yet to perform their respective roles on stage together (that would wait eleven years until London in 1964, although they joined for Act II during the Paris Opera Gala of 1958), an innate interaction existed between the two from the start. One plays to the other, draws strength from the other, and they exchange dramatic blows much like a pair of champions in a title bout. Actually, given de Sabata's mesmerizing influence, the match is a three-sided one. But opera being an arena that makes its own rules, the winner is none of the three but a fourth—Puccini.

**VERDI:** *La traviata.* With Francisco Albanese (Alfredo), Ugo

Savarese (Germont), Ede Marietti Gandolfo (Flora), Alberto Albertini (Douphol), Mario Zorgniotti (Dr. Grenvil and D'Obigny), Ines Marietti (Annina), Mariano Caruso (Gastone), Tommaso Soley (Giuseppe). With the orchestra and chorus of RAI, Turin, Gabriele Santini conducting. [Recorded September 1953, for Cetra, reissued as Fonit Cetra 2.]

This *Traviata* was Callas' last Cetra recording, though both *Manon Lescaut* and *Mefistofele* with her were planned by the Italian firm. But by this point, however, Callas was firmly allied with EMI, and though her contract allowed her to make a certain number of sets for other labels, she exercised that option only for the Ricordi *Medea*. (The date of this *Traviata* is usually given as 1952, but Callas herself emphatically placed it a year later.)

As Callas never remade *Traviata*, the Cetra set is the only commercial recording of one of her principal roles. (EMI's *Traviata* a few years later excluded Callas because of a technicality in her Cetra contract that restricted her from re-recording the opera within a given period of years; Serafin conducted the set with Antonietta Stella, and this led to a temporary break between him and Callas).

The Cetra *Traviata* is, on the whole, a tepid affair: Santini's conducting lacks impetus, and Callas' colleagues range from routine to a good deal less. Though her Violetta is beautifully sung, it never delves very deeply below the surface of the part here with the exception of a handful of moments, which, however touching, do not add up to a finished portrayal. The pallor of sickness, which pervaded the first act of the 1951 Mexico City *Traviata*, is completely missing; in its place, Callas uses her "little girl" voice, which suggests frailty but does not impart a sense of Violetta's impending tragedy.

The first glint of character comes in "Ah! fors'è lui," which is expressed with a haunting hush and then (in "A quell'amor") a rush of wonderment. The cavatina's cadenza is somewhat altered from the Mexico performances, and Callas again chooses an upward ending. The recitatives before "Sempre libera" are curiously empty (especially "Sola, abbandonata") and more thrust is needed for the cabaletta than Callas employs. The two-note phrases toward the end of the cabaletta are magical, but the top Cs have a disturbing tightness beneath their bright veneer; the same is true of the final E-flat in alt.

What with Santini's pale pacing of the second-act duet and Ugo Savarese's singing of Germont with a sameness that cancels out his efforts, a none too fertile ground is laid for Callas to dig into the drama of the scene. She does, however, trim her voice down from the lavish outpouring of the Mexico performances, but with little of the cohesion one might expect as a result. Instead, quite a few sections ("Così alla misera," for example) are sung inexplicably straight, and "Dite alla giovine," while wreathed in melting sound, goes far but not quite far enough. "Amami, Alfredo," on the other hand, is a living moment, filled with urgency and meaning.

Where her voice was reduced in Act II, it is expanded in the next scene, and Violetta's rising cry of anguish (first heard as "Ah perchè venni") is much too heavy as a consequence. Santini's tempo for the finale of the act and throughout most of the last act becomes a millstone about this *Traviata*'s neck; especially deadly is his direction of "Addio del passato" and "Parigi, o cara." The former, though it drags from phrase to phrase, has at least the distinction of containing Callas' most plausible reading of Germont's letter to date. Her most expressive achievements in the last act are "Ah! Gran Dio! Morir sì giovine" and "Prendi, quest'è l'immagine."

**BELLINI:** *Norma.* With Franco Corelli (Pollione), Elena Nicolai (Adalgisa), Boris Christoff (Oroveso), Bruna Ronchini (Clotilde), Raimondo Botteghelli (Flavio). Antonino Votto conducting. Performance of 19 November 1953, Teatro Giuseppe Verdi, Trieste. [Melodram 26031.]

This is a large-scale performance by Callas. Her voice throughout is massive and freewheeling, and where this often results in great heroic statements, it also bruises many phrases, particularly in the last two acts. Callas does sing with an evenness throughout all registers which matches the broadness of her mood on this occasion. I regret that this is one of only three instances of

71

Christoff juxtaposed with Callas, and I also regret (in a different sense) the efforts of Votto, again the *routinier*.

CHERUBINI: *Medea.* With Gino Penno (Jason), Maria Luisa Nache (Glauce), Giuseppe Modesti (Creon), Fedora Barbieri (Neris), Enrico Campi (Captain), Angela Vercelli and Maria Amadini (Handmaidens). Leonard Bernstein conducting. Performance of 10 December 1953, Teatro alla Scala, Milan. [Fonit Cetra 1019.]

Though Callas learned the part of Medea for Florence in record time, one writer observed that she performed it as though she had been born singing Medea. A parallel to her resourcefulness is found in Bernstein's performance in Milan. Like Callas, he learned the score in a matter of days. The Scala production had originally been planned for de Sabata, but he became ill just before rehearsals began. Bernstein, then winding up a series of concerts in Italy, was persuaded to jump into the breach. This *Medea* marked his professional operatic debut. The performance displays Callas in as secure and free a voice as she will be found at any point in her career. The many top Bs have a brilliant ring, and she handles the treacherous tessitura like an eager thoroughbred.

If a parallel is to be found to Callas' Norma, then we must look not to another bel-canto work but to a work of the late eighteenth century, to Cherubini's *Medea*. This parallel is not a question of musical or even dramatic similarities, for the former are slender at best (an Italianate *cantabile* in lyrical lines) and the latter lie on the drama's surface. No, the link is found in historic attitudes towards these roles and the way Callas shifted these attitudes. In her performances of both roles, benign classicism became vibrant emotionalism; friezes of sound evolved into human portraits.

Yet the fascination in Callas' performances of both is the contrast she found in the characters. Her Norma was all woman—proud, vain, vulnerable, loving. But her Medea was a mixture of demi-woman and demi-goddess, with both halves at war within one body for supremacy. Though her Medea was also a character built on primal emotions, there is far less nobility to her than there was to Callas' Norma. After all, Norma contemplated the murder of her

72

children and turned away from the deed. Medea not only took the lives of her infants but gloried in it. This primitivism makes Norma seem of cultured civility in comparison.

This pagan quality is evident at Medea's first entrance. Callas' voice is all venom, and a listener draws back with Jason, echoing with him "Ah, quale voce." The recitative before Medea's first lyric statement, "Dei tuoi figli," runs a gamut of vocal colors from brutal harshness ("Indegna di Giason") to great tenderness ("Senti ancor"). The aria itself is the one truly feminine moment in Callas' characterization. She almost makes us believe that love alone brought Medea to Corinth. From liquid phrases reverberating with deep sentiment, Callas steadfastly builds the aria to affecting heights, though it is robbed of its final punctuating cry from the heart as Bernstein cuts the last "Pietà." Callas overreaches the drama somewhat in the duet that ends Act I. Her first confrontation with Jason is of too savage a nature; I cannot believe Medea would play such high cards so soon in this game of wills. There is, however, a transfiguring moment as shaped by Bernstein during the course of the duet which must not be overlooked. In the canonlike "O fatal vello d'or," he slows down what has been a propulsive tempo to a pace several degrees cooler. Both the orchestra and the two singers reduce their dynamics and thrust as well to create a chilling incantation. This is only one of a dozen or more instances of the influence Bernstein exerts on the performance. In many other moments, his sorting out of dramatic lines brings the music into remarkable relief; one almost feels the surface of the sounds can be touched and the textures felt. As in de Sabata's *Macbeth*, Bernstein's approach to *Medea* is more symphonic than operatic, in that he is a catalyst and not an accompanist.

In the second-act scene with Creon, Callas works within a framework which is again at times too big for the needs of the action; here Medea should be at her craftiest. But she is on a firmer footing in her second encounter with Jason. Now we hear the outward sense of supplication needed in the first-act duet. That Callas achieves it here and not earlier is due, I think, to more of an opportunity to contrast a surface plea with Medea's inward vows of vengeance. Callas' remarkable balancing of this set of contrasts leaves no room for speculation about the fearful course of action Medea will pursue.

The mask she has worn in the previous acts is off entirely in the opening of Act III, where a full sense of the terror of Callas' portrayal is laid bare in Medea's invocation of her gods. Her voice is a caldron of evil in this, our first unretouched look at Medea's blackest side. The sorceress comes to life in Callas' voice as in no other's. Even the ensuing lament for her children (where Bernstein truncates the allegro section) emerges as more a cry of self-pity than self-recrimination and imposes upon a listener for a final time the terrible realization of the inexorable path Medea has chosen. It could well be that Bernstein's strange cut was designed to minimize Medea's preoccupation with the children and to strengthen her resolve of vengeance so that her fury would strike with full force in the final pages of the act. Indeed, this is what happens here.

# *1954* ⌒⇝

DONIZETTI: *Lucia di Lammermoor.* With Giuseppe di Stefano (Edgardo), Rolando Panerai (Enrico), Giuseppe Modesti (Raimondo), Giuseppe Zampieri (Arturo), Luisa Villa (Alisa), Mario Carlin (Normanno). Herbert von Karajan conducting. Performance of 18 January 1954, Teatro alla Scala, Milan. [Standing Room Only 831.]

Odd as a mating of Karajan with Donizetti might at first appear, the Austrian conductor displays a brilliant affinity with the Italian composer's style. His conducting brims with theater, and under his hands the music continually breathes (he also expands the second-act finale by replacing a lengthy cut not heard in Callas' performances of the work without Karajan). The sympathetic partnership of Karajan and Callas launched here in Milan was repeated in *Lucia* a year later in Berlin with even more vivid success, and in Vienna in 1956. They also later collaborated for EMI in *Trovatore* and *Madama Butterfly.*

There is less mystery and neurosis from Callas in this *Lucia* than in any other excepting the Berlin performance. Her voice is bright and flows easily, its top radiant. While all the extraordinary subtleties of rhythm are present which we have come to expect from her singing as a matter of course, there is not as lavish a wealth of tonal colors as in the first EMI set. Yet her singing is of such beauty, and the passagework is of such dazzling freedom, that what is less on the one hand is more on the other. Di Stefano, too, is in fine vocal shape, and his performance of the first-act duet (in which Callas' tracing of "Verrano a te" remains as plaintive as ever) sets off a prolonged volley of applause from the audience.

The tempo for the Mad Scene is of a breadth which might well choke another, but Callas thrived within such spaciousness. She binds the scene tightly together with her unique legato, and her voice is more shaded than elsewhere. Unfortunately some of the Mad Scene was lost in transmission as was a bit of the first act. The cadenza, however, is present and immaculately sung.

GLUCK: *Alceste*. With Renato Gavarini (Admeto), Paolo Silveri (High Priest), Rolando Panerai (Apollo), Silvio Maionica (Tanato), Giuseppe Zampieri (Evandro), Enrico Campi (Herald), Nicola Zaccaria (Oracle). Carlo Maria Giulini conducting. Performance of 4 April 1954, Teatro alla Scala, Milan. [Melodram 26026.]

As in her singing of Medea, Callas entertains no false concepts of "classicism" here, but sings Alceste's music in Italian and in an ample and indispensable declamatory style. She uses the entire voice from chest to a clarion top, endowing the music with an alive, fully theatrical air. Along the way there are many moments to cherish, such as the central, reflective section of "Divinités"— "J'enlève un tendre époux." She makes of it more than something vocally exemplary; it vibrates with warm humanity. In the same vein is her noble approach to "Non, ce n'est point." It is majestically broad and of penetrating dignity, and though a strong dramatic impulse is felt, Callas' good sense has informed her of the aria's special nature. Alceste, after all, is not Medea; she is a devoted rather than an avenging woman, a figure ready to sacrifice herself rather than another. An even deeper sense of her imposing stature comes in "Ah! malgré moi." Here Callas lends the music a sense of endless lines, a quality also lavished on "Grands dieux," especially at the point where Alceste sings "Vis pour garder le souvenir.

BELLINI: *Norma*. With Ebe Stignani (Adalgisa), Mario Filippeschi (Pollione), Nicola Rossi-Lemeni (Oroveso), Rina Cavallari (Clotilde), Paolo Caroli (Flavio). With the orchestra and chorus of Teatro alla Scala, Tullio Serafin conducting. [Recorded in Milan, 23 April–3 May 1954, for EMI, reissued as 47304.]

The character of Norma in this set is even more one-sided than in London, more the warrior than the woman. Callas begins in the guise of the former, with the opening recitatives on an Olympian scale, her voice covered and menacing. But she does not shake all the granite from her voice before beginning "Casta diva," and it is sung with too great a girth of sound. Also the cabaletta is still too public a statement for its private thoughts, and curiously Callas omits the sixteenth-note flourishes just before the cabaletta.

The second-act scenes with Adalgisa are sung by Callas in too much the same manner, with only an occasional shading. Also, the duets are less fine than in London, although, to be fair, a studio microphone hears differently from a broadcast one. This fact possibly has more significance in regard to Stignani, for in the EMI set she sounds less supple of line and her top more brittle. Callas' very vocal approach here finds a proper outlet only in the anger of the act from "Oh! non tremare" through the finale, with "Oh! di qual sei tu vittima" searingly sung. Another contrast to London is the absence of the added high D at the act's end.

The sort of pliable, tinted sound needed in the first two acts is finally encountered at the beginning of Act III with "Teneri figli." The introspection with which this pathetic line is drawn and a draining of pressure from her voice now lifts Bellini's lines into a realm of moving expression. With "Deh! con te," however, there is a return to an over-generosity of sound, but the first half of "Mira, o Norma" glows with repose.

Callas' moment of triumph in this set comes with the exterior emotions of "In mia man." But what gives this section its profile is her balancing the opening outward statement of Norma with contrasting asides, such as the compassion that envelops her voice at "pei figli tuoi." In the finale, "Deh! non volere" is taking shape, and in the final pages Callas' voice now soars in a magnificent arch of sound. Mario Filippeschi is no asset, but Nicola Rossi-Lemeni, however uneven his singing, is a monumental pillar of dramatic purpose.

**LEONCAVALLO:** *I pagliacci.* With Giuseppe di Stefano (Canio), Tito Gobbi (Tonio), Nicola Monti (Beppe), Rolando Panerai (Silvio). With the orchestra and chorus of Teatro alla Scala, Tullio Serafin conducting. [Recorded in Milan, 25 May–17 June 1954, for EMI, reissued as 47981.]

*Pagliacci* is the first of four operas Callas recorded but never performed on stage, and it is easy to forget that she made this recording, for Nedda is not the sort of role one would associate with Callas. In recent years the role has too often gone to a soubrette soprano who makes the part more giddy than not; but what a strong characterization Callas offers, what marvelous application she makes of her theatrical sense. Her portrayal is of a willful young woman filled almost to the bursting point with life ("Io son piena di vita," Nedda herself tells us before the "Ballatella"). The aria's recitative is freely sung and a miniature drama in itself. Callas' voice turns from pensiveness to fear, then shakes off Nedda's fears in the warmth of the morning sun. Though the aria has moments that are too harsh, there is still the unmistakable aura of joy in being alive. No note is glossed over, but all are linked together through the ebullience of her singing.

The Tonio-Nedda encounter which follows is in many ways the heart of Callas' performance. Again we find the strong dramatic interplay which always permeated a Callas-Gobbi encounter. She begins the scene with bemused impatience, but gradually her voice takes on edge as Tonio's passion and insistence grow. With Nedda's whip, Callas' voice lashes out at him. The words "Hai l'animo siccome il corpo tuo difforme" ("You have a soul as deformed as your body") are drenched with loathing. How much is evident minutes later when Callas speaks Silvio's name with a loving lilt. The duet which follows is a rapturous interlude within the storm of the drama, and Callas and Panerai sing it with waves of ardor (Serafin, alas, chooses the traditional cut of forty-six bars, which alters the dramatic balance of the scene).

It is in the second act where Callas' use of her voice for character comes most vitally into play. The throb of emotion in the first act is replaced by a chasteness of sound and a simplicity of approach. She maintains this playful quality until just after Canio's outburst "No! Pagliaccio non son" (magnificently sung by di Stefano, who here gives one of his finest performances on disc; words are deeply felt, his voice is free and here is the rage and jealousy of a young rather than an aging man). After Canio's aria, Callas' voice flashes out in "Ebben! se mi giudichi" with all the fury of her earlier scene with Tonio in Act I. When Nedda tries to restore the comedy, Callas' voice is again lightened but it is more nervous and punctuating than at the beginning of the play; at this point she is only half Colombina. The part that remains is abandoned in "No, per la madre," where Callas' voice rides the orchestra with a pride and defiance that we can easily believe is the final provocation to murder.

VERDI: *La forza del destino.* With Richard Tucker (Don Alvaro), Carlo Tagliabue (Don Carlo), Nicola Rossi-Lemeni (Padre Guardiano), Renato Capecchi (Fra Melitone), Elena Nicolai (Preziosilla), Plinio Clabassi (Marquis), Rina Cavallari (Curra), Dario Caselli (Mayor), Gino del Signore (Trabucco). With the orchestra and chorus of Teatro alla Scala, Tullio Serafin conducting. [Recorded in Milan, 17–27 August 1954, for EMI, reissued as 47581.]

As with *Nabucco, Macbeth,* and *Ballo in Maschera,* Callas seldom sang *Forza del Destino,* yet she brought an indelible quality of her own to the score. This Leonora has little in common with Verdi's earlier Leonora, apart from the fact that both are Spanish and in the grip of a melancholy so dominant that they are robbed of further dramatic dimension. Also, neither lady is a clear-cut protagonist, and both must share the drama and the music equally with the male characters; the same circumstances condition Amelia in *Ballo* as well. Musically, however, the *Forza* Leonora ranges beyond her namesake through Verdi's more ennobling music. In *Forza* we find him securely his own man. His writing is tighter than in the *Trovatore* period, shorn of redundancies of musical convention and freely given over to the needs of the drama. In this Leonora, he has provided fertile opportunities for wide-ranging expression, and Callas seizes and utilizes them like a great tragédienne.

After the first brief scene between father and daughter, in which Callas is duly diffident, a restrained urgency enters her voice during "Me pellegrina." From demureness, she now wavers in her resolve to leave with Alvaro. This is beautifully set forth in "Ti lascio, ahimè," a rising set of two-note phrases expressed by Callas as sighs. The passion Leonora has attempted to subdue surfaces in Callas' voice during the duet with Alvaro. Like Aida, Leonora is torn between love and filial regard. Serafin not only underlines this torment with full, taut orchestral sounds, but makes the scene unusually broad in scope.

The first scene of Act II has little bearing on Leonora musically; her contribution is limited to two onstage lines as she merges with a band of pilgrims. However, it sets her on the path to the monastery, and her arrival there in the second half of the act and her meeting with Padre Guardiano form the apex of this recording. Leonora's opening "Son giunto! grazie, o Dio" bears a great weight of weariness, and the later prayer "Madre, pietosa Vergine" offers an immediate contrast, thanks to the agitation Serafin implants in the orchestra and the sustained line Callas draws above it. The entire scene is among Verdi's most remarkable pages, especially the offstage chorus beneath Leonora's "Deh! non m'abbandonar." Of enormous impact here are the different calibrations Callas finds for each of the three statements of this plea. The first is hushed, the second more outward, and the last almost desperate.

Throughout the aria and in the duet to come, Callas' top voice (particularly Bs) is not consistently stable: indeed, several notes go awry. This was the period when she was emerging from her famous loss of weight, and many have ascribed the tenuousness of her upper range to this physical factor. But this is too facile a conclusion. As we have seen, her top could be precarious in her bulky days, just as it would be rock-solid later when she was even slimmer. So much more was involved in how her voice responded; it was a combination of the inherent physical characteristics of her vocal cords, her own state of health, and her mental well-being or unrest.

The duet with Guardiano is rich in that sort of open contrast that so sparked Callas' dramatic imagination. The principal ones interacting here are Leonora's plea for sanctuary and her fear that it will be denied. With Rossi-Lemeni's magnificent Guardiano we experience the same alive give-and-take as in the Callas-Gobbi relationship, where one artist fed the other theatrically. This scene is a tremendous test for any soprano, for a Leonora must have prodigious reserves of breath and use them cannily in sustaining the high-lying phrases of the music. Callas took to such challenges with relish, and she solves this one by a poised awareness of the music's rhythmic structure; she sings as much on the rhythm of notes as on the notes themselves. The act concludes with the prayer "La vergine degli angeli," sung with a prolonged radiance of sound.

In the final scene of the last act, her delivery of "Pace, pace, mio Dio" is at variance with those who view the aria as an inward reflection. Callas molds it as an outward cry, a plaintive mourning for a lost love and a plea for release from life. Also by not dwelling unduly on the climactic B-flat of the aria ("Invan la pace") she keeps the music flowing and allows its resolution to come in the cries of "Maledizione." This final part of the aria is too often treated as a coda, when actually it is a climax. When it becomes separated from the whole by too great an emphasis on the B-flat, disunity results and Verdi's ending is neutralized. In the final trio, Callas' Gilda voice of "Lassù in cielo" comes into play, that frail sound of slowly depleting life. Her final phrases, "Lieta poss'io precederti," are of a quiet peacefulness, as though Callas wants us to believe that Leonora has found the final release for which she has so yearned.

**ROSSINI:** *Il turco in Italia.* With Nicola Rossi-Lemeni (Selim), Nicolai Gedda (Narcisco), Jolanda Gardino (Zaida), Francesco Calabrese (Geronio), Mariano Stabile (Poet), Piero de Palma (Albazar). With the orchestra and chorus of Teatro alla Scala, Gianandrea Gavazzeni conducting. [Recorded in Milan, 31 August–8 September 1954, for EMI, reissued as 49344.]

This is one of Callas' least discussed sets, yet one of her most absorbing. Not only does it display her inventiveness as a comédienne, but it marks her only participation in what is essentially an ensemble work. Though she thrived on acting the protagonist, her discipline and musicality were flexible enough for this too. While I extravagantly admire her as Rosina in *Il barbiere di Sivi-*

*glia* (her one other comic role), it is *Turco* which offers the most convincing proof of her sympathy for a lighter genre (for the statistically minded, Callas sang a third more *Turco*s than *Barbiere*s). Listening to the concentrated flow of wit and melody in *Turco*, it is only with effort that one recalls that Rossini was barely in his twenties when the opera was written. It is so compactly made that no room has been left for excisions within set pieces, a unique instance in bel-canto music. There are some cuts by Gavazzeni here but they are limited to recitatives and to entire single numbers (Zaida's bolero, Narciso's aria, the ballet music, and the second waltz at the Act III party; I base this on the Rennert-Ricordi edition published *after* the Scala revival and recording of *Turco*).

The role of Fiorilla is that of a scheming vixen who delights in her womanliness and her ability to manipulate men. Callas plays her as thoroughly mischievous, enjoying to the full every ounce of attention extracted from her husband and suitors. Here we again find Callas with the upper hand, but using it in a totally different and disarming manner from previously. Fiorilla begins with an aria ("Non si dà follia maggiore") of simple design by Rossinian standards (*Turco*, with its tight interrelation of music and character, has none of *Barbiere*'s elaborate display pieces). It is an unfettered statement of her attitude towards life and the men in her life. Callas sings it breezily, with a light tone and on a properly small scale.

An opportunity for her to get under the skin of the part comes in the first of two masterful duets for Fiorilla and Selim. The dramatic ploys which stood her in such good stead in more forceful parts, particularly the element of contrast, transfer smoothly to comedy. Callas operates on two expressive levels in this duet, or, one might say, she uses two voices here. The one, out to ensnare Selim, is coy and girlish; the other, which speaks Fiorilla's mind to the audience, is direct and stinging. The results are delicious, from the first lilting aside ("Che bel turco") to the last ("Non è più così difficile questi turchi a conquistar"). Her voice has the scaled-down compactness that so persuasively brought to life Colombina's lines in the *commedia dell'arte* of *Pagliacci,* and this reduced sound puts detail after detail in a magical light. Just as superb is the grave humor of Rossi-Lemeni's singing. It seems incredible that this is the same pair of artists who plumbed such dramatic depths in the Convent Scene of *Forza*.

The spirit of the duet carries over into the scene in Fiorilla's house, where there is an authentic Rossinian smile in Callas' voice as she serves Selim coffee and confides to us "Il turco è preso" ("The Turk is caught"). Here, and later in the quartet with its "Siete turchi, non vi credo," Callas frequently reminds one of the matchless Rossini singing of the late Conchita Supervia; for the wit, brightness of sound, and pointed tone used in *Turco* are remarkably similar to the same qualities Supervia lavished on *L'italiana in Algeri*, though Callas lacks Supervia's charm. With the exception of a dashing scale added to the duet that follows with Geronio, Callas' interpolations in *Turco* are limited to upper endings, such as the top C inserted at the conclusion of the quartet.

One of the prime attractions of this set is the Fiorilla-Geronio duet. Here Callas turns Fiorilla into a professional female, and the duplicity with which she handles Geronio (Fiorilla's husband) is superb. Callas begins with a pout in her voice ("Di voi moi dolgo anch'io che vi siette cambiato"—"My complaint is that you have changed"). Then her voice turns to sticky honey with "No, mia vita, mio tesoro" ("No, my life, my treasure"), as if to show us with a wink how easily a husband is manipulated when a wife so desires. Finally the shrew pops out with Callas' stinging enunciation of "Ed osate minacciarmi?" ("And you dare to threaten me?"), catching Geronio so much off-guard that his only recourse is to beg for forgiveness. Equally funny, and also reaffirming her credentials as a comédienne, is the confrontation between Fiorilla and Zaida, where Callas gives her rival a vocal scratching with the word "civetta" ("flirt"). The two characters are supposedly fighting over Selim, but Zaida could be just as upset over the Fiorilla's appropriation of the lovely line "Ah, che il cor." Another transference comes when Fiorilla's "Se il zefiro si posa" is moved from the party scene to before the next Fiorilla-Selim duet.

This second encounter between Callas and Rossi-Lemeni brings forth a further wealth of wit, especially when their voices declare together "In Italia, in Turchia, sicuramente non si fa l'amor così" ("In Italy, in Turkey, one definitely does not make love like this"). The finale of the scene is one of Rossini's finest, and Callas begins it ("Questo vecchio maledetto") with bright pinpoints of sound, unfurling her full voice only in the concluding pages. Following a repentant aria for Fiorilla not found in the Ricordi score but richly shaped by Callas, the dramatic threads of the plot are tied together in general forgiveness. Fiorilla calls Geronio her "beloved elm" and invites him to return to her "shade"; Callas' voice is flooded by a warmth that suits the reformed Fiorilla.

PUCCINI: *Manon Lescaut:* "In quelle trine morbide," "Sola, perduta, abbandonata"; *La bohème:* "Sì, mi chiamano Mimì," "Donde lieta uscì"; *Madama Butterfly:* "Un bel dì," "Tu? tu? piccolo Iddio!"; *Suor Angelica:* "Senza mamma"; *Gianni Schicchi:* "O mio babbino caro"; *Turandot:* "Signore, ascolta," "In questa reggia," "Tu che di gel sei cinta." With the Philharmonia Orchestra, Tullio Serafin conducting. [Recorded in London, 15–21 September 1954, for EMI, reissued as 47966.]

Callas' first recital disc is a mixture of souvenirs and previews. The souvenirs are of *Suor Angelica* (sung only once on stage, the National Conservatory in Athens, 1940) and the title role of *Turandot* (a part which figured prominently in the first three years of her career in Italy). The previews are of future EMI recordings of *Madama Butterfly* (1955), *La bohème* (1956), and *Manon Lescaut* (1957); there would also be a complete *Turandot* in 1957. Although Chicago saw Callas as Butterfly, her Manon and Mimi remained only studio performances. The rarities on this disc are Callas' only versions of Liù's two scenes from *Turandot* and her first try at the *Schicchi* aria, which would later figure prominently in her concert tours of 1963 and 1973–74.

With the exception of "In questa reggia," this collection of arias is sung with uncommon simplicity. Even such expansive moments as Butterfly's death and Manon's "Sola, perduta" tend to understatement. But as we found with the Cetra 78's, Callas has more often than not scaled down an aria when dealing with it out of context. Interestingly, the excerpts from *Bohème, Butterfly*, and *Manon Lescaut* are in every case later intensified in the complete sets, where they are integrated into the dramatic fibre of the whole.

As these excerpts, apart from "In questa reggia," are all brief, single statements of mind, an emphasis more vocal than dramatic results. Though Callas usually required the large perspectives and dramatic give-and-take of live performance to fill music fully with meaning, there are, nonetheless, rewards within the confines of the disc. Manon's "In quelle trine morbide" has quiet elegance imparted to its broad lines, and especially lovely is the shaping of a pair of turns which appear in the latter part of the aria. "Sola, perduta" provides a broader base of emotions, yet Callas keeps the scene in check; rather than a voice racked with desperation, hers is colored with tired resignation. This is a Manon who has faced and accepted her death. This idea is reinforced later by the sense of release with which Callas frames "Terra di pace mi sembrava questa."

"Un bel dì" is delivered with great delicacy, and Callas' "little girl" sound touchingly etches "Chi sarà, chi sarà." The death scene from *Butterfly* begins drained of life, with "Con onor muore" voiced as if from an automaton; but the scene finishes all the stronger because of this beginning. Though several notes go awry in the two *Bohème* arias, there are many quite personal inflections; this is a Mimì of gentle dignity. Less convincing are the two *Trittico* arias. Callas' tone is too mature for both Lauretta and Angelica, and their music seems too heavily weighted. And the *Angelica* scene confronts us for the first time with an aspect of Callas' singing which became steadily more controversial after this date. This is—for the lack of a more precise word—the "wobble" that crept into her upper voice. It has also been termed a "tremolo," an "undulation," and even—erroneously—a "vibrato." I say "erroneously," because vibrato is the lifeblood of a voice as it is of a string player's sound. It is that slight fluctuation of pitch just above and below the core of a note that lends it color and life. Just where vibrato ends, or becomes excessive, and a wobble begins depends on the individual listener. Edward Greenfield has written of a "wobble tolerance" in regard to Callas and noted that it varies from person to person to a marked degree. The limit of my "tolerance" comes when a note is so out of control that no amount of will or technique can prevent it from being musically intrusive. This is what happens on the A at the conclusion of "Senza mamma."

The two Liù arias are an inconclusive experiment on Callas' part. They are too strong in approach and lack that quality of frail femininity that runs through Puccini's operas like a leitmotif. Turandot's aria, however, is another matter. It is imperious without being steely, imposing without being frigid. Callas' voice rides the scene's high-lying tessitura with brilliance and she sounds as though there is power to soar in reserve; the aria in the complete set will lack as easy a freedom.

CILEA: *Adriana Lecouvreur:* "Io son l'umile ancella," "Poveri fiori." CATALANI: *La Wally:* "Ebben? ne andrò lontana." GIORDANO: *Andrea Chénier:* "La mamma morta." BOITO: *Mefistofele:* "L'altra notte in fondo al mare." ROSSINI: *Il barbiere di Siviglia:* "Una voce poco fa." MEYERBEER: *Dinorah:* "Ombre légère." DELIBES: *Lakmé:* "Où va la jeune Indoue." VERDI: *I vespri siciliani:* "Mercè, dilette amiche." With the Philharmonia Orchestra. Tullio Serafin conducting. [Recorded in London, 15–21 September 1954, for EMI, reissued as 47282.]

A great variety of character and musical styles makes this second recital disc a more rewarding listening experience than the all-Puccini disc recorded in the same six-day period. This record was obviously planned as a showcase for Callas' agility and her dramatic prowess. Of the eight operas represented here, only half were sung by her on stage. In the remainder we are vouchsafed her only versions of music for Cilea's Adriana and Catalani's Wally.

The verismo half of the record is sung with much the same introspection heard in the Puccini album, and while the first Adriana aria is too "umile" in gait and tone (there are also strange breaths taken within phrases), "Poveri fiori" is steeped in pathos. The *Andrea Chénier* and *Wally* excerpts have a rather too slow-burning fire, but the *Mefistofele* aria is most eloquent, with a phrase such as "L'aura è fredda" literally chilled and of wrenching expression. This is the deepest statement on the disc, and it is sung in so well-measured a manner that the two cadenzas are bound into the aria rather than left dangling like pendants, as frequently happens.

The virtuoso side of the record presents an interesting contrast: few singers have ever offered the opportunity to compare their Lakmé with their Wally. The *Barbiere* aria is taken at a very deliberate pace and tends to become arch. It is also a more elaborately decorated version than Callas will employ at La Scala or for her EMI recording. Though her voice is bright, this Rosina is mezzo-soprano in posture, with an interpolated low G. Passagework is deft and closely bound into the whole.

Another remnant of study with de Hidalgo is the *Dinorah* aria, sung in Italian. Callas' performance is highlighted by a superb shaping of scales and the many widely spaced leaps all tightly in tune. Noteworthy is her plotting of the echo effects and her lilting phrasing of the coda. She observes a cut in the center of four pages, and expands the final cadenza, which ends on top D-flat and includes a dialogue with flute. The *Lakmé* aria (also in Italian) is broad but with less freedom than in the earlier RAI performance, and phrases are broken down into smaller expressive units. There are troublesome notes throughout, especially the B at the end of the first section and an off-center E at the end, and the bell imitations are chimed cautiously.

The beauty of this lighter side is Callas' breezy delivery of the *Vespri* Bolero, particularly the lift brought to "O caro sogno, o dolce ebrezza!" by a slight *ritardando* and a further softening of her voice. The final E is fine here and rings with more conviction than the same note at the end of the "Bell Song." Still, it does sound like the very upper limit of her voice at this moment.

SPONTINI: *La vestale.* With Franco Corelli (Licinio), Enzo Sordello (Cinna), Nicola Rossi-Lemeni (Pontifex Maximus), Ebe Stignani (High Priestess), Vittorio Tatozzi (Consul), Nicola Zaccaria (Soothsayer). Antonino Votto conducting. Performance of 7 December 1954, Teatro alla Scala, Milan. [Melodram 26008.]

These *Vestale*s were Callas' only performances of the work and her first collaboration with director Luchino Visconti, a giant who in his way had as great an influence on her art as did Serafin. *Vestale* was followed by a quartet of Callas-Visconti-Scala productions, all preserved in sound: *La sonnambula, La traviata, Anna Bolena*, and *Iphigénie en Tauride*.

The part of Giulia has musical appeal but is of slim theatrical proportions. It has been termed a "junior" Norma, and this easy generalization has a justification of sorts. Both women are in love with Roman soldiers and both are priestesses who betray their calling. What is lacking in Giulia is the transfiguring element of sacrifice, and Spontini's music is minus the range and humanity of Bellini's epic canvas. Only Giulia's music billows out over the otherwise cramped and stilted score. Callas' voice first emerges with force in the act I aria "In nome degli Dei." From this, it is evident she will treat this classic character and score vividly, and indeed throughout she fills Giulia's phrases to the brim with tone and word color. yet Giulia's mooning sentiments are all so similar, with her eyes turned downward to Licinio or upward to Vesta, that we are left with a sense of Callas' superior vocal skill rather than one of penetrating involvement. The words and music of *Vestale* simply do not provide room for the latter.

> **MOZART**: *Die Entführung aus dem Serail:* "Martern aller Arten."
> **MEYERBEER**: *Dinorah:* "Ombre légère." **CHARPENTIER:**
> *Louise:* "Depuis le jour." **ROSSINI**: *Armida:* "D'amore al dolce impero." Alfredo Simonetto conducting. Concert of 27 December 1954, RAI, San Remo. (Fonit-Cetra 5; *Entführung* and *Armida* arias also issued as EMI 54437.)

Callas ended 1954 with a quartet of arias that centers on the major moment of her only onstage Mozart heroine, Constanze (she shared this concert with the veteran tenor Beniamino Gigli, but no duets were performed). "Martern aller Arten" is sung here as "Tutte le torture," and her singing is virtuoso in scope and the most compelling realization of the aria extant. Callas, in superb form, fills the scene with defiance through incisive phrasing and a continual sense of forward motion. The passagework is firm and full, and enveloped in great vaulting phrases. The only challenge Callas fails to meet fully is the sustained top C before the coda; it turns unruly and sounds uncomfortable. But this blemish is minor in comparison to the passionate whole, and is easily engulfed by the excitement generated throughout.

The *Dinorah* excerpt (again in Italian) includes the recitative omitted in her EMI recording, and the scene is more rounded as a result. Also, Simonetto's more jaunty tempos lend greater spirit, and the echo effects are more charmingly made than for the recording. "Depuis le jour" brings the first instance of Callas' performing in French, and even before her residency in Paris, she makes it clear what a fine feeling she has for the language. This aria (later commercially recorded) never worked for Callas in toto; the final B remained an unresolved problem. But the quiet rapture of her intent is never in doubt. She had the rare gift of divulging the inner feelings of a character such as Louise with an immediacy that made one feel privy to something quite personal and real. Listen only to her singing of "délicieusement" to appreciate this. One has to reach back to Mary Garden's Columbia recording to find as touching and enthralled an effect on this word.

Callas' revisiting of *Armida* finds some of its garni trimmed away and a cut taken where the second stanza of the chorus appears. Again Simonetto take a brisker approach than Serafin, and this provokes more propulsive singing from Callas (though the orchestra here and in the Mozart borders on crudeness). While there are some ambiguous notes, especially in the area around top C, a proud brilliance matches the radiance of the *Entführung* aria.

# *1955* ⌒

GIORDANO: *Andrea Chénier*. With Mario del Monaco (Andrea), Aldo Protti (Gerard), Maria Amadini (Countess), Silvana Zanolli (Bersi), Enzo Sordello (Fléville), Mario Carlin (L'incredible), Enrico Campi (Roucher), Lucia Danieli (Madelon), Vittorio Tatozzi (Fouquier), Giuseppe Morresi (Dumas), Eraldo Coda (Schmidt). Antonino Votto conducting. Performance of 8 January 1955, Teatro alla Scala, Milan. [Melodram 26002.]

Maddelena de Coigny was another role learned by Callas in a matter of days. Originally, she and del Monaco were to have appeared in *Il trovatore*, but the tenor asked that *Andrea Chénier* be substituted, and Callas agreed to add yet another verismo heroine to her repertoire. It is an oddity in her career, for there is little substance to Maddelena (Santuzza has more musical and dramatic opportunities). A soprano's contribution in *Chénier* is limited to two duets, an aria, and scattered lines requiring little more than a single vocal color; even in the duets, the tenor tends to dominate. While Callas' singing is strong and involved, there is not much to distinguish her performance from any other well-sung Maddelena. The one moment where she leaves an individual imprint is "La mamma morta." The aria is sung with far more bite than for EMI. The B at its climax goes somewhat wild, but it does hit with force, and Callas follows it with further excitement by digging deeply into the final notes on "l'amor." Callas greatly heightens the very end of the third act by singing with the orchestra its impassioned *larghissimo*, using the words "Andrea! Andrea! Rivederlo!" written by Giordano to be spoken rather than sung. Nothing exceptional marks the singing of the duet which concludes the opera. I only wonder why Callas and del Monaco found it necessary to take the disfiguring transposition of a semitone at the end of the duet, for both seem in secure, easy voice here.

BELLINI: *La sonnambula.* With Cesare Valletti (Elvino), Giuseppe Modesti (Rodolfo), Gabriella Carturan (Teresa), Eugenia Ratti (Lisa), Pierluigi Latinucci (Alessio), Giuseppe Nessi (Notary). Leonard Bernstein conducting. Performance of 5 March 1955, Teatro alla Scala, Milan. [Myto 89006.]

As Callas restored the original strength and humanity embedded in Norma, so she reinstated the quiet hues and passions of Amina. Bellini, after all, wrote both roles for the same singer, an artist to whom Callas is frequently and justly compared—Pasta. Only when one hears Amina in a voice that endows Norma with its proper humane dimensions is one aware of the depth to be found in *Sonnambula.* As Bellini designed the role of Amina, and as Callas reminded us, she is a creature of flesh and meant to move and not merely to delight. That Callas does both is testimony to the fascination of the character she created. Instead of merely giving us the role's plasma, offered by so many, Callas gives us its blood as well.

Nowhere has her voice sounded so fresh and lovely. There is a beguiling maidenliness to phrases without too pointed a use of the "little girl" sound. Her measuring of the recitative before "Come per me sereno" is entirely natural and tinged with shyness. The aria itself is marked by a rare buoyancy of tone, with Callas eliding the short rests after "sereno," "oggi," and "terren" to create longer phrases with which to express Amina's inner joy. The care with which melismatic phrases are bound and the full values given notes contribute to the elegance of the mood. The cavatina ends with a simple cadenza which resolves upward.

This was Bernstein's first encounter with *Sonnambula,* and he works with Callas in an entirely sympathetic manner while maintaining his own and the music's integrity. For example, the short chorus before the first act cabaletta is marked *allegro brillante,* and Bernstein makes it a whirlwind of excitement, with the chorus outwardly seconding Amina's inner rapture. The contrast that results establishes two distinct musical attitudes, two different worlds—one dreamlike and one real. The melodic idea of the cabaletta, "Sovra il sen," occurs three times (a fourth is omitted here), and each time it is a little more elaborately embellished by Callas. The final statement is decorated with two sets of upward staccati written by Bernstein, and ends with an arpeggio which dips to a low A-flat. The success of these additives stems from their firm rooting in Bellini's harmony. The coda is breathtaking in Callas' agile handling of its many turns and scales, yet it, too, retains character, leaving more a sense of Amina's happiness than of Callas' skill.

In the recitatives before the duet "Prendi, l'anel ti dono," she continues to reaffirm the simple, trusting nature of Amina. Listen to the demure way "Il cor soltanto" is delivered, and later the hushed ecstasy brought to "Sposi! oh! tenera parola." Bernstein again jolts us back to reality with the bristling allegro after the duet, which also brings Amina and Elvino out of their reverie. Callas is more open in her singing of the mazurka-like "Ah! vorrei trovar," as though now willing to share Amina's bliss with others. Cesare Valletti is an eloquent Elvino, but he dodges the two high Cs in the section. Perhaps the reason behind Bernstein's lengthy cut of the repeat of this lovely music is to relieve Valletti of this challenge a second time. Surprisingly Valletti does deliver, and quite well, a C with Callas at the end of the first-act duet. Yet so right are his sensibilities in terms of Bellini's music that a pair of notes is a price readily paid for his presence.

The duet "Son geloso del zefiro" is a model of grace and repose. In the section with the descending trills in thirds, Callas exchanges lines with Valletti (a not uncommon practice and one which will be encountered also in Il barbiere), and they return to their parts as written for the "addios." The duality of Amina comes to the fore in the second act (Scene 2 of Bellini's original Act I), where, in her sleep, she wanders into Count Rodolfo's apartment. Like Lucia in her Mad Scene, Amina imagines her wedding day, and Callas' voice takes on the glazed, drowsy sound heard in the Donizetti opera, demonstrating again the accumulative nature of her art. This sound is in contrast to the urgency and fright of her voice when she is abruptly awakened and cannot grasp the situation about her. As in "Come per me," the careful measuring of the beginning of the act's finale "D'un pensiero e d'un accento" is a study in Callas' ability to set a mood with her voice and her patience to take the time needed to implement a musical idea. Nothing is rushed or left unfinished; one phrase is attended to and rounded off before the next evolves. She doubles Elvino's lines in several places during the ensemble, and her full voice burgeons out for the first time as Amina's anguish turns to desperation. The act is crowned by an E-flat in alt, held ringingly for four bars.

The opening scene of the last act belongs principally to the tenor, but in Amina's recitatives Callas continues to create an authentic personage, and her pathetic cry "Ah! il mio anello" adds further depth to the character. The final scene is built around a remarkable brace of arias for Amina which are virtually a summing up of work and its central figure. The recitative and cavatina of this scene are among the most moving pages in operatic literature, and Callas' singing of these alone would be enough to assure a proud place for her in the annals of singing. Again Amina is sleepwalking, but her dreams are now bordered with sorrow. Callas sings the cavatina "Ah! non credea" with stately simplicity using her voice in a half-lit, subdued manner yet with a miraculous range of stresses. The aria is concentrated melody, and Callas' singing of it is the purest sort of vocalism. Profoundly moving are such phrases as "Portia novel vigore il pianto, il pianto mio recarti" ("Perhaps my tears will recall you to me") as cradled in the soft, sombre recesses of her voice. She sustains a pitiful mood which once heard, remains deeply within one, forming a touchstone for future performances. The cabaletta, Amina's awakening to Elvino's renewed love, provides that sort of quick contrast which always winged Callas to soar. Her voice becomes infused with brightness; yet the first verse of "Ah! non giunge," while nimbly sung, retains tenderness thanks to the airiness with which its bravura demands are handled. The second verse is less complete, for Callas' voice turns harsh in several instances. Bernstein has also laden her with too many decorations, especially a volley of intricate *staccati* which fail to sound and which will become legati for the EMI recording.

VERDI: *La traviata.* With Giuseppe di Stefano (Alfredo), Ettore Bastianini (Germont), Silvana Zanolli (Flora), Arturo La Porta (Douphol), Silvio Maionica (Dr. Grenvil), Luisa Mandelli (Annina), Giuseppe Zampieri (Gastone), Antonio Zerbini (D'Obigny), Franco Ricciardi (Giuseppe). Carlo Maria Giulini conducting. Performance of 28 May 1955, Teatro alla Scala, Milan. [EMI 63628.]

This *Traviata* represents an enormous stride forward by Callas in conquering this complex work. It also demonstrates what a product she was of her artistic environment and how responsive she was to the circumstances of a given performance. Amid commonplace surroundings her energies and imagination often took (in part) the attitudes and temper of those about her (the 1952 Mexico *Traviata*, for example). Of course her performances even under the least ideal conditions had rewarding aspects, for Callas' taste and intuition served her well even in artistic adversity. But if this taste and imagination were stimulated by challenging artistic surroundings (exemplified here by Giulini and Visconti) they would flower with rare color and life.

Giulini provides an orchestral voice which sings in broad, expressive terms; yet this lyrical flow is continually channeled into the drama. Giulini leaves no room for applause to interrupt the movement of Verdi's theater; when it comes uninvited, he ignores it and moves quickly forward. Though not an active voice in the performance, the presence of Visconti is also strongly felt, for his pacing of the onstage drama produces a time-continuum which has a direct effect on the unfolding of the music in general and Callas in particular. Obviously playing the work with a firm belief in the viability of its drama, Visconti makes musical moments stand out in relief which in other productions are left unfulfilled or only suggested (this is especially true of Acts II and IV).

In conversational moments of Act I, there is a natural banter between Violetta and her friends; she is deep in a pretense of well-being, attempting to maintain an air of normality. Indeed, the "Drinking Song" is sung almost lustily by Callas, as if to assure all that Violetta is over her tiresome illness. It is only after the first bout of coughing that the pallor of sickness heard in the 1951 Mexico performance begins to creep into Callas' voice and drain her responses of life. The exchange with Alfredo brings a fuller awareness of just how ill she really is, as Callas half-speaks, half-sings many of the lines. Balancing this is a realization of

Violetta's inner misgivings about her way of life and the suggestion that she wishes for something more ("Un cor . . . si . . . forse"). Still to be brought into line are the act's concluding arias. They are still a bit too full, even forceful (the lower, written ending to "Ah! fors'è lui" is, interestingly enough, employed for the first time), and the Cs of "Sempre libera" are sung with steeliness and come under control only towards the end of each. Also a frayed E-flat at the act's end detracts from, rather than peaks, the cabaletta.

In Act II, Callas has begun a scaling down of her voice to meet the needs of the music and the drama. She is working for the most part alone, for Ettore Bastianini sings the Germont-Violetta duet with a single, strong color throughout. This has a particularly damaging effect in "Dite alla giovine," for though Callas sharpens the A-flat of "giovine," she sets a deep and interior mood which is intruded upon rather than reinforced by Bastianini. Left to herself, she reestablishes a mood in the writing of Violetta's farewell to Alfredo, and "Amami, Alfredo" is of such concentrated ardor that one wonders how Violetta's love could be doubted, no matter what she said or did later.

The third-act duet is played at white heat by Callas and di Stefano (he is generally admirable throughout), and the finale ("Alfredo, Alfredo, di questo core") is also successful. But it is the final act that represents Callas at her pinnacle in this performance. Surely Visconti's influence must have been the force behind her by now heartrending reading of Germont's letter. The justness of emotion in Callas' low, sad volume of speech makes this the finest such moment in any of her recorded *Traviatas*. As in the first act, there are bits of half-spoken phrases within the recitative itself ("Oh! come son mutata"), and the aria is full of emptiness and sadness. After a weak response to Annina's announcement of Alfredo's return, there is a sudden surge of strength in Callas' voice at his entrance. The duet is sung with much of the pretended well-being heard in Act I, but in the scene that follows, Callas mixes this with a sense of the truth of the situation. Only with Germont's entry does she drop all pretense, and the phrase "Se una pudica vergine" is sung with a pathetic beauty which gives Violetta's death an almost unbearable reality.

CHERUBINI: *Medea:* "Dei tuoi figli"; SPONTINI: *La vestale:* "Tu che invoco," "O Nume tutelar," "Caro oggetto." BELLINI: *La sonnambula:* "Come per me sereno," "Ah! non credea . . . Ah! non giunge." With the orchestra of Teatro alla Scala, Tullio Serafin conducting. [Recorded in Milan, 9–12 June 1955, for EMI. *Medea* and *Vestale* reissued as 47282; *Sonnambula* reissued as 47966.]

The year 1955 was an active recording year for Callas—an aria recital and three complete operas. The *Medea* and *Vestale* excerpts were recorded to fill half a disc entitled "Callas at La Scala"; side two was to consist of the first- and last-act scenes for Amina from *La Sonnambula.* Though the second side was recorded and tests turned up on private discs, Callas never permitted it to be published during her lifetime (the recordings are discussed below).

A "concert" atmosphere pervades the *Medea* excerpt, what with the omission of its recitative, some drowsy conducting by Serafin, and generally limp singing by Callas. There is far more stuff of the theater in the *Vestale* arias (particularly the cabaletta of "Tu che invoco"), the only commercial souvenirs of her performances of Giulia. The first part of "Tu che invoco" and all of "O Nume tutelar" are exquisitely limned, and "O Nume" in particular is filled with indelible colors. In stark contrast is the cabaletta to the first aria, in which Callas' voice takes fire and mounts to a blazing added top C.

It is difficult to fathom the reasons behind the initial rejection of the *Sonnambula* arias, for Callas' singing is ever lovely and expressive, though a bit less spontaneous than in the live or commercial complete performance. There is, however, more appeal to these excerpts than the *Medea* aria with Serafin which was published, and certainly they deserve a hearing as much as the 1961 first-act *Pirata* scene which remained unpublished for twelve years.

Choral parts are omitted, and "Come per me" is slower than with Bernstein; this provides room to shape the fioritura of the coda with greater gentleness. Also, the ornamentation throughout is reduced to essentials, though the omission of a cadenza between the two verses of "Ah! non giunge" leaves the aria somewhat stark and removes tension from the finale.

BELLINI: *Norma.* With Ebe Stignani (Adalgisa), Mario del Monaco (Pollione), Giuseppe Modesti (Oroveso), Rina Cavallari (Clotilde), Athos Cesarini (Flavio). Tullio Serafin conducting. Concert performance of 29 June 1955, RAI, Rome. [Fonit Cetra 4.]

This *Norma* is closer to the London performance of 1952 than to the commercial recording of 1954, and in several instances betters it. Norma the warrior is less dominant, particularly in the duets of the second and third acts (this was Callas' final Norma with Stignani, who is in remarkable form here). There is also a lightening of the cabaletta of "Casta diva," and it is a more personal statement as a result.

Though there is an edgy quality to top notes at first, especially in the aria's ascent to B-flat, this stridency dissolves by the third act. Callas' most mettlesome moment is found in the confrontation with Pollione, from her dazzling singing of the polonaise in Act II with its clarion top Cs, to the flood of hatred that pours out of "In mia man" in the last act. But again this fury, underlined by her chest voice, is checked in Norma's references to her children; on the line "pei figli tuoi" Callas quiets the bitterness in her voice with a gentle caress of tone. Serafin's conducting is epic in scope and a number of cuts made for EMI are replaced, notably in the trio-finale of Act II, which is again crowned with a top D.

PUCCINI: *Madama Butterfly.* With Nicolai Gedda (Pinkerton), Lucia Danieli (Suzuki), Mario Borriello (Sharpless), Renato Ercolani (Goro), Mario Carlin (Yamadori), Plinio Clabassi (Bonze), Enrico Campi (Commissioner), Luisa Villa (Kate Pinkerton). With the orchestra and chorus of Teatro alla Scala, Herbert von Karajan conducting. [Recorded in Milan, 1–6 August 1955, for EMI, reissued as 47959.]

Many singers in varying degrees have understood the dramatic potential of Butterfly; given a basic sympathy for the role's theater, a certain success is virtually guaranteed, for much of the character's veracity and appeal was built into the music by Puccini. Yet out of the many who have recorded the part, only two—Toti dal Monte and Renata Scotto—have achieved the compelling heights scaled by Callas. The living fibre of her portrayal is all the more impressive when it is remembered that her only active contact with the work prior to this recording was two of its arias.

Her remarkable identity with the part on so short an acquaintance becomes understandable if we realize that Callas' Cio-Cio-San was a composite of previous dramatic factors: Amina's innocence and quiet devotion, Gilda's metamorphosis and betrayal, and Violetta's passion and sacrifice. Yet the whole of this Butterfly is strikingly different from its parts, for the tragedy of Puccini's geisha was a private one; even her maid Suzuki is kept on its perimeter. Callas sensed and absorbed this essential fact on her initial contact with the score, and defined it in inward, concentrated terms, reaffirming her gift of acclimatizing herself to a specific theatrical terrain.

Once past Butterfly's entrance, a largely "vocal" moment, marred in this set only by a dizzying high D-flat, Callas establishes Butterfly as a creature of great delicacy. In her conversations with Pinkerton and Sharpless there is shyness coupled with a questioning eagerness. Both tell us how anxious this Butterfly is to be accepted, to please. Callas' voice is kept light—"on, rather than in, the string," one might say, like a violinist using his bow with a minimum of pressure. This engaging stance is maintained through the wedding scene with the exception of the reference to Butterfly's father. Callas' voice, in that instance, becomes hollow and hushed, as though unwilling to share publicly very private feelings. After the Bonze scene, a bit more body is injected into her voice, and still more and warmer tone is added in the duet with Pinkerton, to encompass the rapture of the moment.

So often, and this *Butterfly* is an excellent case in point, Callas' voice seems a vessel which can be filled or drained to various levels of intensity at will. What controlled this flow was the text, for Callas, when most moving, sang exactingly on the word; note the various stresses used during the course of the first-act duet alone. Of course, she was always dependent upon the amount of room a conductor gave her to make her dramatic points fully. Karajan supplies all the musical space needed while retaining a firm musical unity. Like the other major conductors with whom

Callas was fortunate to collaborate—Serafin, de Sabata, Bernstein, Giulini—Karajan retains his own identity in the process. This is felt in the strong symphonic approach he takes to *Butterfly*; this full orchestral outlook is another characteristic all five conductors had in common. Karajan seems to view *Butterfly* as an orchestral poem with voices as much as an opera. I am only sorry he chose the standard cut after the wedding ceremony; this five-page excision saves little time, robs Butterfly's friends and relatives of what dimension Puccini allotted them, and reduces them to a chorus rather than individuals.

The three years that lapse between the first two acts are reflected from the outset of the second by Callas. Gone is the girlish sound of Act I (though it returns for an instant in "Un bel dì"); in its place, her voice takes on a dull cast, a weary sound without sheen, full of uncertainty. As Suzuki's doubts mount, intensity is added to Callas' voice, as if she can quell Butterfly's fears by answering Suzuki's. "Un bel dì" is greatly tightened over the earlier recording; here Callas creates a miniature drama within Puccini's larger one. She acts out three roles for Suzuki—Butterfly as narrator, as herself, and as Pinkerton. She pictures his return with moving simplicity and child-like conviction, and by the aria's conclusion we are made to believe, like Suzuki, that Pinkerton will return to Butterfly.

A flood of lightness suffuses Callas' voice at Sharpless' entry, but the shyness of Act I is replaced with a new self-assurance in the Consul's presence. The charm of the atmosphere set by Callas is broken only after the reading of Pinkerton's letter, when Sharpless suggests Butterfly marry Yamadori. The blunted sound of her response carries vividly her pain and even anger at such a suggestion. "Che tua madre," on the other hand, has a composed dignity in place of the hysteria which often grips this moment. Callas' voice is that of a woman rather than a girl, one in whom irony is only just suppressed. An interesting contrast comes later in the encounter with Goro after the Consul's departure. Callas realized it was Butterfly's respect for Sharpless which directed the words of "Che tua madre" to the child and not the Consul. But a caustic edge of her voice leaves no doubt as to where her words are truly aimed. On the other hand, Goro is an equal, and Butterfly can (and Callas does) lash out at him with directness and uncontrolled fury. The sighting of Pinkerton's ship after Goro flees is one of those moments in *Butterfly* that is always effective no matter who the protagonist. Callas handles it with less outward emotion than most; by fully measuring its notes she produces a calm deliberateness which gives a deeper thrust than usual to "Trionfa il mio amor." The flower duet is lightly sung, and the soft, reflective cast Callas brings to "Non son più quella" ("I am no longer the same") is in beautiful contrast to the joy of "Vo' che mi veda indosso il vel del primo dì" ("I want him to see me as I was the first day").

The child in Butterfly comes to the fore a last time in Callas' voice after Pinkerton's "Addio." With the exception of her fury at Suzuki's silence, there is an imposing solemnity during the scene with Kate Pinkerton and Sharpless. Again, there is more scope to the death scene than on the recital disc, and Callas, in an almost stately way, fills Butterfly's final action with inevitability.

**VERDI: *Aida*.** With Richard Tucker (Radames), Fedora Barbieri (Amneris), Tito Gobbi (Amonasro), Nicola Zaccaria (King), Giuseppe Modesti (Ramfis), Franco Ricciardi (Messenger), Elvira Galassi (Priestess). With the orchestra and chorus of Teatro alla Scala, Tullio Serafin conducting. [Recorded in Milan, 10-24 August 1955, for EMI, reissued as 49030.]

Callas' final Aida was for EMI. Her voice is lighter here than in either Mexico performance, and in general there is greater calm and less intensity than was the case in the theater. While this lends a noticeable depth to certain phrases (particularly those expressing Aida's private thoughts), there is a corresponding loss of excitement and momentum in other places. It is in the big sections of the opera that Callas oddly does not bring the full force of her dramatic personality to bear. The heat generated in the Mexico performances flares only in the Nile Scene with Gobbi, a high-strung, involved stretch of singing. Elsewhere, there is a studied and almost tepid character to her performance, which is as curious as it is ineffectual. "Vedi la morte" in the final scene is touching, but "O patria mia" continues to rankle, particularly given a flapping high C through which the Egyptian army could have marched.

VERDI: *Rigoletto.* With Giuseppe di Stefano (Duke), Tito Gobbi (Rigoletto), Nicola Zaccaria (Sparafucile), Adriana Lazzarini (Maddalena), Plinio Clabassi (Monterone), Renato Ercolani (Borsa), Elvira Galassi (Countess Ceprano), Giuse Gerbino (Giovanna), William Dickie (Marullo), Carlo Forti (Count Ceprano), Vittorio Tatozzi (Usher), Luisa Mandelli (Page). With the orchestra and chorus of Teatro alla Scala, Tullio Serafin conducting. [Recorded in Milan, 3–16 September 1955, for EMI, reissued as 47469.]

Three weeks after her farewell to Aida, Callas took leave of Gilda, a part for which she had a greater sympathy. Where her scaling down of voice and emotions worked against her in the recorded *Aida*, it gives the *Rigoletto* set an uncommon dimension. Her performance of Gilda for EMI is essentially that heard in Mexico City three years before, but there is a finer finish to phrases and a further depth of character. The changes come in small details; for example, in Act II when Gilda cries "Oh Dio! nessuno" ("Heavens, none to help me"), Callas caresses the word "nessuno," as though Gilda is secretly elated that she is at last alone with the young man of whom she has so long dreamed. There are many such accents, implications and colors, which make this recording a never-ending source of dramatic enlightenment. Of immeasurable help to Callas' penetrating portrayal are Serafin's collaboration, full of wisdom and song, and the exactingly intelligent singing of Gobbi in the title role. Like Callas, Gobbi draws strength from the text, and he does so with such model diction that we all but taste Piave's words.

Verdi termed *Rigoletto* a "long series of duets," and Callas and Gobbi compellingly demonstrate that *Rigoletto*'s heart beats in the duets for father and daughter. So strong is the sense of musical integration in this recording that Rigoletto's "Pari siamo" and Gilda's "Tutte le feste" seem not so much arias as opening solo sections of an extended duet; both are bound into the scene rather than set apart from it. There are also several other musical aspects to this recording worth noting; chief of these is Serafin's inclusion of virtually all of "Ah! veglia o donna." Though seven bars are still omitted, this small cut was obviously made in the name of theater. There is a stronger dramatic pull when Rigoletto interrupts Gilda rather than himself. Also Callas has simplified her approach to the coda of "Caro nome." With a less fulgent use of her voice than in Mexico City, and with Verdi's original ending taken (a long rapturous trill), the proper note of reverie is now struck. Another, more musical solution is the written, quiet ending to the quartet. The only disturbing aspect of this set is that it signaled Callas' final Gilda—a loss for Verdi and a loss for opera as drama.

DONIZETTI: *Lucia di Lammermoor.* With Giuseppe di Stefano (Edgardo), Rolando Panerai (Enrico), Nicola Zaccaria (Raimondo), Giuseppe Zampieri (Arturo), Luisa Villa (Alisa), Mario Carlin (Normanno). With the RIAS Orchestra, Herbert von Karajan conducting. Performance of 29 September 1955, by La Scala at the Berlin Städtische Oper. [EMI 63631.]

The powerful alchemy which existed between Callas and Karajan finds its most finished and exciting outlet in this *Lucia.* Both give inspired performances, carrying the splendor of their 1954 La Scala collaboration to a new glory. As penetrating as were the *Lucia*s Callas sang with Serafin, her performances with Karajan are as remarkable, though quite different. Where there is brooding melancholy with Serafin, there is more a sense of a young girl with Karajan. With this shift in emphasis—and it is fascinating to compare the two approaches—there is a corresponding shift in Callas' vocal attitude. Under Karajan there is a greater lightness, more forward placement of tone throughout, and the length of phrases is prodigious. Though the maidenly quality of the Karajan performances conveys less of a sense of tragedy, Lucia does become more vulnerable, more fragile. Callas' singing of the Mad Scene is painted in paler shades than was the case with Serafin; yet there is a return to the strong verismo of the Mexico performance of 1952, with a snarl on the words "Il fantasma." Contrasting with such vivid moments are hushed ones in which Callas seems dazed and uncertain of where she is or what has taken place. The cadenza is finely drawn, though Callas misjudges her breath in one spot and a flicker of strain is felt. She takes a downward ending to the cadenza, saving an E-flat in alt (and a good one) for the conclusion of the scene. Elsewhere in this performance, di Stefano is in enviable form and his singing handsomely shaped. The high point in Karajan's conducting is the finale of the second act, where all dramatic stops are pulled out, bringing the excitement to fever pitch (he also opens a cut here as he did at La Scala). If I could own but a single Callas set, it would be this one.

BELLINI: *Norma*. With Giulietta Simionato (Adalgisa), Mario del Monaco (Pollione), Nicola Zaccaria (Oroveso), Gabriella Carturan (Clotilde), Giuseppe Zampieri (Flavio). Antonino Votto conducting. Performance of 7 December 1955, Teatro alla Scala, Milan. [HRE 1007.]

This *Norma* came on the heels of Callas' second season in Chicago, the site of her American debut the year before. She obviously came from America as she had arrived there from Berlin—in stupendous voice. The second La Scala *Norma* builds on the RAI performance in the sense that more and more of the woman is emerging in Callas' portrayal. This places the cabaletta of "Casta diva" in a more revealing light and makes the second-act duets more moving. With a more careful shading of her tone and a lighter approach to inner moments, sections of rage take on a new force in comparison, notably the finale of Act II from "Oh! non tremare" onward (again a mighty D crowns the finale). However, "Deh! con te" in Act III still lacks the play of light and shadows which so transforms the other duets. Simionato brings much more profile to Adalgisa than in Mexico, for the role is now more practiced. Her voice is firm and glowing, and the easy response of her top requires no alterations in Adalgisa's vocal lines.

# *1956* ∽

VERDI: *La traviata.* With Gianni Raimondi (Alfredo), Ettore Bastianini (Germont), Silvana Zanolli (Flora), Arturo La Porta (Douphol), Silvio Maionica (Doctor Grenvil), Luisa Mandelli (Annina), Giuseppe Zampieri (Gastone), Dario Caselli (D'Obigny), Franco Ricciardi (Giuseppe), Carlo Forti (Messenger). Carlo Maria Giulini conducting. Performance of 19 January 1956, Teatro alla Scala, Milan. [Myto 89003.]

The cultivated singing of Gianni Raimondi as Alfredo is the principal difference between this La Scala *Traviata* and the one the year before. Though Callas' performance sounds less detailed and spontaneous (especially in the first and third acts), she brings "Ah! fors'è lui" more in line with the character and achieves a further cohesion in the scenes with Germont, thanks to greater finesse from Bastianini.

ROSSINI: *Il barbiere di Siviglia.* With Tito Gobbi (Figaro), Luigi Alva (Almaviva), Nicola Rossi-Lemeni (Don Basilio), Melchiorre Luise (Dr. Bartolo), Anna Maria Canali (Berta), Pierluigi Latinucci (Fiorello), Giuseppe Nessi (Official). Carlo Maria Giulini conducting. Performance of 16 February 1956, Teatro alla Scala, Milan. [Melodram 26020.]

Those who value the Callas-EMI recording of *Barbiere* will find this live performance a surprise, though not altogether a pleasant one. Callas was too strong a Rosina on stage, overplaying many moments and often creating more of a shrew than a vixen. She also approached the part very much as a soprano, changing lines which dip below the stave and even taking entire phrases up an octave. This creates the nagging feeling that she was not as yet certain of what she wanted from the part. But then comedy was not a métier for which she had the best instincts. She could, of course, make capital of a comic role given time. The polished recording of *Turco in Italia*, after all, came four years after Callas had first sung the part on stage. The recording of *Barbiere*, which followed the Scala performances by a year, would reflect the lessons taught by her experience as Rosina in the theater.

Though Rosina makes a brief appearance in Act I of *Barbiere* in answer to Almaviva's serenade, her first full singing comes in the second act (or Scene 2 of Rossini's original Act I) with the aria "Una voce poco fa." Callas begins in rather thick voice, with narrative phrases sung heavily and lacking in spontaneity. Scales and *gruppetti* are lighter, however, and more focused, though several staccato notes are split and off-center. The final B of the aria is driven, and it is not until the delightful dialogue before "Dunque io son" that she begins to settle into the performance.

In the breezy exchange between Rosina and Figaro just after "La calunnia," she handles her part of the banter with just the right mixture of coyness and curiosity, and "Dunque io son" is magically launched by a lilting, soft laugh. The duet ripples along easily at first, for Callas keeps her voice free and Gobbi is one of the few baritones of this century technically equipped to sing Figaro's music without cheating. But the airiness of the scene is destroyed by a raucous peal of laughter from Callas when she produces Rosina's note, and by her vast oversinging of the second statement of "Fortunati affetti." She takes the soprano variants in the last section of the duet, rising to a D in alt, a note which she returns to and sustains for the climax of the scene. The ensuing recitatives with Bartolo are witty and spontaneous, but again there are a number of exaggerations in the scene with Almaviva disguised as a soldier; a simple "grazie" becomes a *scena*, and "Ecco qua! sempre un'istoria" is too broadly played. All principals are guilty of rushing Giulini in the finale, where he gives us more music than most conductors, taking only a comparatively short cut of five pages at the very end of the stretta.

For the Lesson Scene, Callas sings Rossini's original aria, "Contro il cor," a tone higher than written. She begins heavily, even forcefully, and lightens her voice only for the asides to Almaviva. It was, no doubt, Giulini who conceived the charming idea of having the aria accompanied only by harpsichord, saving the orchestra for the exchanges between Rosina and Almaviva. The repeat of "Cara immagine" is cut here, and Callas uses a rather too elaborate solo cadenza to finish this truncated version of the aria, a cadenza sung cautiously and concluding on a wobbly A above the stave. After polite applause, Almaviva's next line "Bella voce, bravissima") expresses a sentiment ("What a beautiful voice") with which not all in the theater are prepared to agree. A noisy protest breaks out but is eventually shouted down by the pro-Callas faction. However, the next line is Bartolo's "Certo, bella voce," and Melchiorre Luise accents "Certo" and throws it out into the theater with unmistakable meaning. A single voice yells back "Ah! no," and Luise hurls a second "Certo, bella voce!" settling the matter. The quintet with Basilio goes along fairly well, but Giulini takes the usual cut of some ten pages out of the shaving scene, and again all rush his beat. Happily, only nine bars are lost from "Ah! qual colpo," which is suavely sung. For the "Zitti" trio, Callas and Gobbi exchange lines (as they had in "Buona sera" during the quintet), and each of its three statements is sung as a solo. It is not surprising that Giulini removes Almaviva's aria after the wedding ceremony; not only is the cut standard, but Alva's limited technique could not have coped with it. It is strange, however, that Giulini elects so wide a cut in the finale, taking out both Rosina's and Almaviva's flourishes. Callas manages a final gesture, however, with an added D in alt at the very end. The curious thing about this set is that it is one of the very few performances by Callas which does not in some way improve on her commercial set of the same work.

**DONIZETTI:** *Lucia di Lammermoor.* With Gianni Raimondi (Edgardo), Rolando Panerai (Enrico), Antonio Zerbini (Raimondo), Piero de Palma (Arturo), Anna Maria Borrelli (Alisa), Pietro Moccia (Normanno). Francisco Molinari-Pradelli conducting. Performances of 22 March and 24 March (excerpts only) 1956, Teatro San Carlo, Naples [Myto 90319.]

This *Lucia* and its two repeats were Callas' farewell to Naples. As a musical and dramatic statement it lies midway between her *Lucia*s with Serafin and those with Karajan, neither as dark as the former nor as open and free as the latter. While this compromise furnishes no new insights, it does offer Callas in a markedly introspective vein during the Mad Scene. This section is sung with unusual sustained calm, with phrases such as "Del ciel clemente" almost more felt than heard. As in Berlin, Callas ends the cadenza on the lower E-flat.

I have a special affection for this *Lucia*, for it unites Callas with the sympathetic Edgardo of Gianni Raimondi. The performance is also among the most sympathetic I have encountered from Molinari-Pradelli, who provides his singers with luxuriant musical settings. The CD edition of this Naples *Lucia* includes a set of previously unknown excerpts from the second performance on 24 March—the entire second scene of Act I and the first scene of Act II. Whether the entire second performance was recorded is unknown.

Following these *Lucia*s, Callas returned to La Scala for more *Traviata*s with Raimondi and a new role—Giordano's Fedora. Lamentably, *Fedora* was not broadcast, though there continue to be rumors of the existence of a transistor recording of one of the performances.

**VERDI:** *Il trovatore.* With Giuseppe di Stefano (Manrico), Fedora Barbieri (Azucena), Rolando Panerai (di Luna), Nicola Zaccaria (Ferrando), Luisa Villa (Inez), Renato Ercolani (Ruiz), Giulio Mauri (Gypsy). With the orchestra and chorus of Teatro alla Scala, Herbert von Karajan conducting. [Recorded in Milan, 3–9 August 1956, for EMI, reissued as 49347.]

For EMI's microphones Callas takes leave of yet another Verdian role. Her final appearances as Leonora came the autumn before in Chicago and marked her only performances with Jussi Björling. The second of the two *Trovatore*s (where Claramae Turner substituted for Ebe Stignani) was recorded, but the known copy was destroyed. One hopes the tape will resurface;

in the meanwhile this EMI set demonstrates that Callas' musical
ideas about *Trovatore* had by now been honed down to essentials. There are few additions here (both "Tacea la notte" and its
cabaletta are performed as written), and though Callas still
includes a D-flat at the end of Act I, she omits the same note at
the conclusion of "D'amor sull'ali rosee." A minor point of interest is the inclusion of both verses of "Di quella pira" and with
them Leonora's brief responses in between. However, of major
importance is the inclusion of Leonora's rich cabaletta to
"D'amor," or rather one verse of it plus coda. At last we hear
this fourth-act scene intact in Callas' voice. She sings the noble
strains of "Tu vedrai che amore in terra" with all the quiet power
she has long lavished on Leonora's two cavatinas. Though her
top is minus some of the solidity heard in the Naples and La
Scala performances of *Trovatore*, and though the cabaletta to
"Tacea" has an almost studied air about it, what remains is the
most beautiful concentration of sound and poignancy ever
brought to Leonora's music by Callas.

Unfortunately, di Stefano lacks the proper heft for Manrico's
heroics, and Panerai and Barbieri are not at their known best.
But Karajan is again a lofty partner, especially his illumination
of the finale of Act II through a careful shifting of dynamics.
The close rapport between himself and Callas, and between the
pair and Verdi's music in this, their last collaboration, gives this
set its importance and justification. (Giulio Mauri is a *nom de
guerre* for Nicola Zaccaria.)


**PUCCINI:** *La bohème.* With Giuseppe di Stefano (Rodolfo),
Rolando Panerai (Marcello), Anna Moffo (Musetta), Nicola Zaccaria (Colline), Manuel Spatafora (Schaunard), Carlo Badioli (Benoit
and Alcindoro), Franco Ricciardi (Parpignol), Carlo Forti (Soldier).
With the orchestra and chorus of Teatro alla Scala, Antonino
Votto conducting. [Recorded in Milan 20 August–4 September
1956, for EMI, reissued as 47475.]

There has never been a scarcity of sopranos for Puccini's Mimì,
while Medeas will always be in short supply. This, no doubt,
helps to explain why Callas did not perform *Bohème* on stage.

Fortunately, Legge had the vision to arrange for her to perform the opera on records, and from these EMI sessions emerges one of the most affecting portrayals of this loveliest of Puccini heroines.

Callas' first words as Mimì are muted by fatigue, as though speaking were an effort. The parallels here and elsewhere between Callas' Violetta and her Mimì are inescapable and show once more how cumulative was her art. The fact that Violetta and Mimì are young, French, of a questionable morality, and consumed by the same disease probably linked them less in Callas' mind and throat than did the fate they shared in common. Mimì, of course, contains none of the musical complexities of Violetta, nor is she as finely drawn a character. Mimì is forthright and of a single color. Yet, within this limit, Puccini created a character so sympathetic that she makes the most direct appeal possible to a listener's sensibilities. This is the appeal Callas so thoroughly exploited.

There is more tone and point to her sound after Rodolfo's ministrations, and "Sì, mi chiamano Mimì," like Callas' singing of "Un bel dì," is more a narrative than an aria. Her tale is told simply, with a touch of hesitancy at first, but this is only part of her careful measuring of the scene. When the rapturous "Ma quando vien lo sgelo" arrives, Callas does not slur into it; her voice is gradually flooded with a warmth which at full tide is a match for Puccini's music. The whole has more shape and movement than the version of her recital disc; crucial here is her stressing of the four As during the aria. As Puccini directs, Callas lingers only on the final one, keeping the aria's profile intact. The duet that ends Act I is rich in nuance, from the deep legato with which Callas molds "Tu sol commandi, amore" ("You alone command, love") to the meaningful coloration of "V'aspettan gli amici," which implies "Take me with you" before Mimì has the courage to speak the words.

It is Act III that brings Mimì's drama into the open. Often this act is sung with the same intensity and inflections as the first, or vice versa; but the music and the dramatic situations cry for a sharp distinction to be made, for by the third act Mimì is despondent over her relationship with Rodolfo and her imperiled health. Not only does Callas make this important difference, but the scene with Marcello is the crux of her performance as it is of Mimì's dilemma. We are taken into Mimì's innermost fears and longings, and Callas not only conveys a sense of waning strength, but of the embarrassment of laying bare private feelings to a third person. There is no doubt, however, of Mimì's commitment to Rodolfo, given the ardor with which Callas speaks his name and the hush with which she begs Marcello "Fate voi per il meglio" ("Help us, I beg you"). Her farewell a few moments later is sung with a composure and dignity broken only on the word "bada," where her voice becomes suffused with urgency. In the final act, her singing is as much a vocal sunset as the dramatic one of Giacosa and Illica's text: fragile vocal colors are used to recall Mimì's first meeting with Rodolfo and the pallor of death lies unmistakably over the half-spoken final lines.

Callas is surrounded by a cast of distinction (excepting Anna Moffo's unformed Musetta) performing with optimum sincerity and sensitivity. Di Stefano is an ideal Rodolfo, in superb voice and with little of the tightness that often crept into his upper register. While Votto was not entirely the right conductor for so dramatically attuned a cast (what a collaborator Karajan might have been!) he is mindful of his singers' needs and supplies thoughtful support. It is principally in the solo orchestral moments of Acts III and IV that he fails to carry his share of Puccini's theater.

> **VERDI:** *Un ballo in maschera.* With Giuseppe di Stefano (Riccardo), Tito Gobbi (Renato), Fedora Barbieri (Ulrica), Eugenia Ratti (Oscar), Ezio Giordano (Silvano), Silvio Maionica (Samuel), Nicola Zaccaria (Tom), Renato Ercolani (Judge and Servant). With the orchestra and chorus of Teatro alla Scala, Antonino Votto conducting. [Recorded in Milan 4–12 September 1956, for EMI, reissued as 47498.]

A month after divesting herself of Verdi's first Leonora, Callas added to her repertory his second Amelia. This set marks her last recording of a complete Verdi opera, though in the future lay three discs of Verdi extracts. In *Ballo* we find Verdi striving

110

for a more supple operatic structure by making divisions between sections of his music less pronounced. Also felt is a widening of his harmonic spectrum and a greater individuality in the orchestra's voice. Like the second Leonora still three years away, Amelia is a more modern musical figure than previous Verdian heroines, and also one of the most consistently human. Verdi arouses strong compassion for Amelia's conflict, torn as she is between a secret love and a husband, by expressing it in flights of superb musical imagination. Almost as soon as we meet Amelia, Verdi introduces one of those magnificent vaulted phrases such as he had provided for Violetta in Act III of *Traviata* and would fashion for Leonora in the Convent Scene of *Forza*. It is a broad gulf of sound ("Consentimi, o signore") which Callas' voice spans masterfully.

It is not until the second act of the opera, however, that we come into direct contact with Amelia's personal drama. Callas once again gives an impressive account of the opening scene, and she is careful to shape the few cantabile sections as small islands of expression within the turbulent storm that threatens to engulf Amelia. Though Callas makes a majestic statement of "Deh! mi reggi," her top C is less than majestic, but she does leave it in splendid fashion, phrasing down to and through "O signor." If her credentials as a Verdian soprano of first-rank ability are in need of further support, her singing of the expansive duet that follows supplies them, particularly the phrases "Ah! deh soccorri," "Ma, tu nobile me difendi dal mio cor," and "Ahi, sul funereo letto." At the conclusion of the duet, on which Votto keeps rather too tight a rein, di Stefano not only joins her for the final high C but decides to pocket the B just before as well; in general his lyrical singing in *Bohème* transfers intact to *Ballo*. The trio and the finale are presented with only minor excisions, and Callas begins the former ("Odi tu come fremono") in a whispered sound which gradually builds to the point of hysteria.

The third-act aria "Morrò, ma prima in grazia" is the least successful aspect of her Amelia and recalls the imbalance found between her singing of Aida's two arias. Callas seems to have no greater sympathy for the single sentiment of "Morrò" than she had for "O patria mia." As a piece of singing *per se*, it is plausible, but it is disengaged from Callas' finer dramatic instincts. Her best

111

moment in the act comes with the trio of conspirators where her voice is flushed with apprehension and desperation. The final scene belongs prinicipally to the tenor, but Callas, with di Stefano's help, makes a telling bit of theater with the duettino "Ah! perchè qui," which both sing half-voiced up to the moment Riccardo recognizes Amelia; the final part of the scene is sung by Callas with impressive drive and passion which resolves itself in the death of Riccardo.

SPONTINI: *La vestale:* "Tu che invoco." ROSSINI: *Semiramide:* "Bel raggio." THOMAS: *Hamlet:* "A vos jeux." BELLINI: *I puritani:* "Vieni al tempio." Alfredo Simonetto conducting. Concert of 27 September 1956, RAI, Milan. [*Vestale, Semiramide, Hamlet* in Fonit-Cetra 5; *Puritani* in Fonit-Cetra 4.]

Though the next seven years would bring a flurry of activity from Callas in concert halls in Europe and America, this was her last aria program for Radio Italiana. (She appeared with tenor Gianni Raimondi.) The *Vestale* aria varies little from the EMI recording except that the cabaletta seems less propulsive. The cavatina, however, retains a beautiful length of line. The *Semiramide* aria, on the other hand, is surprisingly inconclusive. Though later versions exist, this was the closest Callas came to achieving a cohesive statement of "Bel raggio." The problem lies chiefly in her moving by individual phrases instead of by groups of phrases; the scene is thus broken into pieces and remains earthbound. While I admire Callas' chasteness in regard to ornamentation, it is carried too far here. Her most prominent embellishment is a modest trill and a scale made to serve as a cadenza midway through. It only draws further attention to the stark quality of her performance and its lack of vocal scintillation.

Her cautiousness with "Bel raggio" is all the more mystifying next to her certain and controlled singing (in Italian) of the *Hamlet* Mad Scene. If anything the *Hamlet* excerpt is even more episodic, yet Callas sings through its phrases with accustomed authority making a convincing whole. Furthermore, there is more elasticity and color here (particularly in scale passages), not to mention ease on top. It is as if the two excerpts had come from two different concerts. The *Puritani* scene begins with Elvira's "La dama d'Arturo." As in the *Semiramide* and *Hamlet* scenes, choral parts are included, and two unidentified singers handle the lines for Riccardo and Giorgio; only the first part of the finale, "Vieni al tempio," is performed. While Callas' singing of these melancholy lines is as touching as ever, the ensemble as a whole is shoddy.

PUCCINI: *Tosca:* Excerpt Act II. With George London (Scarpia) and the orchestra of the Metropolitan Opera, Dimitri Mitropoulos conducting. The Ed Sullivan Show, New York, 25 November 1956. [Melodram 36513.]

Callas completed 1956 with a series of performances at the Metropolitan Opera, New York, where she made her overdue debut, on 29 October, as Norma. She claimed to have been offered a contract with the company in 1946 by Edward Johnson after auditioning with arias from *Trovatore* and *Norma* but refused the offer of *Fidelio* (in English) and *Madama Butterfly*. Johnson's successor, Rudolf Bing, opened negotiations with Callas for the Met as early as 1951, but it took five years for them to arrive at a mutually agreeable contract. In addition to Norma, her first season with the company included Tosca and Lucia. This brief tape taken from television is more a souvenir than a pertinent document. The second-act scene begins with the line "Salvatelo" and cuts come fast and furiously, reducing the music by a good third and omitting the character of Spoletta. Neither singer had the opportunity to get inside the music, and both are at less than their best vocally. (A kinescope of this performance has been preserved.)

DONIZETTI: *Lucia di Lammermoor.* With Giuseppe Campora (Edgardo), Enzo Sordello (Enrico), Nicola Moscona (Raimondo), Thelma Votipka (Alisa), James McCracken (Normanno), Paul Franke (Arturo). Fausto Cleva conducting. Performance of 8 December 1956, Metropolitan Opera, New York. [Melodram 26034.]

113

Callas' only Metropolitan Opera broadcast is, unfortunately, one of her most uneven Lucias, one in which prose dominates poetry. She is trapped within unsubtle surroundings; the orchestra plays poorly for Cleva, and Campora and Sordello do little more than bawl their parts. Neither was she in confident voice; there is a shortness of breath, her top is unsteady (neither E-flat is attempted in the Mad Scene), and there is rarely that buoyancy of phrase which is normally a Callas hallmark.

# *1957*〜

ROSSINI: *Il barbiere di Siviglia.* With Luigi Alva (Almaviva), Tito Gobbi (Figaro), Nicola Zaccaria (Don Basilio), Fritz Ollendorf (Dr. Bartolo), Gabriella Carturan (Berta), Mario Carlin (Fiorello). With the Philharmonia Orchestra and Chorus, Alceo Galliera conducting. [Recorded in London, 7-14 February 1957, for EMI, reissued as 47634.]

EMI's *Barbiere* is as joyful as the Scala performance was unsettled. Among complete recordings of Rossini on disc only two others (EMI's *Turco* and *L'italiana in Algeri*) serve this composer as sympathetically. This set—comedy, not farce—was also Callas' first EMI opera since the 1953 *Lucia* not made under the aegis of La Scala. Her playful, sedate performance of Rosina sets a high-water mark for the role, and she holds its musical and dramatic elements in beautiful balance. Although there are still a number of alterations made within melodic lines (Callas and Gobbi continue to exchange lines in several places), she now sings the part with more of a mezzo-soprano character. Her voice also holds more subtle shades and is used with greater spirit. Recitatives continue to be a delight and ensembles have an effervescent bounce, a Rossinian smile rather than a belly laugh. In the Lesson Scene, the written accompaniment is used, Galliera includes more music than did Giulini, and Callas' voice is employed with striking bravura but without the heaviness of the Scala performance. Galliera also opens up the finale, restoring to each of the three principals their solo flourishes; Callas trades her line for Alva's and tosses it off with virtuoso aplomb and brilliance.

BELLINI: *La sonnambula.* With Nicola Monti (Elvino), Nicola Zaccaria (Rodolfo), Fiorenza Cossotto (Teresa), Eugenia Ratti

(Lisa), Giuseppe Morresi (Alessio), Franco Ricciardi (Notary). With the orchestra and chorus of Teatro alla Scala, Antonino Votto conducting. [Recorded in Milan, 3–9 March 1957, for EMI, reissued as 47378.]

The voice which so expressively limns Amina's music in this recording is unmistakably the same as that which dealt so trippingly with Rosina's for EMI a month earlier. Yet how unalike the two voices are, even though deployed with similar lightness and elegance. They offer striking testimony to Callas' uncanny gift for changing the basic characteristics of her sound to encompass the spirit of differing dramatic figures. It is not just a question of her recognizing that Amina and Rosina, while musical cousins, are the classic masks of comedy and tragedy, but rather the manner in which so obvious a distinction is imparted. This can be partly explained by the slight edge and greater point to her tone as Rosina, while a more hollow, rounded sound is used for Amina. Yet these are only surface indications of a strong force at work. Too frequently, opposing feelings are conveyed on the operatic stage by a mere change of vocal weight; how often are these distinctions drawn by an actual alteration within the timbre of a voice? While actors on the legitimate stage change their voices as they do their dress, and are expected to do so, singers tend to follow their native vocal bent, remaining more dependent on the exterior mood of the music to set character than on their own sound. The marvel of Callas lies not so much in the way she colors Rosina's banter with playfulness while framing Amina's utterances with shyness, but in the fact that she makes one hear and feel the difference in the two attitudes. With Callas happiness is one thing to Rosina and quite another to Amina. It cannot be readily explained, but neither can it be missed.

So moving is the poetry of Amina given us by Callas in this set, it is regrettable that the recording was made under the prosaic direction of Votto rather than the more eloquent baton of Bernstein or Serafin. Though Votto is generally respectful of his singers (except for his haste in "Ah! non credea") he brings little of himself to the music. EMI has given us a beautiful painting minus its frame. Votto also makes a number of cuts beyond those taken by Bernstein: especially regrettable is the omission of yet another statement of "Sovra il sen," a good half of "Ah! vorrei trovar" and a large part of the finale of Act II. Nor is Monti's Elvino as cultivated as Valletti's, and the more dramatic moments of the role (particularly the opening scene of Act III) are not comfortably within his grasp. A tape is said to exist of the 2 March performance at La Scala, in which a number of changes not employed in the recording were made for the sake of Monti, but I have never encountered it.

**DONIZETTI**: *Anna Bolena.* With Giulietta Simionato (Jane Seymour), Gianni Raimondi (Percy), Nicola Rossi-Lemeni (Henry VIII), Plinio Clabassi (Rochefort), Luigi Rumbo (Hervey) Gabriella Carturan (Smeton). Gianandrea Gavazzeni conducting. Performance of 14 April 1957, Teatro alla Scala, Milan. [EMI 64942.]

Through Callas' performances as Anna Bolena were limited—a dozen in all—the role stands as one of her most exacting characterizations. Her remarkable identification with Anna's tragedy comes as a culmination of all the wronged, wounded characters she had previously portrayed, for the emotions of one role provided fuel to ignite another. But here the qualities of conflict, melancholy, and sacrifice are changed and chastened: Callas is aware that she is not dealing with a personal drama, but with the fate of a woman judged by history. This understanding both limited Callas' performance and at the same time strengthened it.

The Scala revival of *Bolena* was presented in an edition prepared by Gianandrea Gavazzeni, who freely cut, and even provided bridges within some sections to tighten the score and its action. In the process, whole set pieces were removed (the overture and Percy's aria "Vivi tu" from the last act), as well as from two to two-dozen bars within the parts that were retained. While Gavazzeni's motives are understandable, a measurable amount of Donizetti's personality and a good deal of musical vitality were lost by his wholesale pruning and patching. What helps to offset these alterations is the overriding presence of Callas and Simionato;

Rossi-Lemeni and Raimondi are less convincing here than we have encountered them elsewhere.

We meet the two protagonists head-on, first Simionato in a brief arioso, then Callas. Anna's opening recitatives are given a pale shading suggesting her troubled state of mind. The aria "Come innocente giovine" takes us behind her courtly mask to dark, inner fears. The cavatina, while short, is demanding, for it continually circles that area of the stave on which Callas' voice pivoted. But with a sure sense of the problem, she paces the aria knowingly, clinging closely to Donizetti's marking of *larghetto*. Her voice is kept free of pressure and imparts the air of a confidence rather than an open statement of mind. The introduction and second verse of the cabaletta are removed by Gavazzeni, and Callas, while more giving in tone, remains gentle. The finale of the second scene completes our introduction to Anna by juxtaposing her for the first time with Henry. Callas continues her contained interpretation, with both her voice and Anna's emotions held in check, until she adds a top C at the end of the scene to heighten the impact of the finale.

Her voice takes on more character in the final scene of the act where Anna is alone with Percy. Though Callas allows more of the woman to surface here (Anna, naturally, is concerned for her and Percy's safety), she still manages to impart a sense of composure up to the discovery that her confidences have been overheard by the page Smeton. After her wounded cry of "Deh! fermate, io son perduta" ("Ah, stay, I am lost"), dignity returns to her voice in her supplication to Henry, "In quegli sguardi," a moving length of cantabile which introduces a sextet of extraordinary imaginativeness. Though quite different from the more sweeping and better-known sextet of *Lucia*, the *Bolena* ensemble is its peer. When Henry rebukes Anna, admonishing her to save her pleas for her judges ("I giudici la tua discolpa udir"), Callas brings the queen's worst fears to the fore as her voice flashes with anger on the word "giudici." On this single word the drama shifts, for Anna is now in open conflict with Henry, and Callas etches it with all the importance it deserves. The fire kindled by her voice bursts into a conflagration in the spirited finale, mounting to a blazing high D at the act's end.

After the quickening of tension created by "giudici" and its threat to Anna's sovereignty, the drama comes to a head in the first scene of Act II where Anna learns the identity of her rival for Henry's love. Together with this dramatic ploy is a rivalry of another sort, the vocal argument which was sparked between Callas and Simionato. Though the original score of *Bolena*, like that of *Norma*, describes both the principal distaff roles as sopranos, custom has come to prefer a mezzo-soprano voice for Jane as for Adalgisa. Having voices of strongly contrasting timbres does make for greater musical variety, and with Simionato no special consideration is required, for her top was splendid and unusually free and full for a mezzo. This she amply demonstrates at the duet's conclusion by joining Callas on a prolonged high C.

This extended duet is among Donizetti's most dramatic and skillfully made pages. It begins quietly with Anna in prayer ("Dio, che mi vedi") and mounts steadily in tension. The crux of the scene is Jane's disclosure of her involvement with Henry ("Dal mio cor punita io sono"). Against her plea for pardon, Callas' voice stabs Jane's eloquent lines with hollow disbelief ("Ella . . . mia rivale"). But Anna, like Norma, ennobles herself through forgiveness, and Callas' haunting delivery of "Va, infelice" is an affecting mixture of sadness and tenderness set within a magical buoyancy of phrase. The exciting conclusion of the scene (sung with brilliance and fiery commitment) foreshadows by a year the stretta of "Mira, o Norma." In the second scene of the act, Anna is brought into deeper conflict with Henry, and Callas' voice now lashes out in opposition to the king, as though Anna is no longer concerned for his waning affection but rather for her name and history's judgment.

The final section of the opera belongs entirely to Anna, awaiting death in the tower. A contemporary review of *Bolena* described her first aria "Al dolce guidami" as "the swan song of a tired person, touched by the sweet memory of love." This is the exact mood in which Callas sings Anna's elegiac cavatina, lavishing on it beautiful proportions of color and rubato, especially the spiraling chain of turns built on the words "del nostro amor" (though she loses for a second the A at the top of the line). A final melancholy effect comes with an attractive cadenza built on the rhythmic figure of an eighth note and two sixteenth notes heard earlier in the aria. Separating the cavatina and cabaletta is a scene between Anna, Smeton, Percy, and Rochefort as the latter are led to their deaths, and an unexpected and original arioso based on "Home, Sweet Home," with which Anna makes her final peace. The repose and spaciousness with which Callas sings this brief moment are in direct contrast to the force of voice and strength of stride with which she delivers the cabaletta. Her voice rises with full security to its top Cs, and there are many stirring embellishments employed throughout to heighten the power of Anna's defiant farewell. A mighty effect is achieved midway by Callas with a set of rising trills, which she elongates by a broad *ritardando*. The return of the principal theme resounds with even greater intensity and caps one of her most inspired achievements in wedding the needs of drama to the resources of her voice.

GLUCK: *Iphigénie en Tauride.* With Francesco Albanese (Pylade), Anselmo Colzani (Thoas), Fiorenza Cossotto (Diane), Dino Dondi (Oreste), Stefania Malagù and Eva Perotti (Priestesses), Edith Martelli (Greek Slave), Constantin Ego (Servant). Nino Sanzogno conducting. Performance of 1 June 1957, Teatro alla Scala. [Melodram 26012.]

Iphigénie was the second of Callas' two Gluckian roles, and as with Alceste, she performed the role in Italian. Vocally, it is one of her least distinctive achievements, for though there is always ample line and taste to her singing, the static theater and music of Gluck's heroine confound even her expressive gifts. Callas responds with a single color throughout—forceful, dark and thick. Even "O malheureuse Iphigénie," the prime, moving moment for soprano, lacks those subtleties of rhythm and grace one expects from Callas. The one place where the urgency of her singing makes itself felt appropriately is in the turbulent opening pages of the opera, where her voice rides the orchestra like a boat in full sail on a stormy sea. No doubt Callas, so chameleon-like in her response to her musical surroundings, was influenced by the rude hand of Sanzogno and the uniform unsuitability of her colleagues.

DONIZETTI: *Lucia di Lammermoor.* With Eugenio Fernandi (Edgardo), Rolando Panerai (Enrico), Giuseppe Modesti (Raimondo), Dino Formichini (Arturo), Elvira Galassi (Alisa), Valiano Natali (Normanno). Tullio Serafin conducting. Concert performance of 26 June 1957, RAI, Rome. [Melodram 26014.]

Though this concert *Lucia* is a more finished performance than the broadcast of the opera from the Metropolitan the year before, it is, nonetheless, not one of Callas' more notable performances and underlines the fact that her days in the role were numbered. Her top sounds uneasy and is approached with great care. The cadenza to the Mad Scene is particularly precarious and again ends on the lower E-flat. Her most supple singing comes in the first-act duet, especially the lilt brought to "Deh! ti placa." The opening arias, on the other hand, are in much the same thick sound as her Iphigénie earlier in the month, and the mood Callas conjures in the duet is frequently marred by the hard, graceless singing of Fernandi. There is also uncertainty from Serafin, who from time to time displays an unusual impatience and pushes his singers unduly, especially at "t'infiammi il petto" during the first-act duet.

BELLINI: *La sonnambula.* With Nicola Monti (Elvino), Nicola Zaccaria (Rodolfo), Fiorenza Cossotto (Teresa), Mariella Angioletti (Lisa), Dino Mantovani (Alessio), Franco Ricciardi (Notary). Antonino Votto conducting. Performance of 4 July 1957, Grosseshaus, Cologne. [Melodram 26003.]

Two performances of *La sonnambula* were given in Cologne by the touring Piccola Scala forces and supposedly both were taped. The cast is, with one minor difference, the same as the Edinburgh performances in August and the EMI recording in March. Yet the results are arrestingly different and vividly testify to the degree of chance and variance that exists in the act of making music even with so professional and practiced a group of performers.

The principal drawback of the commercial set was the prosaic conducting of Votto, especially in comparison to the Bernstein/ Scala *Sonnambula*. But on this particular night in Germany the alchemy between the pit and the stage yielded gold, with Votto not only poetic but mesmerizing. No doubt it was the riveting presence of Callas that raised him to such singular heights, for she is inspired here. The Cologne *Sonnambula* (a nonbroadcast recorded cleanly and naturally, probably from a microphone hung in the house rather than above the stage or orchestra) was a mythic night in her career where voice, intent, and technique were in miraculous balance.

The only other consistent examples of such complete unity of expression and will from Callas are her live performances of *Lucia di Lammermoor* from Berlin and *Medea* in Dallas. These, plus this *Sonnambula* are, in themselves, enough to justify the idea of pirate discs, and taken together the trilogy forms the ultimate testimony to the greatness of Callas.

Of special interest here is the extraordinary insouciance with which Callas delivers the *fioriture* in the cabaletta of "Come per me sereno," framing it within prodigious, even for Callas, legato phrases. Just as astounding is the vaulting cadenza between the two verses of "Ah! non giunge," which is couched in a single phrase and flung out to the German audience with what amounts to ecstatic arrogance. She also brings the cadenza to a head with an immense swell on F at the top of the stave, a capping device not used by her in other *Sonnambula* performances with quite so blinding a result.

But eventually, as is usually the case with Callas, it is not the pyrotechnics of this performance which burn the brightest in one's mind, but the simpler, inward moments, such as the shy responses to Elvino in "Prendi, l'anel ti dono," the light step with which she treads through the dance-like "Ah! vorrei trovar," the expressive suppleness of the second-act finale "D'un pensiero," and her ever-profound realization of "Ah! non credea."

**PUCCINI:** *Turandot.* With Eugenio Fernandi (Calaf), Elisabeth Schwarzkopf (Liù), Nicola Zaccaria (Timur), Giuseppe Nessi (Emperor), Mario Borriello (Ping), Renato Ercolani (Pang), Piero de Palma (Pong), Giulio Mauri (Mandarin). With the orchestra and chorus of Teatro alla Scala, Tullio Serafin conducting. [Recorded in Milan, 9–17 July 1957, for EMI, reissued as 47971.]

A good measure of Callas' early reputation in Italy was based on her portrayal of Turandot, a role she set aside in 1949 after nearly two dozen performances, returning to it only for this EMI recording. It is too bad that an entire live *Turandot* has not survived, for there is an element of strain to high-lying passages in this recording which would not have been as strongly felt eight years earlier. Also, the whole of this recording has an artificial atmosphere, especially Schwarzkopf's arch Liù and Fernandi's unformed Calaf. But there are marvelous compensations from Callas. First, her intense declamation of this comparatively short part gives her performance an imperious power, as she offers not only the ice of the character, but the fire which Turandot tells us burns beneath. In other words, we experience a more layered Turandot than other singers have chosen to reveal. The womanliness of the Princess is unmistakably conveyed by the vibrancy of Callas' voice, the fullness of her phrasing, and the insinuations of her lower register. The first key of Turandot's vulnerability comes in the many moods Callas pursues in the Riddle Scene. Impatience turns to anxiety as Calaf successfully solves Turandot's puzzles. Then, anxiety flares to anger ("Percuotete quei vili") before she is unmasked and begs the Emperor not to give her away "come una shiava morente di vergogna" ("like a slave dying of shame"). This rising phrase is lifted into sharp profile by Callas' strong emphasis of "vergogna," a summation of Turandot's fears and a final crumbling of her haughty exterior. When at last she is subjugated by Calaf's kiss, there is no need for a great shift of color in Callas' voice, for she had become a credible figure by the end of the Riddle Scene. There is, however, a softening of phrase plus an air of mystery at her discovery of first love. Fortunately, Turandot's second aria, "Del primo pianto," is included (it is often cut), providing the needed room to make Turandot's awakening to passion fully effective. This Callas does superbly. (Again Giulio Mauri is a pseudonym for Zaccaria.)

PUCCINI: *Manon Lescaut.* With Giuseppe di Stefano (Des Grieux), Giulio Fioravanti (Lescaut), Franco Calabrese (Geronte), Dino Formichini (Edmondo), Carlo Forti (Innkeeper), Vito Tattone (Dancing Master), Fiorenza Cossotto (Musician), Giuseppe

Morresi (Sergeant), Franco Ricciardi (Lamplighter), Franco Ventriglia (Officer). With the orchestra and chorus of Teatro alla Scala, Tullio Serafin conducting. [Recorded in Milan, 18–27 July 1957, for EMI, reissued as 47393.]

Callas' fourth EMI set of this year was of a further Puccini heroine, another she was never to perform on stage. This recording was also her final EMI collaboration with di Stefano. The issuing of the set was delayed three years, perhaps because of the uncertain state of Callas' top voice here; there are some alarming flaps on top C and even on the B-flat of "In quelle trine morbide." But what a wealth of insight and beauty of characterization is also to be had from this set. Of recorded *Manon Lescauts*, only Callas achieves a full poignant sense of Prévost's French heroine in her Italian setting. Far too often this Mediterranean Manon is sung with a gusto more appropriate to Tosca. But the simplicity of line and gentleness of tone, in all but Callas' top, touchingly suggest more of the vulnerability of the character than her fickleness. This is what Puccini sought to convey. Another factor that sets Callas' Manon apart is her sensibility in invoking rhythmic license without distorting the music.

In the first act, Manon's part consists of two extended exchanges with Des Grieux, the second of which is one of the composer's least dramatically attuned stretches of music. Callas delivers her dialogue with modesty rather than coquetry, though eagerness enters her voice at Des Grieux's suggestion that they escape to Paris together. In Act II, Callas' voice sheds demureness for melancholy, for Manon now lives with the aging Geronte; Puccini, in telescoping Manon and Des Grieux's affair, omitted their brief idyll in Paris. "In quelle trine morbide" is taken a bit faster than on the recital disc and emerges more expressive. It is still sung more to Manon's inner self than to her (in the Puccini version) brother Lescaut, and an engaging effect comes with the unaccompanied words "Come un sogno gentile"; charm derives from Callas' heeding of Puccini's request for *senza rallentare* and aiming the line directly to the fermata before the final phrase. Again, the arietta "L'ora, o Tirsi," meant for Geronte, seems more a comment by Manon on herself through Callas' introspective singing of its graceful lines. The admirable restraint which permeates this *Manon* extends into the great duet of the second act "Tu, tu, amore? Tu?," which is kept closely in check by Serafin and imparts an unprecedented reflective air even within a broad orchestral framework. Passion, to be sure, is plentiful, but it is of a controlled rather than an unbridled sort. During its course, Callas makes a fine resolution of "Cedi, son tua," singing the line meltingly and with meaning. She then builds the arching, "Ah! vieni," the climax of the scene, into a single but multicolored phrase.

In the third act, Callas exchanges Manon's melancholy for a deeper weariness which drains her brief lines of life in an act that belongs principally to the tenor. By the last act, profound sadness envelops her singing, and "Sola, perduta, abbandonata" is more a self-pitying realization of her hopelessness than a desperate cry. In the final pages of the opera, particularly "Ho freddo; era amorosa la tua Manon?" ("I am cold; was your Manon loving?"), there comes that lifeless sound heard in both Callas' Mimì and Butterfly. It is the hollow, dead-before-dying coloring of notes and words that is so unique and so moving.

VERDI: *Il trovatore:* "D'amor sull'ali rosee"; *La forza del destino:* "Pace, pace, mio Dio." WAGNER: *Tristan und Isolde:* "Liebestod." DONIZETTI: *Lucia di Lammermoor:* "Regnava nel silenzio . . . Quando rapito in estasi." THOMAS: *Hamlet:* "A vos jeux." With the Athens Festival Orchestra, Antonino Votto conducting. Concert of 5 August 1957, Arena Herodes Atticus, Athens. [Hunt 537.]

In September 1944, Callas sang for the only time Beethoven's *Fidelio*, in Greek, in the ancient outdoor Herodes Atticus Theater at the foot of the Acropolis. This August 1957 concert signaled her return not only to that site, but to Greece itself. Later at the theater of Epidaurus would come performances of *Norma* and *Medea*. Callas is not in her best voice for this concert; she had postponed it earlier because of the intense heat and dryness of Athens during the summer. Her top notes are especially wavery, and she tends to attack them forte and then pull back to piano.

Nor are matters helped by the pedestrian conducting of Votto and miking that is much too close.

The *Trovatore* aria is sung with a heavy legato. Its most distinguishing characteristic is Callas' single-breath singing of the cadenza, whose ending is altered since previous performances; she still seems to be unable to make a decision about the conclusion of this music. Her voice remains thick in the *Forza* excerpt, and the opening "Pace" is sorely pushed. Early on, she forgets the text and covers with some indeterminate vowel sounds and a final "ahimè," always a good solution for a memory slip. There are some remarkable long phrases here as in the *Trovatore* aria, notably the descent from the B-flat of "Invan la pace" which is carried over into the next phrase. Again she points the aria towards the final "Maledizione," making it an integral part of the whole.

The *Tristan* "Liebestod" is once more sung in Italian, and is less tranquil and more urgent than on the Cetra disc. It is curious that even without the confines of a 78-rpm disc, Callas moves the music along comparatively fast, whereas her inclination was usually to broader tempos. There is very little that is exceptional in her singing of either the *Lucia* or *Hamlet* scenes; much of this has to do with Votto's square accompaniments. In the *Lucia* cabaletta, scales are uneven and the whole is sung much too strongly to be graceful. Furthermore, she uses her top voice with continued caution; the final D is glassy and threatens to shatter.

The *Hamlet* excerpt, also in Italian, begins roughly with some shoddy orchestral playing. Callas' voice is heard at its lightest during this concert, but Votto's sing-song accompaniment calls forth only matter-of-fact singing. In fact, at certain points Callas sounds downright bored. The audience, however, is appreciative, and in response, Callas repeats the final half of the *Hamlet*. This second go-round has a bit more life and lift, but Callas gives out on the final top note.

**BELLINI:** *La sonnambula.* With Nicola Monti (Elvino), Nicola Zaccaria (Rodolfo), Fiorenza Cossotto (Teresa), Edith Martelli (Lisa), Dino Mantovani (Alessio), Franco Ricciardi (Notary).

Antonino Votto conducting. Performance of 21 August 1957, by La Piccola Scala, King's Theatre, Edinburgh [Virtuoso 2697252.]

Callas agreed to this series of *Sonnambula*s under strong pressure from the management of La Scala and against her doctor's wishes; he had certified her as exhausted and on the verge of physical collapse after the appearance in Greece. The Edinburgh engagement, however, was a prestigious one for La Scala, and it sorely needed Callas' name. She was persuaded to sing four performances. This recording of the second performance (the third was also broadcast) makes it obvious that she is working under adverse vocal conditions; not only is her top uncertain, quite white and without resonance, but her middle voice is used cautiously and is not consistently steady. She sounds relaxed and able to cope only in the Sleepwalking Scene of Act II and in the recitatives of the third act. The single most expressive moment of singing comes with "Ah! non credea," which is more heartfelt than in the EMI recording.

**CHERUBINI:** *Medea:* With Mirto Picchi (Jason), Renata Scotto (Glauce), Giuseppe Modesti (Creon), Miriam Pirazzini (Neris), Lidia Marimpietri and Elvira Galassi (Handmaidens), Alfredo Giacommotti (Captain). With the orchestra and chorus of Teatro alla Scala, Tullio Serafin conducting. [Recorded in Milan 12–19 September 1957, by EMI, for Ricordi, reissued as 63625.]

If Callas had been unwise in accepting the Edinburgh performance when she was so fatigued, she compounded this error by attempting a recording of *Medea.* The opera was taped quickly with Callas in uneven voice and more apart from the drama than a part of it. There is the sound of evil in moments of the second and third acts, but never quite enough to make as potent and rounded a characterization as either the Scala or the later Dallas performances. Nor is she anywhere as vocally secure as in these other landmark *Medea*s. The air of this recording is one more of the concert hall than the theater, and Serafin is partly at fault. As with Callas, there is often sharp realism and detail to his work, but just as often vital scenes are set within too slow a tempo for theater's sake. Also the sound of the strings throughout is curiously thin, of chamber rather than symphonic dimensions. Serafin has provided his own edition of the score with extensive cuts which differ from those of Bernstein and Nicola Rescigno (who conducted the work for Callas in Dallas and London). In general Serafin's cuts make sense, though he does take a good deal out of the first Medea-Jason duet, and his cutting creates an awkward moment in the recitative before Medea's last-act "Del fiero duol." However, he does allow Callas the *allegro moderato* of this aria, which Bernstein had suppressed, though Serafin removes two pages of music from it; Callas caps it with an added B-flat.

**MOZART:** *Die Entführung aus dem Serail:* "Martern aller Arten." **BELLINI:** *I puritani:* "Qui la voce." **VERDI:** *Macbeth:* "Vieni! t'affretta!"; *La traviata:* "Ah! fors'è lui . . . Sempre libera." **DONIZETTI:** *Anna Bolena:* "Al dolce guidami." With the Dallas Symphony, Nicola Rescigno conducting. Rehearsal of 20 November 1957, State Fair Music Hall, Dallas. [Legato 131.]

With this program, Callas inaugurated the Dallas Civic Opera, and in the following two years appeared with the company as Medea, Violetta, and Lucia. Though the actual concert was not recorded, its rehearsal was and forms a fascinating document of Callas at work. She has obviously had sufficient rest after the ordeal of Edinburgh and is *in gamba* (in fine fettle), with her voice firm and ringing yet with ample caress. She begins the *Entführung* scene in half-voice, but the urge to sing out soon engulfs her (Callas was never happy simply marking in rehearsal). By the first scale runs, she is using her full voice. The aria goes along well with even more shadings and felicities than the earlier RAI performance. There are only two trouble spots which require reworking. The first is the sustained high C; this is solved by less pressure on her voice and a tempo increased a fraction by Rescigno. The second problem is one of ensemble between Callas and the orchestra in the aria's final set of rising scales. This section is repeated three times as Callas attempts the second of the two phrases in one breath. After her second try, Rescigno comments, "Long breath, huh?," and Callas replies with a low moan. But on the third try, she builds the huge phrase to the cadential A-flat in one musical sentence.

The *Puritani* aria is sung with a plaintiveness and plasticity of phrase which recall her early Cetra disc rather than the EMI recording. Though *Lucia*s and *Sonnambula*s earlier in the year seemed to indicate a shrinking of her upper register, here she delivers an easy, full E-flat in alt which belies previous difficulties. The explanation of this enigmatic feat probably lies in the fact that she is not before an audience but in a relaxed and closed rehearsal situation, at ease and free from performance pressure. The cavatina is performed in toto, then Rescigno returns to the final ten bars to work out its *rubati*, so natural to Callas and so difficult for the orchestra. At the end of the cabaletta, which Callas sings out, although easing up on the downward scales, the orchestra breaks into spontaneous applause. Rescigno returns to the end of the cavatina again, singing along with the orchestra as he further irons out the *rubati*; this portion of the rehearsal ends with another run-through of the cabaletta without Callas.

The *Macbeth* aria is sung without cabaletta, and the cavatina again gets off to an unpromising start with Callas' peculiar voicing of its spoken lines. Once past this section, her voice is ripe in meaning, with dark colors and fiery thrust, even though high notes are held back during the recitative. Rescigno has to repeat the brief passage for orchestra between the recitative and the cavatina to correct a rhythmic problem, but once into the aria proper, he and Callas go without a stop and at a brisker pace than de Sabata's at La Scala. An animated exchange follows between Rescigno and Alberta Masiello (who served as Dallas' first choral mistress) in which it is decided that the orchestra needs more body to match the force of Callas' voice. On the repeat of the cavatina, the tempo and sound are more suitably weighted. Callas begins the second run-through holding back her voice, but soon she is unable to resist singing out, which she does at "Di Scozia a te," though she checks herself at the cadenza and takes most of it down an octave.

Oddly enough, this rehearsal is the only instance preserved in which Callas programmed the first-act *Traviata* arias in concert.

This scene poses the least trouble of all during the rehearsal. Only the connecting recitative between cavatina and cabaletta needs to be repeated. Callas keeps her voice down, singing out only during portions of the cabaletta, and taking its first C and final E-flat down an octave. Alfredo's serenade is omitted along with the second verse of "Sempre libera," a normal occurrence in concert performances. Rescigno's conception of *andantino* for "Ah! fors'è lui" is a quicker pulse than was usual for Callas, but nonetheless effective.

The most interesting segment of this marathon program is the preparation of the final scene from *Anna Bolena*; a chorus is used that delivers not only its own part but many of the lines of Percy, Rochefort, and Smeton. The first recitatives and the cavatina are sung more heavily than at La Scala; this is curious, as Callas usually tended to understate in concert. It could well be that this more black-and-white approach was for the benefit of the orchestra, which was not at this time accustomed to the peculiarities of bel canto. In 1957, American interest in bel canto was largely confined to *Lucia, Barbiere*, and the occasional *L'elisir d'amore* or *Norma*, and none of these had been played by the Dallas Symphony. This was also a period in which literalness in musical performance was still a fact to a great degree in America, so the sort of bending, shaping, and shading that Callas practiced as a matter of course was not easily assimilated by an orchestra in Texas. This became a problem in the working out of the *Bolena* cabaletta after Rescigno and Callas have fixed the cadence of the cavatina and a cut following the "Home, Sweet Home" quote. The snags come quickly—the rising chain of trills, the ins-and-outs of tempo at "favor, pietà," and finally the elongation of "Tacete, tacete, cessate." This final problem brings the orchestra to a halt, and Rescigno returns to the beginning of the cabaletta to straighten it out. Callas follows along in half-voice, but gradually sings out more and more as the problems arise. The trills with their spacious ritardandos are again a hurdle for the players, and Callas sings the final one by herself to show how it should be phrased back into tempo. When she finishes, Rescigno observes, "Now you've heard it, you know what the problem is," and the stretch is tackled again. This time, the ritardandos at "favor, pietà" are given special attention. After reaching the end of the scene, where Rescigno cut the postlude to its final chords, attention is turned once more to the trills. Callas, working like a member of the ensemble and not as a soloist, sings the section *a cappella* a second time before two more run-throughs with the orchestra in full voice. So deep are her interest and concentration, her mind is taken from her own challenges, and the top Cs roll out with breathtaking ease, bringing this extraordinary document to a full-throated conclusion.

VERDI: *Un ballo in maschera.* With Giuseppe di Stefano (Riccardo), Ettore Bastianini (Renato), Giulietta Simionato (Ulrica), Eugenia Ratti (Oscar), Giuseppe Morresi (Silvano), Antonio Cassinelli (Samuel), Marco Stefanoni (Tom), Angelo Mercuriali (Judge), Antonio Ricci (Servant). Gianandrea Gavazzeni conducting. Performance of 7 December 1957, Teatro alla Scala, Milan. [Hunt 519.]

Although Callas was unusually gifted in her ability to create the atmosphere of a theater in the recording studio, there nonetheless remained a gap between her performances in these two arenas. She said that on records one has "to reduce everything to a minimum because everything is so exaggerated in sound." Just how wide this gap could be is clear when a comparison is made between this live *Ballo* and the EMI set. While the commercial recording stands as an entity, even with its less than complete realization of Amelia's third-act aria, the Scala performance is sung with more vivid colors, with accents more etched and a general intensification of Verdi's drama. In the grips of actual theater, before an audience and with the need to act visually as well as vocally, Callas' voice pours out with greater openness. Even "Morrò, ma prima in grazia" fulfills itself in a more convincing way, though it still lacks an inevitability of line. However, the great second-act duet is lifted to compelling new heights, and the final scene with Riccardo has a spontaneous rather than charted veracity. This *Ballo* was the last operatic collaboration of Callas and di Stefano, who apart from a few pinched notes is once more an ardent Riccardo, one happier in the lyrical sweep of the part than in its more introspective, tragic moments. Furthermore,

Gavazzeni ranges further and deeper than did Votto for EMI. Without wishing to minimize Gavazzeni's contribution, it is something else again to imagine what this performance might have been under Serafin's direction.

# *1958* ∼

BELLINI: *Norma.* Act I. With Franco Corelli (Pollione), Miriam Pirazzini (Adalgisa), Giulio Neri (Oroveso), Piero de Palma (Flavio). Gabriele Santini conducting. Performance of 2 January 1958, Teatro dell'Opera, Rome. [Melodram 16000.]

This new year began with the major "scandal" in Callas' career, an event that continued to dog her throughout her life, even after the matter was legally resolved in her favor. During the rehearsals for this *Norma*, the opening night of a new Rome opera season, Callas caught a cold in the unheated theater. The cold developed into flu, and she wanted to cancel the performance. But the theater had no substitute and prevailed upon her to sing against her better judgment. After "Casta diva" Callas realized it was useless, that her voice was slipping away from her and she would never be able to finish the evening; she canceled after the first act. The outcry from the audience and the press was tremendous, and the management of the theater said nothing in Callas' defense. Callas took action in the form of a lawsuit against the house, and after nearly a decade was awarded damages in the case. The tape of the first act shows that Callas was in obviously uncomfortable form. Her breath is uneven, a good deal of pushing is going into her singing, and her mind seems more intent on survival than on the music. This labored quality is felt even more in the recitative after the cavatina and in the cabaletta. Whether or not she could have continued cannot be deduced from this recording. However, it seems certain that had she gone on, the results would have been minor Callas.

VERDI: *La traviata.* With Alfredo Kraus (Alfredo), Mario Sereni (Germont), Laura Zannini (Flora), Alvaro Malta (Douphol), Alessandro Maddalena (Dr. Grenvil), Maria Christina de Castro (Annina), Piero de Palma (Gastone), Vito Susca (D'Obigny), Manuel Leitao (Messenger). Franco Ghione conducting. Performance of 27 March 1958, Teatro Nacional de São Carlos, Lisbon. [EMI 49187.]

Though not a major performance in the Callas chronology, this *Traviata* derives importance from the fact that it was among her final Violettas, and it was her only appearance with Alfredo Kraus, a tenor, who like Cesare Valletti, was an artist who complemented Callas' patrician sensibilities. While Kraus' singing here is not always the work of the super-suave, elegant artist he was to become, it is fascinating to encounter him at the outset of his career and listen to his Alfredo with the hindsight of what was to be.

The fault that Callas is not given fuller rein to create a more dimensional Violetta rests with the pedestrian conducting of Franco Ghione. Yet, within this structure, there are moments to cling to, from the soft-textured and arcing delivery of "Ah! fors'è lui" to, the pathetic beauty with which she endows "Addio del passato" and "Parigi, o cara." In many ways her voice is firmer and more pliable in Lisbon than it would be for the Covent Garden *Traviata* broadcast three months later. But the superiority of the latter performance is due in large measure to the support and presence of Nicola Rescigno, who makes a crucial difference in Callas' overall performance and characterization.

PUCCINI: *Tosca:* "Vissi d'arte." ROSSINI: *Il barbiere di Siviglia:* "Una voce poco fa." John Pritchard conducting. Concert of 17 June 1958, London. [Legato 162.]

After appearances in Bellini's *Il pirata* at La Scala (which was not broadcast) and a brief rest, Callas returned to England for appearances at Covent Garden, first in its Centenary Gala (singing "Qui la voce") and then as Violetta. In between came a television appearance with performances of a pair of arias. The first, Tosca's "Vissi d'arte," is the better—broad and pensive in mood.

The second, Rosina's "Una voce poco fa," is in nearly every respect disappointing. Though Callas' voice remains steady enough throughout, her singing lacks life, and there are moments which sound like a motor running down, or as if Callas is about to fall asleep on stage. Many of the scales and other filigree are tentative and lacking in body, as though she were in a rehearsal marking the music rather than in a performance singing it. Also, *fioriture* are broken up into many little phrases and sound choppy as a result. It would be difficult to believe from this appearance that Callas was on the eve of a series of the most masterful performances of her career.

VERDI: *La traviata.* With Cesare Valletti (Alfredo), Mario Zanasi (Germont), Marie Collier (Flora), Forbes Robinson (Douphol), David Kelly (Dr. Grenvil), Leah Roberts (Annina), Dermot Troy (Gastone), Ronald Lewis (D'Obigny), David Tree (Giuseppe), Keith Raggett (Messenger), Charles Morris (Servant). Nicola Rescigno conducting. Performance of 20 June 1958. Royal Opera House, Covent Garden, London. [Melodram 26007.]

While this performance uncovers some pronounced vocal problems (the top C's are more willed than sung and the now inevitable E-flat at the end of "Sempre libera" is thin and precarious), Callas' use of her voice to expressive ends amounts to an amalgamation of the best in previous *Traviatas*. For even though her voice betrays her at times, her intellect and spirit have now conquered the part in a manner that outdistances all others. The first act remains largely as heard in the first season of the Visconti production for La Scala, though the A-flats of "Ah! fors'è lui" have a new floating quality and the general mood of the aria is more fragile. Despite the hurdles posed by "Sempre libera," the scale passages remain as supple as ever, and Callas makes no concessions to the difficulty of the cabaletta; when the going is roughest, she maintains an even tempo and a proper length of line.

The Germont of Mario Zanasi is quite different from the memorable one of Giuseppe Taddei in Mexico—of a lighter sound and more distant in an aristocratic sense. Yet it is, in its contrasting manner, a performance of almost parallel importance. Zanasi's intrinsic musicality combines with Callas' wealth of insights to bring the lengthy second-act scene between Germont and Violetta to a living realization. This duet is a study in contrasts, tensions and releases on the highest expressive level. Callas' voice is scaled down to essentials; there is no dross. "Dite alla giovine" especially has been refined to a frail, rending thread of sound. The slight hesitation Callas makes before "pura" in its second phrase is deeply affecting, as though Violetta, thinking of her own life, is unable at first to pronounce the word.

But it is in the final act that Callas makes the tragedy of Violetta most immediate. Only her reading of the letter—plausible but not as revealing as at Scala—stands apart from the indelible quality of the rest. The opening recitatives and "Addio del passato" are from another world. The aria is enveloped in memory, and its final high A evaporates into a sigh of nothingness. There is less of a pretense of well-being in "Parigi, o cara," to a better effect, and Callas' responses to Valletti (a near-ideal Alfredo) are drained and hollow. The one show of strength in this act comes with "Gran Dio! Morir sì giovine." The top G which launches this phrase is built to white-hot intensity, but this momentary burst of self-pity quickly subsides, and Callas' Violetta is summed up in the strain "Se una pudica vergine," sung in a half-lit legato of heartbreaking eloquence. Rescigno brings sanity and song to the performance, and was remarkably one with Callas in the ends she sought.

VERDI: *Macbeth*. "Vieni! t'affretta!,," "La luce langue," Sleepwalking Scene. *Nabucco:* "Anch'io dischiuso." *Ernani:* "Ernani! Ernani involami." *Don Carlo:* "Tu che le vanità." With the Philharmonia Orchestra, Nicola Rescigno conducting. [Recorded in London, 19–24 September 1958, for EMI, reissued as 47730.]

This is the first of what would eventually be three recitals of Verdi heroines, and it is the only commercial representation of two major Callas stage parts: Lady Macbeth and Abigaille. The prime fare on the disc is an entire side devoted to *Macbeth*. The side begins auspiciously with "Vieni! t'affretta!" and Callas' finest reading of Macbeth's letter. Though still not entirely spontaneous, her speech has a more natural rhythm and is minus those odd stresses which had previously distorted this decisive moment. The recitative is darkly weighted, and its cadenza an urgent flash of sound. Callas strongly accents the cavatina throughout but within a framework of rhythmic exactness which retains Verdi's *grandioso*; it is a pointed example of what she meant when she spoke of establishing a slow "attitude" within a moving tempo. Rescigno removes twenty-two bars from the *allegro* bridge to the cabaletta, cutting to "Duncano sarà qui?" The tempo for the cabaletta is excellent—well balanced between *allegro* and *maestoso*. On the first upward surge to high B, Callas shifts Verdi's markings of staccato to a more binding non-legato; a sense of separation is still felt but without a loss of line. Particularly striking is her "under the breath" delivery of "Tu, notte, ne avvolgi," which descends malevolently on the word "immortal," as Lady Macbeth invokes night's "immortal darkness." The second verse of the cabaletta is cut, and the tempo is urged forward in the coda, with Callas' voice rising triumphantly to the B.

There is less mystery and more earthiness to the singing and conducting of "La luce langue" than at La Scala, but again Callas' prodigious low register, with its dramatic Bs, is used to enormous effect. Her performance is once more strengthened by the contrasts of the text—the whispered "nuovo delitto" with its thundering answer "E necessario," and the chorale, which Callas fills with evil, followed by the rousing "O voluttà del soglio!" The heart of the disc, however, is really the Sleepwalking Scene (one of two versions she made with Rescigno; the other remains unpublished). It is more than one of the most descriptive moments of singing ever captured on record; it is a summary of Callas' unparalleled power to give words shape and dimension through vocal colorations. Throughout she brings myriad inflections and unearthly tints into play to create the other-world atmosphere heard here. She begins with a touch of awe in her voice, as though Lady Macbeth were standing apart from herself looking at the spots of blood. When she realizes that the stains are actually on her own hands ("Via, ti dico") amazement shifts to disgust, as if her abrasive singing of "O maledetta" could clean away the spots. The words "Una, due" have a distant sound; in contrast her voice swells out with "Tremi tu?" ("Do you tremble?") and then cuts with "Non osi entrar?" ("Do you not dare enter?"). Her full voice is used in the next lines where Lady Macbeth upbraids her husband in her mind for his cowardliness; particularly important to the shape of the line is the strong emphasis given to "O vergogna!" ("O shame!").

Using the *sforzando* markings on "tanto sangue immaginar," Callas reiterates Lady Macbeth's obsession with Duncan's murder, his blood, and with the final "immaginar" (a stifled, almost choked sound), she retreats once more into conscience. Callas' Lady Macbeth is more or less in control of herself in the next section, and her voice is again let out. But this is only momentary; soon her sound is contracted to a whisper with "No, mai pulire io non saprò" ("I shall never know how to clean my hands"). Of great expressive power are the two vocal attitudes contained in the phrase "Arabia intera rimandar si piccol mano." The first two words are sung with force, while the last four are hushed and edged with fright. This section ("Co' suoi balsami non può") of this episodic scene ends on a note of despair, as though Lady Macbeth has finally accepted her guilt. In her mind, she returns to her husband, and Callas' voicing of "A letto, a letto" is as sensual as her voice earlier was obsessed. One last foray into fear comes with "Batte alcuno," and the rest is serene, as though the Lady is at last reconciled with conscience. Callas' voice moves ethereally to the D-flat in alt with which Verdi closes the scene, then dissolves into the mist of the postlude. The entire prelude to the scene is included, though the parts of the doctor and the serving woman have been omitted. Rescigno's brooding tempo is superb and serves Callas and the music's atmosphere far better than de Sabata's nervous pace at La Scala.

Side two of the disc opens with Abigaille's second-act aria from *Nabucco*. The recitative, while exciting in many respects, is hard-driven and seems not as comfortably seated in Callas' voice as before. The cavatina, however, has been wonderfully deepened, but the cabaletta, like the recitative, is problematic, with an unruly cadential trill on top G and a pair of off-center high Cs (the final tremulous one is especially difficult to countenance). Yet there is undeniable thrust and involvement even when her voice is overtaxed.

In marked contrast to *Nabucco* is the very graceful, suave per-

138

formance of "Ernani, involami." Though Callas did not perform more of *Ernani* than this aria, her feeling for the piece is extraordinary. Her voice trippingly dispatches the enormous difficulties posed by Verdi, and the music takes on a lilt which makes it sound far less difficult than it is in actuality. Of special note is Callas' gentle voicing of Ernani's name; this fleeting moment, filled with quiet ardor, sets the mood for the entire aria. This loving beginning carries over into the cabaletta, which is sung, as Verdi directs, to Elvira herself, expressing inner rather than outer thoughts. The chorus is eliminated, as is the second verse of the cabaletta.

Rescigno has recalled that the aria was not rehearsed in advance and the recording was made in one take:

> I took the cavatina rather quickly, and Maria looked up at me; her eyes became very big as they always did when something new was being pulled on her. But good trouper that she was, she went along with my tempo. As we went into the control room to hear the playback she said, "My God, Nicola, that was on the fast side." But Legge greeted us saying, "Rescigno, what a wonderful tempo! It was just right. After all Elvira is a young woman and the text is one of elation." That was all Maria needed. She said "OK, if you two like it, it is all right with me," and she approved it on the spot. But she was so flexible in this regard. I have conducted for many fine singers for whom this was not so. I remember in particular Schwarzkopf's "Mi tradi" in *Don Giovanni*, which she sang superbly, but it had to be measured exactly the same way every time or she'd run out of breath. It was the way she had prepared it. Whereas with Maria you could do anything, you could play with the music. She often did this herself, and I always went along with her as she did with me.

The final extract is from *Don Carlo*, which Callas performed on stage only at La Scala in 1954. Though Verdi marks "Tu che le vanità" a *scena ed aria*, this description only hints at the unusual structuring of this broad, sustained stretch of music for soprano. It is, in actuality, an aria, recitative, arioso, two-part scene, and a recapitulation of the initial aria. This concentration of form was needed to house the five separate states of mind which preoccupy Elisabetta. First, she philosophizes on the vanity of the world, then anticipates Carlo's arrival, recalls her native France, reflects on her love for Carlo, bids farewell to that love and returns to her original thoughts. The piece is one of Verdi's most original designs; by *Don Carlo* he had reached a point of confidence in his career and felt free to tailor music to the mind of a character rather than force it into a prescribed form.

The variety of emotional responses here was guaranteed to trigger the most imaginative side of Callas' artistry. She begins the scene deep in line and legato, majestically forming the broadness of phrase Verdi asks for at the beginning of the section. In contrast, the recitatives are as disjunct and agitated as the aria was resolute and sustained. Callas begins to plot her eventual return to the aria itself by gradually building in intensity with each succeeding section. In the third part, which grows from Elisabetta's memory, her singing is serene yet longing. She gives special emphasis to "Francia" and to "Fontainebleau," as the orchestra quotes from the love music of the first act of the original five-act version. Unrest enters her voice with the realization that her love for Carlo is an "illusion perduta, il nodo si spezzò, la luce è fatta muta!" ("a lost illusion, a broken knot, a light now dumb!"). The turbulence here quiets itself only in Elisabetta's cry for death and in Callas' heavy-chested utterance of "La pace dell'avel" ("the peace of the tomb"). This dark, sombre sound propels us back into the aria proper, as Callas' gift for binding diverse thoughts into a single expression finds one of its most complete outlets.

**DONIZETTI:** *Anna Bolena:* "Al dolce guidami." With Monica Sinclair (Smeton), John Lanigan (Percy), Joseph Rouleau (Rochefort), Duncan Robertson (Hervey). **THOMAS:** *Hamlet:* "A vos jeux." **BELLINI:** *Il pirata:* "Col sorriso d'innocenza." With the Philharmonia Orchestra and Chorus, Nicola Rescigno conducting. [Recorded in London, 19–24 September 1958, for EMI, reissued as 47283.]

Callas had hoped to record *Anna Bolena* and *Pirata* complete, but this disc containing the final scene of each, plus a further *Pirata* aria, was the closest she came. The *Bolena* excerpt is more pathetic in sound and of more subtle colors than those heard in the La Scala broadcast, though Callas' top voice was more focused in the live version. Her phrasing of the cavatina for EMI is one miracle after another of lengthy breath and molded line. The ultimate in this regard is an extended set of melismas on "del nostro amor," which proceeds by groups of turns to a top A; there, Callas lingers a moment and then phrases through into the next section. Another rare effect is achieved with the echo on "un sol."

It was during the recording of this cavatina, Rescigno recalls, that he closeted himself with the English-horn player of the Philharmonia to work out the long solo which commences the cavatina. As the player went over this passage in an effort to achieve the right musical mood, Callas, in response to the music, came into the room. At first she listened quietly, then entered actively into the work, singing the line for the player. A discussion followed on the quality of the music and how a Donizetti line or embellishment differs from a Bellini line, how one should approach and leave a trill in this period of music, and many other technical considerations. As in the rehearsal in Dallas, once again she was a musician at work with another musician, rather than a passive prima donna who arrived, sang, and departed.

The section between the *Bolena* cavatina and the arioso on "Home, Sweet Home" is presented intact, though palely sung by Callas' colleagues. After the arioso, Rescigno cuts from a roll of drums and peal of bells to "Suon festivo?" The cabaletta is sung with a bite that borders on the venomous. The ascending chain of trills and the *ritardando* at their zenith produce enormous excitement and a sense of suspension. Callas' top is better here than in any given place in the Verdi disc, and the controlled abandon of her singing has far more of the theater than was usual in a studio situation.

Though we have encountered the *Hamlet* scene twice before, this is the first time we hear Callas sing it in the original French, and the dividends are many. Her sound is brighter, more forward, and of a greater purity and innocence. This was also her first commercial recording in French, and she demonstrates (as in the RAI *Louise* aria) how well her legato stayed intact when transferred to another language. Instinct must have told her that

141

the question of singing on the vowel is no less a consideration in French than in Italian. French music is not music to be crooned, spoken, or whispered as many singers would have a listener believe.

The beginning of this most gentle of mad scenes has a relaxed and pastoral air. There is never an intruding scene of tragedy in Callas' performance, only the quiet melancholy of Ophelia lost in reverie, grasping neither the sadness of her plight nor her impending death. The tranquil mood Callas imparts throughout stems in large measure from her careful, full phrasing of the aria's florid section. She never allows the *fioriture* to break off from the whole but binds them internally as mental flights of fancy. In this, she is aided by Rescigno's unhurried *tempi*.

The final scene of *Pirata* poses special problems to a singer, for it opens with a long and complex recitative mixed with islands of arioso. Callas solves the challenge by dividing the section into two halves, building the first to the outcry "E desso, Ernesto," and allowing the second to melt into the flute solo which precedes the cavatina. The body of this scene contains one of the most appealing cavatinas and cabalettas written by Bellini. The first is elegiac and of long-spun melody, while the second is dashing and built of short flashing motives. They are a brilliant foil for one another. The cavatina is not unlike that of *Bolena*'s final scene, and Callas adopts a similar dimly lit sound, with floating melismas and wonderfully arched scales. She chooses an upward ending for the conclusion of the cavatina, as she had at the end of the opening recitative. Her voice takes flame in the bridge between the two arias and flares out in the cabaletta where all manner of scales provide fuel for the ensuing blaze. The cabaletta centers on the lines "Là . . . vedete . . . il palco funesto" (There, see the grim scaffold") in which Callas pulls from her throat the most portentous of her sounds. The second verse of the cabaletta is included and embellished in elaborate style but within the spirit and harmonic framework of the whole. The final chorus is omitted, and Callas rides a scale up, and peaks with a brilliant, slashing high C. As she resolves the C downward, Rescigno leaps ahead to the final eight bars of the postlude, condensing the ending and bringing the scene to a more convincing and rousing finish than the one Bellini has written.

BELLINI: *Norma:* "Casta diva." PUCCINI: *Madama Butterfly:* "Un bel dì." John Pritchard conducting. Concert of 23 September 1958, London. [Legato 162.]

Callas' return to London in September for a set of aria discs was followed by a television concert which included a short interview. The uncertain voice heard here does not match the controlled singing of the EMI sessions, and of greater interest than these weak performances is Callas' statement in the interview that in about a year "I will give up singing"—if not completely then she will only sing "very rarely, and on occasions that will be worth my while. I really feel I am wasting my energy, wasting my own young life just for the sake of celebrity, which I feel I have obtained." I wonder if she realized then how prophetic these words were to be.

CHERUBINI: *Medea.* With Jon Vickers (Jason), Elizabeth Carron (Glauce), Nicola Zaccaria (Creon), Teresa Berganza (Neris), Judith Raskin and Mary Mackenzie (Handmaidens), Peter Bender (Captain). With the Dallas Symphony, Nicola Rescigno conducting. Performance of 6 November 1958, Dallas Civic Opera, State Fair Music Hall. [Melodram 26016.]

Dallas was the scene of yet another eruption of "scandal" within the stormy year of 1958. Just hours before Callas was to sing her first Medea in America, a telegram arrived from Bing dismissing her from the Metropolitan's 1958–1959 season over a contractual disagreement. If any good could be said to come from Bing's precipitate act, it was the fire he helped to kindle in Callas' only American Medeas. To those who witnessed any one of them or have heard this recording of the second, there is little doubt that her vitriolic sounds are directed as much to Bing as to Jason. The dramatic imbalances heard in Callas' La Scala Medea are neatly resolved in Dallas, and while Rescigno's conducting does not have as wide an emotional range as that of Bernstein, his performing edition is more compact and swift-moving. Finally, a stronger cast from top to bottom was provided. Of primary importance is her first appearance opposite Jon Vickers. This complete artist (a musician rather than a tenor) was one of the few ideal artistic matches Callas had during her career. He stood for the same aims and standards in singing as Callas, and one regrets that he was never Pollione to her Norma. Another outstanding piece of casting was Teresa Berganza, making her American debut as Neris.

Throughout, Callas' singing is marvelously free, with the role's many top B-flats and Bs sung solidly. After a searing entrance, the feeling again persists that Medea has come to recapture Jason's love. Mark the loving two-note phrases at "splendeva a me" in the first-act aria, the frustration, not anger, of "ho dato tutto a te" and the sensual caress of "Torna a me." Even in the fierce duet that follows, Callas is not as brutally forceful as at La Scala. Everything is in better proportion; the first act is one of hope, the second of intrigue, and the last of vengeance and triumph.

Callas begins the second act impulsively, plunging into her recitatives before the prelude has died away. Here is Medea in the greatest of torment. Though her anguish is suppressed in the duet with Creon, where she is a supplicant, it remains a strong tide under their scene together and bursts out in Medea's asides, notably "Re, degli Dei!" There are two especially memorable moments in the course of the duet; first is the place where Medea agrees to her exile but asks for one day more in which to prepare ("Ebben! tutto mi manca"). This is sung with such sustained pitiableness; it melts not only Creon but a listener as well. Five pages later, Rescigno restores a moving lament cut by Serafin, in which Medea calls out to her homeland in great sorrow. The second duet with Jason, always well-charted by Callas, continues on its strong course (though the microphone placement makes Vickers as overdominant here as Callas was in the first-act duet). Callas' voice now becomes that of a furious, caged animal striking out at the bars that hold it; there is an awkward silence in the next recitative, where she forgets her words momentarily, and a garbled sound follows until her memory triggers the correct text. With the martial music heralding the wedding of Glauce and Jason, one can all but see the wild jerk of Callas' head in the direction of the offstage sound ("Ah! triste canto!"). She becomes a lioness who has picked up the scent of prey. Her voice stalks the ceremony, cutting into it with fearsome asides ("Quei canti, ahimè . . . Ah! mal trionfi tu") and bringing the act to a climax with an added high C.

The agitation in Callas' voice is gone by the beginning of the final act. There remains in its stead a steely certainty and resolve. Her seething delivery of "Numi, venite a me" is a frightening prelude to denouement, and nowhere has her voice expressed greater evil of purpose than when she repulses her children with "Lontan! Lontan! Serpenti, via da me" ("Away, away serpents, leave me"). Her voice dominates the terrifying tessitura of the final scenes with magnificent ease, especially the allegro of "Del fiero duol" (Rescigno, like Serafin, takes a two-page cut here). Callas shapes her part in the finale in two quite different moods. In the first, Medea is dazed, asking who she is, where she is; this is her final moment of misgiving. In the second, doubts are set aside as her resolve mounts to frenzy at the death of Glauce. That hollow, eerie sound, heard in *Macbeth*, is brought into play for the first, while her full voice carries the second in a splendid sprint to the murder of the children. She makes a final pitiless appearance as the tragedy's *deus ex machina*, an appearance made more effective by Rescigno's reduction of it to an essential half-dozen lines.

BELLINI: *Norma:* "Casta diva." With Jacques Mars (Oroveso). VERDI: *Il trovatore:* "D'amor sull'ali rosee . . . Miserere." With Albert Lance (Manrico). ROSSINI: *Il barbiere di Siviglia:* "Una voce poco fa." PUCCINI: *Tosca:* Act II. With Tito Gobbi (Scarpia), Albert Lance (Mario), Louis Rialland (Spoletta), Jean-Pierre Hurteau (Sciarrone). Georges Sebastian conducting. Concert of 19 December 1958, L'Opéra, Paris. [Rodolphe 32495.]

The year 1958 came to a close for Callas with her debut in Paris, her future home, at this gala Legion of Honor concert carried live throughout Europe on television (a kinescope has been issued on EMI 91258 (laserdisc).] She is in much less steady voice than in the Dallas *Medea* (five strenuous concerts under the auspices of S. Hurok in the United States had come in between). Nor is she provided with encouraging support by the fitful conducting of Georges Sebastian. The *Norma* scene especially seems poorly prepared. The chorus goes off badly in a number of places, and the orchestra sounds as if it were sight-reading. After a noncommittal stretch of recitative, Callas begins the aria rather well, and her singing of the cabaletta has great spirit, though a number of crucial notes turn wiry. However, Sebastian chokes off the build-up in excitement by cutting the cabaletta's postlude to a single, thudding chord.

The *Trovatore* sequence, minus cabaletta, lacks the full sense of night and mystery Callas usually wove into the music, nor are her top notes too steady. The cadenza is pushed and the final note held more by Callas' throat than her breath. The chorus is again wretched in the "Miserere," and Callas' voice takes flight only in the second verse. But, as was frequently the case with Callas, *seeing* her makes hearing her more exciting, and the kine-scope of the "Miserere" is riveting. The best of the arias is "Una voce poco fa." Callas lets her voice ride its lines easily; there are a few new twists to her ornamentation, but the aria as a whole retains largely the mood and shape of the second EMI version.

The concert part of the evening finished, Callas returned for a staged performance of *Tosca*'s pivotal act. This united her for the first time on stage with Gobbi's Scarpia. Neither singer achieves his best, given the intrusive conducting of Sebastian; their inter-play is sketchy and minus the subtleties that would come later. However, when engrossed in the action of a scene rather than trapped by the ambience of a concert, Callas is more giving and certain of herself. In *Tosca*, her voice is more assured and com-pelling than at any other point in the evening.

# *1959* ⌒

BELLINI: *Il pirata*. With Pier Miranda Ferraro (Gualtiero), Constantino Ego (Ernesto), Glade Peterson (Iturbo), Chester Watson (Goffredo), Regina Sarfaty (Adele). Nicola Rescigno conducting. Concert performance of 27 January 1959, American Opera Society, New York. [EMI 64940.]

The cancellation of Callas' Metropolitan Opera contract by Bing provided the time to accept an invitation from the American Opera Society for this concert *Pirata*. The performance was not broadcast but was captured privately from a microphone hung in Carnegie Hall. Despite the many problems encountered here—chiefly the provincial singing of Pier Miranda Ferraro and Constantino Ego—it is fortunate that the recording was made, as the Scala *Piratas* (her only other performances of the work) were not broadcast.

Imogene is not the most interesting or complete of Bellini's heroines, but there is a good deal of musical meat here, notably the final scene, and Callas' committed performance in general minimizes the part's lack of character. Her voice, however, is unruly and rather thick at the outset, and it takes the initial scene to warm up and come under control. The opening cavatina is of an interesting design and is heard nearly intact. What lends this aria its individuality is an unexpected burst of energy before the recapitulation (*più mosso* beginning "Quando a un tratto"). Callas frames a handsome cadenza for its conclusion before proceeding to a much altered cabaletta. Rescigno has cut three bars from its introduction, and Callas makes a *ritardando* at the end of the cadenza on "mio cor," then phrases through the rest into the next section ("Ah! sarai"). The repeat is omitted, and she pours out a lusty top D at its conclusion. Yet, despite her agile handling

147

of scale passages, the predominant feeling is one of caution. It is not until the first duet with Gualtiero that she appears to relax and begins to make music. Here her voice comes together, and her top remains forceful and compact throughout the remainder of the evening.

This long duet is not of the best quality, and Rescigno, no doubt with this in mind, contrives to tighten it by removing transitional material, making it more of a single piece. Ferraro is incapable of the simplest *gruppetti* and is rhythmically vague throughout. Callas, however, has moments of great expressive beauty, particularly the haunting line in C minor beginning "Ah! tu d'un padre antico." This section lifts into C major for its conclusion, and the ending taken is not found in the Ricordi score. Twenty-eight bars are removed from the *stretta,* and Callas and Ferraro interpolate a pair of high Cs at its end. The recitatives between Imogene and Adele which follow are cut, and we next hear Callas after Ernesto's scene. Again Rescigno strives to bind the loosely made finale into something more shapely. The best music in this rather mechanical piece is the *stretta,* which Callas digs into with tremendous force. Only half of it, however, is retained, and the momentum of the scene suffers as a result. There are, as if in compensation, a dazzling four bars of rapid scales on the word "scoppia" delivered by Callas with glittering virtuosity. Rescigno recalls that at the rehearsal he took these scales at an unusually fast pace, one which required

a machine gun rather than a singer. Maria looked at me a bit frightened when the passage was coming up and she didn't make it. I told her that the next time I would put on the brakes just before her entry. "No, don't do that," she answered. "I like the tempo very much; it is valid and I don't want you to help me." "Well," I said, "what if you don't make it in the performance?" "That's my business, not yours," she countered. However, out of her fantastic will came this superb, astonishing thing at the performance, all in order!

The duet for Imogene and Ernesto in the second act is another patchy affair and underlines the uneven nature of *Pirata.* Again Rescigno dovetails its sections, as well as weeding out some additional hundred bars. Part of this was done, no doubt, to eliminate redundancies, but part must have been done to accommodate Ego's great vocal limitations. Like Ferraro, he is most comfortable in half notes. In the *larghetto* section of the duet he turns his written sixteenth-notes into quarter notes, and Callas has to sing alone an elaborate passage written in sixths. Again, the *stretta* is too heavily pruned, and simplifications are needed for Ego. Callas is heard to dazzling effect despite Ego's problems, as she brilliantly etches Imogene's whiplash lines and darts up to a full, fine B. The second duet between Imogene and Gualtiero is almost a total loss because of Ferraro's continued clumsy singing, but Callas saves what she can with her breadth of line at "Taci, taci, rimorsi amari." Rescigno takes six bars from the end of the duet and segues it into the upcoming section, but what is written as a trio becomes almost a solo for Callas, as line after line for Ferraro and Ego are removed in the interest of musical sanity. Numerous cuts truncate both halves of the trio, and Callas exchanges lines with Ferraro at the end of the *più mosso*. He joins her for a final high C, and the trio's postlude is omitted entirely.

The final scene is more pressed in the cavatina than was the case for EMI; also, the cabaletta seems a good deal faster. Callas employs the same variants and manages to keep details intact under the pressure of Rescigno's quicker tempo. The scene is once more crowned with a sustained top C, which Callas attacks head-on and with a commanding show of force.

**DONIZETTI:** *Lucia di Lammermoor.* With Ferrucio Tagliavini (Edgardo), Piero Cappuccilli (Enrico), Bernard Ladysz (Raimondo), Leonard del Ferro (Arturo), Margreta Elkins (Alisa), Renzo Casellato (Normanno). With the Philharmonia Orchestra and Chorus, Tullio Serafin conducting. [Recording in London, 16–21 March 1959, for EMI, reissued as 47440.]

The next twenty months of recording activity by Callas were a period of remake, as she concentrated on stereo versions of *Lucia*, *Gioconda*, and *Norma*. In each instance, she was competing only against herself; the one bout she loses is *Lucia*. This is one of her few commercial sets in which the velvet of her middle voice sounds frayed, and her upper register is used with extreme care; steady, controlled top notes are in short supply. Though "Soffriva nel pianto" in Act II and the Mad Scene up to the cadenza have plaintive moments and fresh insights, they are better realized in the first set. There are two noteworthy variants here from her usual practice as Lucia. The first is slight, but strange; in the Sextet, Callas approaches her solo B-flat midway through from A-flat instead of the written G. The second change is more crucial and underlines her many vocal insecurities in this recording. For the Mad Scene, the same cadenza is employed, but Callas now eliminates five of its phrases and alters a sixth.

Another nagging drawback to this set is the extreme curtness of phrase in Tagliavini's singing. Though capable of suavity, he was obviously out of sorts here. The few felicities of line he musters (the opening of "Verrano a te," for example) are not enough to compensate for his slovenliness elsewhere. The remainder of the cast sings neutrally excepting Margreta Elkins, who oversings. Only Serafin holds to his course with an unerring sense of dramatic direction.

SPONTINI: *La vestale:* "Tu che invoco." VERDI: *Macbeth:* "Vieni! t'affretta!" ROSSINI: *Il barbiere di Siviglia:* "Una voce poco fa." VERDI: *Don Carlo:* "Tu che le vanità." BELLINI: *Il pirata:* "Col sorriso d'innocenza." With the orchestras of the North and South German Radio Networks, Nicola Rescigno conducting. Concerts of 15 May (Hamburg) and 19 May 1959. (Stuttgart) [Hamburg on Arkadia 410.1; Stuttgart on Eklipse 37.]

Callas' activities in concert remained limited until 1958, when she began an eleven-city tour of America under the Hurok banner. From then until 1964, her time was equally divided between concerts and opera; in fact, 1962 and 1963 were years of only concerts. The program heard in Hamburg and Stuttgart was repeated in Munich and Wiesbaden, all within a month.

Though the *Vestale* scene does not scale the heights in Hamburg that it would during Callas' appearance in Amsterdam, like most of this German concert it shows her in steady form, rested after the rigors of the *Lucia* recording sessions. An advantage to *Vestale* in Hamburg as opposed to Amsterdam, however, is that Callas manages to remember more of the text. Again she makes alterations in the vocal line, most noticeably to accommodate the driving high Gs on "Deh! ti basti" in the cavatina. She also elects, as in Amsterdam, to bypass the final, interpolated high C.

The *Macbeth* aria in general goes well, from the reading upward to secure, easy high notes. The omission of the cabaletta probably explains the punctuation of a sustained A-flat added at the cadence. A little too much of the weight from *Macbeth* seeps into the *Barbiere* aria, but otherwise it is handsomely, though not always clearly, sung. The *Don Carlo* extract, however, lacks the organic wholeness of the EMI recording, and Callas dwells too long on the "Francia" section.

For concert purposes, Rescigno has cut a page of recitative between the two halves of the *Pirata* scene, and Callas jumps to "Gualtier! oh periglio!" Tempos here are less hurried than at Carnegie Hall, and curiously (for Callas is in good form), the final C is omitted. She goes instead for the G, and this lame substitution takes the edge off of what had been an exciting performance. (The Hamburg concert was televised and a kinescope has been issued on Pioneer Laser Disc PA 85–150.)

It is remarkable the concert in Hamburg went as well as it did considering Callas was battling a severe cold. She had obviously shaken it by the time of her Stuttgart appearance, four days later, for there she exercised a finer control of details within her program. There is more abandon and a broader use of chest voice in the *Vestale* excerpt, the opening cadenza in the recitative to the *Macbeth* scene is untrammeled where it had been messy in Hamburg, the ornaments of the *Barbiere* aria are neater and more spontaneous and the mood lighter (although Callas still runs short of breath at a few phrase endings), and the *Don Carlo* scene holds together better. The one part of the concert that remains essentially the same as in Hamburg is the *Pirata* scene.

CHERUBINI: *Medea*. With Jon Vickers (Jason), Joan Carlyle (Glauce), Nicola Zaccaria (Creon), Fiorenza Cossotto (Neris), Mary Wells and Elizabeth Rust (Handmaidens), David Allen (Captain). Nicola Rescigno conducting. Performance of 30 June 1959, Royal Opera House, Covent Garden, London. [Melodram 26005.]

The Dallas *Medea* production traveled to London in exchange for Covent Garden's mounting of *Lucia di Lammermoor*. This *Lucia,* designed and directed by Franco Zeffirelli, was seen in Texas five months later; in it, Callas made her final appearances in a role with which she had become particularly identified. This English *Medea* is a pale copy of the Callas original; it is more akin in its lack of spirit to the Ricordi recording. The first act lacks drive, and though her portrayal springs to life at the beginning of Act II, neither duet is as brimming with meaning as in Texas. The tempos are unaccountably slow, and the section beginning "Ebben! tutto mi manca" threatens to grind to a halt at any moment. While the last act has gripping moments, there are also many stretches so reduced in pace that Callas sounds as if she is singing in slow motion (the pitch of the discs is correct, incidentally). Vickers and Zaccaria, however, are superb, but the orchestra under Rescigno is less surefooted than was the Dallas Symphony.

SPONTINI: *La vestale:* "Tu che invoco." VERDI: *Ernani:* "Ernani! Ernani, involami"; *Don Carlo:* "Tu che le vanità." BELLINI: *Il pirata:* "Col sorriso d'innocenza." With the Concertgebouw Orchestra, Nicola Rescigno conducting. Concert of 11 July 1959, Amsterdam. [*Don Carlo* and *Pirata* in EMI 49428; *Vestale* and *Ernani* in Legato 162.]

With this concert, Callas is back in full stride. She made her debut in Holland in superb voice, and, in most instances, the arias performed here go beyond her EMI recordings of the same material. She brings an even more compelling contrast between serenity and tumult to the *Vestale* scene. The second-half allegro is now sung without an interpolated top C—a great improvement. Callas retains the same approach to the *Ernani* aria as on EMI, but endows it with a further suavity and lilt. Notable here is the breezy lift given to the scales and cabaletta. As in Stuttgart, Callas makes "Tu che le vanità" spacious, but here it holds more convincingly together, and its final section is delivered with greater import. Finally, the *Pirata* finale has a finer softness to phrases and flow throughout. Rescigno and Callas retain all recitative between cavatina and cabaletta, omitting only four bars of unaccompanied chorus before "Gualtier! oh periglio." The one stretch which is more effective in its commercial counterpart is the cabaletta. While the Amsterdam performance is filled with rage, it is not as exciting as the commercial disc, and the final C not as convincing.

**PONCHIELLI:** *La gioconda.* With Pier Miranda Ferraro (Enzo), Piero Cappuccilli (Barnaba), Fiorenza Cossotto (Laura), Ivo Vinco (Alvise), Irene Companeez (La Cieca), Leonardo Monreale (Zuane), Renato Ercolani (Isepo), Carlo Forti (Singer and Pilot), Bonaldo Giaiotti (Barnabetto). With the orchestra and chorus of Teatro alla Scala, Antonino Votto conducting. [Recorded in Milan, 5–10 September 1959, for EMI, reissued as 49518.]

The Cetra *Gioconda* of 1952 and the stereo remake for EMI seven years later both demonstrate Callas' scrupulous care with music and her deep involvement with words. But the EMI set also shows how much wisdom she drew in a decade from diligence and experience. The full abandon of Cetra is tempered on EMI and with more fascinating, less violent vocal emphases and a greater steadiness of approach. There are some surprises along the way, for in several instances Callas is in better control of her wayward top than she was many years and many pounds earlier. For instance, the pitfalls of "Enzo adorato" in Act I are more skillfully skirted, and the top B climax of "Suicidio" is more certain and is bound into the overall phrase. This is particularly impressive, as this set was made during a difficult conflict in her personal life, the separation from her husband; perhaps the *Gioconda* sessions were just the escape valve needed for the pressures which were building off-stage. The glory of this set is found in the last act. Callas once remarked that this section was among the most satisfying of her records, adding quietly, "It's all there for anyone who cares to understand or wishes to know what I was about." The magic begins with "Suicidio," and rather than moving from one outburst to the next as she had on Cetra, Callas creates a sense of wholeness by closely linking dramatic ideas together. What is designed as a soliloquy becomes one in reality. Also improved over Cetra is the rising phrase "E un dì leggiadre," especially her floating leave-taking of the top A in the phrase. She still makes important use of her chest voice, but it is now less of a feature unto itself. Another fleeting touch of magic is her soft delivery of "Enzo, sei tu" in the following scene, and her legato in "A te questo rosario" is unequaled.

The EMI cast supporting Callas makes one feel more charitable towards the Cetra singers; where Callas had at least professionalism from her male colleagues earlier, plus the vibrant Laura of Fedora Barbieri, here she must go her way alone. Ferraro is blustering, Cappuccilli neutral. Vinco does not measure up to Neri and Votto is more distant and less rhythmically exact than on Cetra. As to Cossotto's Laura, a role which will later suit her well, it fits too loosely here. Her rhythmic inexactitude in the duet "L'amo come il fulgor" stretches the beginning of this fiery encounter out of shape and blunts its impact.

VERDI: *Macbeth:* Sleepwalking Scene. BELLINI: *Il pirata:* "Oh! s'io potessi." With the Philharmonia Orchestra, Nicola Rescigno conducting. Concert of 23 September 1959. Royal Festival Hall, London. [*Pirata* LP only.]

This is the only material to have survived from Callas' 1959 London concert, an evening which also included "Tu che le vanità" from *Don Carlo* and "A vos jeux" from *Hamlet*. It provides an interesting footnote to the Callas legacy, for here was the first instance of her being recorded from the audience by means of a transistor recorder (a hand-held machine operating on battery power).

Though common today and often yielding sophisticated results, it was a primitive attempt in 1959. Yet the sound is clear and forward enough for us to be aware of the vivid colors with which Callas is tinting the music. Accents are more violent and the performance scale is broader than either the Scala broadcast or the EMI recording. Here is a Lady Macbeth bordering on a Medea.

From the remainder of the concert, all that could be salvaged was the recitative to the *Pirata* finale. Though most of the scene exists, the cavatina and cabaletta are a maze of distortion resulting from a loss of power in the recorder, whose ebbing can be heard during the opening measures of the excerpt. In what remains, it is obvious that Callas is continuing much in the same mighty frame of mind which had illuminated the *Macbeth* scene in so strong and fresh a light.

PUCCINI: *La bohème:* "Sì, mi chiamano Mimì. BOITO: *Mefis-tofele:* "L'altra notte in fondo al mare." With the Royal Philhar-monic, Sir Malcolm Sargent conducting. Concert of 3 October 1959, London. [Legato 162.]

These two arias were included as part of a television gala which also featured Tito Gobbi, José Iturbi, and Dame Alicia Markova. The *Bohème* aria remains as disarming in its simplicity as "L'altra notte" continues haunting in its complexities. The only disquiet-ing thing is a momentary lapse of memory in the second verse of the *Mefistofele* aria, which Callas covers with vague vowel sounds.

# *1960* 〜

BELLINI: *Norma.* With Franco Corelli (Pollione), Christa Ludwig (Adalgisa), Nicola Zaccaria (Oroveso), Edda Vincenzi (Clotilde), Piero de Palma (Flavio). With the orchestra and chorus of Teatro alla Scala, Tullio Serafin conducting. [Recorded 5–12 September 1960, for EMI, reissued as 63000.]

The first realization of how serious Callas was in London when she spoke of curtailing her career came in 1960. There were no appearances during the first seven months of the year, and the remaining five months were devoted to only two works: *Norma* and her final stage creation, Paolina in Donizetti's *Poliuto*. This second EMI *Norma* was prefaced by a pair of performances of the work in the arena of Epidaurus. These reunited Callas and Serafin in a stage performance. Despite their steady string of records together, they had not worked as a team in the theater since 1953, *Aida* in Verona. The Greek *Norma*s and this recording were their final collaborations.

In many ways, the development of Callas as an artist in the 1950's is most immediately exemplified by a comparison of the two EMI *Norma*s. The emotions of the part are stated in 1960 with less exterior emphases, and details are colored more by the shape and peculiarities of the words themselves. This multi-faceted Norma is more giving, more complex and drawn in finer lines. "Casta diva," for example, is quieter, more mesmerizing (with phrase endings exquisitely tapered into silence), as are the second-act scenes with Adalgisa. The true depth of this Norma, however, is sounded in the final two acts; phrases such as "Teneri figli" and later "Ah! perchè, perchè" in "Mira, o Norma" are carried not only to a lofty level of musical awareness and vocal control but of expression that transcends technical polish. Along with this, the fearsome Norma remains intact; indeed she draws a new strength through the gulf of contrast Callas meticulously establishes. There are other reasons to value this recording—the renewing presence of Serafin and the often noble Pollione of Franco Corelli. While Christa Ludwig rides Adalgisa's music in greater comfort than did Stignani, there is a loss of authority as there is with Nicola Zaccaria's Oroveso, although his sounds are more buttery than those of Rossi-Lemeni.

**DONIZETTI:** *Poliuto.* With Franco Corelli (Poliuto), Ettore Bastianini (Severo), Nicola Zaccaria (Callistene), Rinaldo Pelizzoni (Felice), Piero de Palma (Nearco), Virgilio Carbonari and Giuseppe Morresi (Christians). Antonino Votto conducting. Performance of 7 December 1960, Teatro alla Scala, Milan. [Melodram 26006.]

This opening night performance at La Scala heralded Callas' return to the company and the addition of yet another role to her gallery of operatic personalities. While there are attractive musical aspects to Paolina, there is very limited dramatic tension to this tale of third-century Christian martyrdom, and Paolina is of secondary importance to Poliuto. Of greater interest is the influence the work must have exerted on the young Verdi. In *Poliuto*, Donizetti extended his stylistic boundaries to forge a number of original musical units. In Paolina's first scene, for example, the recitative to her cavatina is separated from it by an offstage chorus, over which she comments before her aria begins. Later, Votto turns to the original five-act version of *Poliuto* written for Paris, restoring a duet ensemble between cavatina and cabaletta. The resulting structure stretches traditional aria design in much the same fashion as Verdi in the unusual scene for Leonora that opens Act IV of *Trovatore*. Another point of interest, especially in terms of Callas, is Donizetti's elimination of the final, summing-up scene for soprano. In its place comes an ensemble that was later echoed in *Ballo*, just as the monumental second-act finale of *Poliuto* prepared the way for the more famous Triumphal Scene in *Aida*.

Callas' voice sounds considerably trimmed down at her

entrance; her careful singing was no doubt conditioned by nerves at her reentry to La Scala. She does not handle the opening flourishes and scales of Paolina's cavatina with great conviction; rather, she seems to be still feeling her way into the performance. Callas removes a bar from the cadence and substitutes in its place a rising, higher ending. The cabaletta that follows the interpolated duet-ensemble is cut by half, and four of its final spirals of eighth notes are omitted to prepare for the one high C out of three Callas chooses to retain. This scene is the extent of Paolina's participation in Act I. In the opening of Act II, a duet between Paolina and Severo, Callas' voice is more steady and in control. There are several appealing strains of melody here, all well sung—"Ei non vegga il pianto mio" and later "Quest'alma è troppo debole." In the first half of the duet there are small, tightening cuts made by Votto, and in the second half there is an enormous one of over two pages that stems the flow of the scene. Paolina's entry into the finale ("Qual preghiera al ciel") is treated as a solo with Severo's interjections omitted. In the *allegro* of the finale, Callas plunges in headlong; her voice is given full rein here and the temperature of the scene rises by several degrees. She tries a top D at the end of the ensemble, but releases it quickly when it threatens to go out of control.

The last act, like the second, involves Paolina only in a duet and the finale. The beginning of the first ("Ah! fuggi da morte") is shaped by Callas in a gentle, pleading way, and she ends this quasi-arioso with a cadenza of her own making. Later, Callas skirts the difficulties of "Un fulgido lume" with masterful ease and lightness (those leaps upward of a tenth to top Bs). She is unequal here only to the top B at the outset of the allegro vivace which must be sustained for five bars. But she turns the acid memory of this note to sweetness in her delicate tracing of "Il suon dell'arpe." Three pages are lost from the remainder of the duet as Votto dovetails it into the final scene where Paolina's contributions are of little consequence. The role's one aria and two duets recall the limited possibilities that *Andrea Chénier* offered Callas, though Donizetti's language offers more to her understanding and is, no doubt, more to her liking than Giordano's. Still it is as curious that she was willing to undertake

Paolina as it is that she sang Maddelena. The answer could well be that Callas wished to return to La Scala as free from nervous tension as possible and thus was willing to share honors with, and even take a back seat to, Corelli.

# *1961* ❧

**GLUCK:** *Orphée et Euridice:* "J'ai perdu mon Euridice"; *Alceste:* "Divinités du Styx." **BIZET:** *Carmen:* "Habanera," "Séguedille." **SAINT-SAENS:** *Samson et Dalila:* "Printemps qui commence," "Amour! viens aider ma faiblesse!", "Mon coeur s'ouvre à ta voix." **GOUNOD:** *Roméo et Juliette:* "Je veux vivre." **THOMAS:** *Mignon:* "Je suis Titania." **MASSENET:** *Le Cid:* "Pleurez, mes yeux." **CHARPENTIER:** *Louise:* "Depuis le jour." With the Orchestre National de la Radiodiffusion Française, Georges Prêtre conducting. [Recorded in Paris, 28 March–5 April 1961, for EMI, reissued as 49059.]

This LP is the French equivalent of Callas' "Lyric-Coloratura" disc of Italian arias made for EMI in 1954. The range here, however, is even wider, but not without historic precedents. One need only recall Pauline Viardot (who sang Lucia and Orphée and for whom Dalila was written) or Adelina Patti (both Amina and Carmen) to realize that Callas has not roamed as far afield as might seem the case. Distinctions between soprano and mezzo-soprano (and even between mezzo-soprano and contralto) were much hazier in the nineteenth century, the age to which Callas' singing continually harks back; certain parts now assumed by mezzo-sopranos were originally designed for contraltos or even sopranos. It was in our century that lines were more sharply drawn. As Callas was mistress of both Isolde and Violetta (as was Lillian Nordica), it should come as no surprise to find her singing music for Carmen and Philine (also Nordica roles).

The record opens with one of Callas' most impressive performances on disc, the *Orphée* aria. It is a true lament. Phrases are laden with sorrow; the second statement of "Rien n'égale mon malheur" is particularly rich in its deep note-to-note legato, and just as telling are the three different weights of voice she finds for each statement of "J'ai perdu mon Euridice." Her cry midway of

160

"Euridice, Euridice réponds" and the intense sadness which follows in "Quel supplice!" linger with one long after hearing the recording. Again, as in the *Alceste* aria which follows, her unique ability to seem to suspend time through rhythmic flexibility is an indelible feature of the whole.

But where Orphée is an abandonment to grief, Alceste's invocation is supreme dignity in the face of loss. As Callas drew distinctions among the three recurring statements of the opening line of Orphée's aria, so she achieves three quite separate ways of coloring "Ministres de la mort" in "Divinités du Styx." The first is hushed, as though Alceste is fearful of summoning death's ministers; Callas makes us believe that Alceste's courage builds in mounting nobility with the music, and the second of these phrases is filled with greater strength and even defiance. Also, as was ever the case with Callas, small details become matters of great eloquence, such as the *appoggiatura* on "époux," when Alceste first mentions the husband she alone can save. This leaning note imbues the word with tenderness and lifts the phrase into prominence, as does her caress of "Mourir pour ce que j'aime." The B-flats of the aria are admittedly driven, but never intrusively so.

The two *Carmen* selections are sung with pointed directness and with more subtlety of rhythm than of vocal colors. She begins both forte rather than piano, and this dynamic level remains fairly consistent throughout. There is, however, the counterbalance of long phrases, sensual *portamenti* and a colorful use of words—the bite of "Il n'a jamais, jamais connu de loi" in the "Habanera" and the humor of "Il est au diable" in the "Séguedille." Callas builds both arias upward, saving gustier inflections for the final phrases. These performances, however, signal a beginning rather than a culmination in realizing this elusive music.

Interestingly enough, there is greater shape and finish to the three Dalila arias, which she would not sing again. Her voice is silky and persuasive in "Printemps qui commence," a mixture of allure and irony, with an easy, full use made of her low voice. A contrast comes with "Amour! viens aider," sung as a stirring invocation, revealing the malevolence behind the irony sensed in "Printemps."

During her lifetime, Callas withheld the aria "Mon coeur s'ouvre à ta voix" because she objected to two descending phrases

on the words "tendresse" and "ivresse." These low-lying passages caused her to take breaths she felt were inappropriate and
unmusical. What was a minor problem in 1961 was by 1982,
when the aria was first issued, a negligible one in light of Callas'
overall sensual delivery of this famous operatic moment. She
makes the aria silky and sexy—the very essence of seduction—
tinting it with shades of pastel rather than the heavier hues often
employed by others.

She sings the piece exactly as written, eliminating Samson's lines,
including his B-flat at the end of the aria. This note is usually
included when the scene is performed without a tenor, but this
addition went against Callas' musical taste. Despite her feelings
to the contrary, she delivers the fullness required throughout
the extremes of these contralto arias, and happily EMI chose to
disregard her wishes, making "Mon coeur" available following
her death.

The remainder of the disc is even more a mixing of vocal light
and shadows. The *Roméo* extract was not really a suitable aria
for Callas' voice. However great her charm in several sections,
she sounds too mature a Juliet, and her voice does not coruscate
as one might have expected. But with Callas there is always
something of interest; here it can be found in the grace of the
*acciaccature* on "Je veux vivre," in the uncanny manner with
which she makes the aria seem to float, the elegance of two-note
groups and the miraculous fades at the end of phrases in "Loin
de l'hiver morose, laisse-moi, laisse-moi sommeiller." Offsetting
these is the by now predictable flap on the final high C; and a
set of three downward scales from top A near the close come
perilously close to war whoops.

By contrast, the *Mignon* fulfills itself with only minor blem-
ishes, though many might well prefer a more bravura attitude and
a more scintillating sound. However, the beginning is beautifully
modeled, with lilt and femininity. The filigree in general is lovely
in its finish and relationship to the whole, and a set of repeated
scales, similar to those which went wild in Juliet's aria, is suavely
managed. The only real moment of concern is a wayward final
trill on A and a recalcitrant B-flat which follows.

Vying for honors with the *Orphée* aria on this disc is Chimène's soliloquy from *Le Cid*, "Pleurez, mes yeux." All those
dark, Greek-theater forebodings Callas knew so well by instinct

and heritage are brought into play in this powerful scene, along with her great technical ability to make such feelings credible. Her identity with Chimène's anguish and her resignation to death is monumental. Once more, this extraordinarily expressive moment can be traced to her many-faceted legato, her response to words (a gift as inexplicable as it is moving) and her use of both to impart texture to musical lines.

"Depuis le jour" is another matter. Though Callas unerringly captures the mood of Louise's mounting ecstasy, her performance is badly flawed by a continual unsteadiness above the stave culminating in a notably tremulous top B. But her intent remains ever clear and on target even when her voice is not.

MASSENET: *Le Cid:* "Pleurez, mes yeux." VERDI: *Don Carlo:* "Tu che le vanità." BOITO: *Mefistofele:* "L'altra notte in fondo al mare." Sir Malcolm Sargent, pianist. Concert of 30 May 1961, St. James's Palace, London. [Legato 162.]

This occasion was a benefit appearance for the Edwina Mountbatten Trust. Also included on the program but not recorded was "Casta diva." Callas is in more even voice here than for the EMI French recital, though, of course, a studio microphone does tend to be a microscope, unnaturally exposing a voice in a manner live performance does not. Her singing is excellent as far as it goes, except that the *Cid* aria lacks the full commitment heard on her recording. Without the buoyancy lent by an orchestral sound, Callas' voice sounds curiously disembodied; the total effect, together with Sargent's unexplainable rhythmic vagueness, is somewhat hazy. The *Don Carlo*, incidentally, was not captured complete; it ends just before the final phrase.

BELLINI: *Il pirata:* "Sorgete, è in me dover," with Alexander Young (Iturbo and Gualtiero), Monica Sinclair (Adele). ROSSINI: *La cenerentola:* "Nacqui all'affanno"; *Guglielmo Tell:* "Selva opaca"; *Semiramide:* "Bel raggio." WEBER: *Oberon:* "Ocean! Thou mighty monster." DONIZETTI: *Lucrezia Borgia:* "Com'è bello." VERDI: *I vespri siciliani:* "Arrigo! ah parli a un cor." VERDI: *Don Carlo:* "O don fatale." With the Philharmonia Orchestra and Chorus, Antonino Tonini conducting. [Recorded in London between July 1960 and April 1962, for EMI. *Pirata* reissued as 47283; *Cenerentola, Guglielmo Tell,* and *Semiramide* arias issued as 49428; *Lucrezia Borgia, Oberon* and *Don Carlo* issued by EMI in 54437; *Vespri* unpublished.]

The issuing of the *Pirata* scene was delayed a little over eleven years and finally coupled with Verdi arias recorded in 1964 (also long suppressed by Callas). This signaled the fact that a cache of unpublished Callas material existed. The majority of it is from sessions in London with Antonino Tonini, an assistant conductor at La Scala. Walter Legge recalls that the sessions were originally set up to record a complete *Traviata*, and the project was canceled at the last minute. In order to "rescue" the sessions and use the contracted orchestra, a recital disc of arias was undertaken.

All of the above arias, except that from *Pirata*, were redone with Nicola Rescigno in late 1963 and early 1964 (with the *Vespri* aria recorded a third time in 1969, also with Rescigno). These earlier versions of the Rossini and Donizetti arias, however, are more attractive vocally, more convincing as musical statements, and the miking of Callas' voice is more becoming than in the remakes. As for the *Pirata* excerpt, which was the first recording from the Tonini sessions to be issued, there is more composure to Callas' singing here than in the complete New York *Pirata*, although her voice is not at its freshest and a final added top D is faltering. The scene is heavily cut, including the introduction to the cavatina.

In 1992 to mark the fifteenth anniversary of Callas' death, EMI issued a CD titled "Callas Rarities"; it contained three further items from the Tonini sessions: Callas' first recordings of "Ocean! Thou mighty monster" from *Oberon*, "O don fatale" from *Don Carlo* and "Com'è bello" from *Lucrezia Borgia*. The record was also supposed to have included the Callas-Tonini version of "Arrigo! ah parli a un cor" from *I vespri siciliani*, but when the CD was put together, the previously published, 1969 version of the *Vespri* aria with Rescigno was used by mistake. The 1960 version remains unpublished.

Compounding this error was another that substituted the 1969 "Te, Vergin santa" from *I Lombardi* for the announced and unpublished 1964 version. Along with the still unavailable *Lombardi* and *Vespri* excerpts, there are two other items from the Tonini sessions that appear to have been lost – "Come innocente giovine" from *Anna Bolena* and an incomplete test recording of "D'amor al dolce impero" from *Armida*.

A comparison of Callas' two versions of the *Oberon* and the *Don Carlo* arias (or the Tonini vs. the Rescigno) is of special and endless fascination, for it demonstrates that Callas was no creature of routine. She continually looked for and found new colors and emphases in the music she sang and opened new windows of interpretation and meaning.

She had made her 1963 recording of the great scene from *Oberon* an heroic statement of grandiose proportions, filling the aria's pages with great urgency. The aria as a whole was delivered as an impassioned narrative. The earlier version with Tonini is winged for swifter flight, with some telling adjustments to the text; it amounts to another face of the same coin. Of equal interest are the contrasting calibrations of accent and tints in the two studio versions of "O don fatale." They are powerful evidence of how Callas' curious and seeking mind never rested.

**CHERUBINI:** *Medea.* With Jon Vickers (Jason), Ivana Tosini (Glauce), Nicolai Ghiaurov (Creon), Giulietta Simionato (Neris), Edith Martelli and Maddalena Bonifaccio (Handmaidens), Alfredo Giacometti (Captain). Thomas Schippers conducting. Performance of 11 December 1961, Teatro alla Scala, Milan. [Hunt 34028.]

Callas' second series of *Medea*s at La Scala served as her farewell not only to the house, but to Italy itself. These five performances (three in December and one each the following May and June) plus two *Medea*s at Epidaurus were her only operatic appearances from 1961 through 1963. This performance is slow to take off, as Callas is working against weak support from Schippers; he tends to isolate set pieces by *tempi* which divide instead of join. Callas' entrance and her first aria are pale indeed, and she sounds somnolent. She infuses some life into the first duet with Jason, but does so in an inconsistent fashion, as though she could not muster the strength to provide all the tension needed. There are few such problems in Act II (though Schippers draws out "Ebben! tutto mi manca" to interminable lengths). The principal alteration here is Callas' eschewing of her usual high C at the end of Act II and taking Cherubini's written B-flat. Act III is compelling throughout, though less venomous than the earlier Scala or Dallas performances. Nonetheless, it is more balanced and more vocally secure than her singing elsewhere during 1961.

# *1962* ⌒

WEBER: *Oberon:* "Ocean! Thou mighty monster." VERDI: *Macbeth:* "La luce langue." ROSSINI: *La cenerentola:* "Nacqui all'affanno." MASSENET: *Le cid:* "Pleurez mes yeux." DON-IZETTI: *Anna Bolena:* "Al dolce guidami." With the Philhar-monia Orchestra, Georges Prêtre conducting. Concert of 27 February 1962, Royal Festival Hall, London. [Melodram 36513.]

1962 was a year of concerts beginning with an appearance in London during February and followed a few weeks later by a return to Germany. This newly unearthed London concert (a nonbroadcast) is of prime importance not only because Callas is in exceptional vocal and expressive form (superior to the Ham-burg concert in March), but because it contains a public perfor-mance of the *Oberon* aria, her finest singing of the *Cenerentola* finale, and her final thoughts on music from *Macbeth* and *Anna Bolena.*

The *Oberon* aria is captured here nearly a year before the issued commercial recording was made for EMI. This unusual scene, originally written in English and performed in that lan-guage by Callas, is in effect a chain of ariosos and recitative which Callas binds together with her always remarkable and instinctive sense of form. The commercial version of the aria for EMI will prove more heroic (in fact, Wagnerian) and deliberate, but it will lose some of the abandon of this performance, and the sense of the music being flung to the winds which buffet Huon's ship. Another major difference in the two performances is Callas' top; in London, it was solid up to high C (and that note is under better control than it will be for EMI) and responsive to her every wish. Exciting, too, are the attacks to phrases lying above the staff; they are dead center in their precision.

It is instructive to have a third version by Callas of "La luce langue." Compared to those of 1952 and 1958, it is apparent how interior Callas' response to the music has become. In London her singing of this incantation amounts to a greater refining and concentration of the expressive values heard in the EMI recording. So telling are these, however, that one literally aches when realizing the opportunity had been lost forever for further stage performances by Callas in this part.

If only one aria had survived from this concert, however, I would have wished it to be the *Cenerentola* rondo-finale, for no other performance of this *scena* by Callas is a match for the spontaneity and joy of this, her first public performance of the aria. Those who have been mystified by her stilted and calculated commercial recording of "Nacqui all'affanno" knew that she was capable of better, and here is the reward for their faith. Where the commercial and the live versions from Hamburg and Paris remain rooted to the ground, in London the aria soared with airy deftness. Callas' singing there was all fantasy and delight, and *abbellimenti* (particularly downward scale passages) are colored with a wonderful variety of weights and dispatched almost with arrogance. As in the *Oberon* and *Macbeth* arias, her top remains obedient and bright.

Also like the *Macbeth* excerpt, Callas' performance of Chimène's monologue "Pleurez mes yeux" is being tuned to finer dramatic essentials, and she now projects it with a more inward and personal sense of longing and resignation. In contrast, the *Bolena* extract adds little to our insights into this work, for the Callas of 1962 was unable to best the Callas of five years earlier. In one instance, in fact, she takes a step backwards by her rejection of the *oppure* line at "in quest'ora tremenda" during the opening moments of the cabaletta, opting for the first time for Donizetti's original, lower, and less effective couching of the phrase.

The cavatina, however, remains garlanded in sadness, with Callas tapering the ends of phrases into a nothingness which continues to command sympathy for the doomed Bolena. The mood created here is breached only in the rising melismas of "del nostro amor." In this phrase, so magical in the EMI recording, Callas resorts to an intrusive breath which leaves a blemish on an otherwise telling portrait in sound.

MASSENET: *Le Cid:* "Pleurez, mes yeux." BIZET: *Carmen:* "Habanera," "Séguedille." VERDI: *Ernani:* "Ernani! Ernani, involami." ROSSINI: *La cenerentola:* "Nacqui all'affanno." VERDI: *Don Carlo:* "O don fatale." With the orchestra of the Norddeutschen Rundfunk, Georges Prêtre conducting. Concert of 16 March 1962, Hamburg. [Arkadia 410.1.]

Callas' second Hamburg appearance was the same program heard in Munich, Essen, and Bonn during March. The *Cid* excerpt, while strong, lacks the concentration of drama and color heard on EMI and the probing of the London concert a month earlier, though the *Carmen* excerpts are carried a step further, despite Prêtre's rushing and Callas' continual lapses of memory in the "Habanera." "Ernani, involami" is sung without cabaletta and without the bounce and freshness of phrase which made previous performances of it by Callas so singular. Oddly enough after the sparkle of her performance in London, she fails to capture the smile in the florid phrases of the *Cenerentola* aria. It is heavily sung, and its many scales and *fioriture* lack spontaneity, tidiness, and grace. Prêtre, following normal practice, cuts the chorus part between the two halves of the scene and removes two pages from the end, where Callas interpolates a watery high B.

The finest moment comes with "O don fatale," an aria new to Callas' repertory. Among Verdi arias this is an amazing creation which telescopes into one compact unit recitative ("O don fatale"), cavatina ("O mia regina") and cabaletta ("Sia benedetto il ciel"). Callas makes the aria a whirlwind of self-recrimination, tearing into the opening lines with a Medea-like ferocity, cooling the heat of the center section with luxuriant lines before returning to her original drive, which brings the final phrases to a brilliant conclusion. Though several top notes are off center here, the message is unmistakable and outweighs all else. (This concert was

televised and a kinescope has been issued on Pioneer Laser Disc
PA85-150.)

**BIZET:** *Carmen:* "Habanera," "Séguedille." Charles Wilson,
pianist. 19 May 1962, Madison Square Garden, New York.
[Ornamenti 109.]

This recording provides more of a footnote than an entry.
Callas was one of many figures from the world of entertainment
who honored the then President of the United States, John F.
Kennedy, on his forty-fourth birthday. Her singing, like her
appearance, was token, and it was poorly recorded.

**VERDI:** *Don Carlo:* "Tu che le vanità." **BIZET:** *Carmen:*
"Habanera," "Séguedille." Georges Prêtre conducting. Concert of
4 November 1962, Royal Opera House, Covent Garden, London.
[Verona 27058; EMI 91283 (laserdisc).]

Callas was one of several artists who took part in this "Golden
Hour" program televised from Covent Garden. She is not in her
best form, having fallen prey to a serious sinus infection that
developed about the time of the Scala *Medea*s, as well as having
damaged the muscles of her abdomen. When these two infirmities
were checked, Callas realized serious work was needed on her
voice, and during the latter part of 1962 well into 1963 she
began working, in her own words, "from the beginning, like
a student."
Though the *Don Carlo* scene is unsettled, even labored in
places, the "Francia" section is again affecting. The *Carmen*
excerpts are less demanding and far more relaxed. In introducing
Callas, Sir David Webster, administrator of Covent Garden, asks,
"If any one of you will send me a telegram tomorrow morning
telling me how I can lure Miss Callas to play Carmen in this
house, I will be a very happy man." The closest Webster or any
other manager came to hearing Callas as Carmen was the complete recording made by EMI two years later. The arias as sung

169

in London are the most tantalizing promise yet of what was to materialize in the complete set. They are more bewitching and insinuating than on the EMI disc or at the Stuttgart concert. (A kinescope of this concert has been preserved.)

# *1963* ⌐

GLUCK: *Iphigénie en Tauride:* "O malheureuse Iphigénie."
BERLIOZ: *La damnation de Faust:* "D'amour l'ardente flamme."
BIZET: *Les pêcheurs de perles:* "Comme autrefois." MAS-
SENET: *Manon:* "Adieu, notre petite table," "Je marche sur tous
les chemins"; *Werther*: "Air des lettres." GOUNOD: *Faust:* "Le
roi de Thulé . . . Ah! je ris." With the Orchestre de la Société
des Concerts du Conservatoire, Georges Prêtre conducting.
[Recorded in Paris, 2–7 May 1963 for EMI, all but *Werther* and
*Faust* arias reissued as 49059; *Werther* and *Faust* reissued as 49005.]

While working on her voice, Callas restricted her activity in
1963 to concert and recording dates. The first of the EMI sessions
produced yet another fascinating excursion into the French repertory which included only one aria sung previously in public, "O
malheureuse Iphigénie"; for this recital she relearned the aria in
French. Unfortunately her voice still carries traces of her ill-
health, and her singing of this demanding aria and the lack of
vocal plushness at the time are both magnified by very close
miking. This disturbing factor masks a crucial shift in her association with EMI. This French record was produced by Michel
Glotz of EMI's Paris branch, who oversaw all her discs from
1963 through 1964 (Legge's collaboration ended in 1962 with the
final Tonini session). Glotz gradually became a force behind the
scenes in Callas' career in and out of the studio for the next few
years, and it is no coincidence that a break with him in 1965
coincided with the beginning of her exile from the stage.
Callas is less cruelly exposed in Marguerite's "D'amour l'ardente flamme," as it lies mostly in the middle voice. There are
great moments of beauty in her singing of this melancholy

171

romance—the broad measuring of its lines, the ever-lifting phrasing of the *più animato* section like rapid heartbeats, and the poignancy of the altered return of the melody at "O caresses de flamme." What an extraordinary Dido or Cassandra she would have made in *Les Troyens*. Here and elsewhere much of the orchestral playing is neither polished nor always exact.

In Leila's "Comme d'autrefois," Callas seems to be on the outside of the music looking in, for an air of caution permeates this aria. Far more involved is Manon's "Adieu," though Callas strangely avoids the first of its recitatives, perhaps to sidestep the B-flat; she begins instead with "Je ne suis que faiblesse." The aria is sung with model simplicity and exemplary diction, and her tone is warmer than elsewhere on the disc. The inclusion of yet another *Manon* aria, "Je marche sur tous les chemins," is inconclusive not only because the Gavotte is omitted, leaving the aria hanging in midair, but because this recitative-like section exposes many vocal uncertainties at this time; furthermore she omits the D at its conclusion. This patchy bit of singing leads into the finest moment of the record, the Letter Scene from *Werther*. Here, she holds one intensely from her first sad uttering of Werther's name through the final tearful accusation "Tu frémiras." It was no doubt the scene's many shifts of mood that engaged Callas so deeply, and her rapport with the music binds its varying attitudes into one deeply felt and compelling whole.

Who would have imagined that one of the revelatory performances here would be Marguerite's worn "Roi de Thulé" and "Jewel Song"? The first is sung with a simplicity of quite a different order from Manon's "Adieu"—demure rather than sad. Callas makes careful differentiations between Marguerite's thoughts ("Je voudrais bien savoir") and her singing of the ballad while spinning; the former are distant and almost clouded, while the latter is more open and conversational. The transformation in her voice when the jewel case is discovered is miraculous, with the recitatives full of disbelief and awe. The "Jewel Song" itself is radiant, the scales of a lovely finish, and the manner in which she floats "Comme une demoiselle," beginning with a slight *ritardando*, spoils one for other performances. Only a final wavering high B goes astray and breaks the ebullient mood she has so well established.

ROSSINI: *Semiramide:* "Bel raggio." BELLINI: *Norma:* "Casta diva." VERDI: *Nabucco:* "Anch'io dischiuso." PUCCINI: *La bohème:* "Quando m'en vo"; *Madama Butterfly*: "Tu? tu? piccolo Iddio!" Georges Prêtre conducting. Concerts of 17 May (Berlin, Orchester der Deutschen Oper), 23 May (Stuttgart, Orchester des Süddeutschen Rundfunk), 31 May (London, Philharmonia Orchestra). [Stuttgart on Melodram 26035; Berlin on Eklipse P-3.]

Callas' 1963 concert tour of central Europe included appearances in Düsseldorf, Copenhagen, and Paris. Comparing the fare for this tour with previous concert programs (and noting especially the missing cabaletta in the *Nabucco* aria) makes it obvious that Callas is now performing almost a minimal amount of music and that a good deal of vigor is lacking in those appearances as a result. Only in the Paris concert that followed was her programming reminiscent of her more adventurous days in concert. The Berlin, Stuttgart and London appearances also speak of the great unevenness of her singing during this period as compared with the consistency of even five years earlier. Her voice is only sporadically used with its familiar élan, freedom and technical sureness. "Bel raggio," freest in Stuttgart, continues to puzzle through Callas' languorous approach and to disappoint in the inequality of *gruppetti* and other *abbellimenti*—not to mention the almost total lack of ornamentation and the omission of a cadenza before the reprise of "Dolce pensiero." "Casta diva" is missing from my copy of the Berlin concert, and while more securely sung in London than in Stuttgart, neither performance is up to Callas' standards. Melismas lack polish, she misses the first high C of the cabaletta in Stuttgart, loses the end of the cavatina in London, and eliminates her former interpolated C in the cabaletta's conclusion, taking instead Bellini's written B-flat. Much the same tentativeness is felt in the *Nabucco* aria; only in Stuttgart does the recitative have a semblance of its former flash and thrust.

I have never quite understood the allure that Musetta's Waltz holds for singers who are quite obviously unsuited for it (Ljuba Welitsch and Renata Tebaldi, among others), and I am amazed that Callas succumbed to it, because of the way it exposes a voice. Her approach is far too overblown and the final top B is never quite in focus. The most involved, all-out response to an aria in these three concerts is the Death Scene from *Butterfly*. Her top sounds well here, and there is passion and surge to her singing which is sorely missed elsewhere.

ROSSINI: *Semiramide:* "Bel raggio"; *La cenerentola:* "Nacqui all'affanno." MASSENET: *Werther:* "Air des lettres"; *Manon:* "Adieu, notre petite table." VERDI: *Nabucco:* "Anch'io dischiuso." PUCCINI: *La bohème:* "Quando m'en vo"; *Madama Butterfly:* "Tu? tu? piccolo Iddio!"; *Gianni Schicchi:* "O mio babbino caro." With the Orchestre Philharmonique de la Radio-Télévision Française, Georges Prêtre conducting. Concert of 5 June 1963, Paris. [Melodram 16502.]

While Callas' top is no more certain in Paris than it was at other points on this tour, she seems more willing to let her voice out and let the chips fall where they may. Consequently there is more life to all she does along with more glaring wobbles (particularly the Bs at the end of the *Cenerentola* and *Bohème* arias). The pair of Rossini arias have greater finish but still tend to droop. However, the *Werther* scene has greater poignancy than the EMI recording, with Callas' voice more supple and the words more fully savored. This is the prize of these 1963 concerts. In much the same manner, the *Manon* excerpt is more meaningfully shaped, though Callas again skirts the B-flat in its recitative. Her voice goes wild in the *Nabucco* recitative, and she later compromises the high C of the cadenza to the cavatina, holding instead to the lower A. *Butterfly* continues effectively, and the *Schicchi* aria, sung as an encore, is lovely in every way.

BEETHOVEN: *"Ah! perfido!"* MOZART: *Don Giovanni:* "Or sai chi l'onore," "Non mi dir," "Mi tradì"; *Le nozze di Figaro:* "Porgi, amor." WEBER: *Oberon:* "Ocean! Thou mighty monster." With the Orchestre de la Société des Concerts du Conservatoire, Nicola Rescigno conducting. [Recorded in Paris, 6–23 December 1963, and 8 January 1964, for EMI, all but "Ah! perfido" reissued as 49005; "Ah! perfido" reissued as 54437.]

Though this disc is a collection of hits and misses, it does show the results of diligent, close work by Callas on her voice. Her top has been smoothed to a greater degree after the spring tour, and little of the cautiousness that marred the second French recital comes into play here. Rather, she gives as a mighty demonstration of willpower, technique, intellect and, in her middle voice, beauty. The best of the disc comes on the first band of each side—Beethoven's "Ah! perfido!" and Weber's "Ocean! Thou mighty monster." The text of the Beethoven concert aria deals with a dramatic situation almost identical with that faced by Mozart's Donna Elvira. The Beethoven scene is in the same key as the Mozart, and in its recitative the clarinet virtually quotes the opening of Elvira's aria, "Mi tradì." Furthermore, Beethoven's unnamed lady and Elvira have a bond of betrayed love, and though each lashes out at her beloved, each is still deeply committed to her love.

Callas launches into the opening lines imperiously, her voice biting into the end of the orchestral introduction. Only Elisabeth Schwarzkopf comes close to matching the fire and recrimination that lights up Callas' voice or her scalpel-sharp attacks. By the infusion of warmth and the softening of phrases at "Risparmiate quel cor, ferite il mio!" ("Spare that heart, strike at mine"), Callas makes us aware that this is a woman still intensely in love. This first recitative is manic in its abrupt shifts of tempo; Beethoven indicates seven different "attitudes" from *allegro con brio* through *andante grave* and finally *adagio,* and Callas unerringly follows, without losing a sense of the whole. The cantilena beginning "Per pietà, non dirmi addio" is ravishing in sound, and the long lines prove that her phenomenal breath control remains unimpaired. She pleads without groveling, and the rising two-note phrase to G on "d'affanno morirò" ("I shall die of sorrow") flows freely, without the constriction which frequently stemmed the tide of Callas' singing on the EMI French recitals. In each instance where "d'affanno morirò" recurs, Callas is careful to head the phrase to "morirò," accenting its first syllable and quietly phrasing away from it. It would seem self-evident, given such a sentiment, that the seminal idea is "die." But so few singers think in literate terms, and what should be a natural part of expression is more an exception with singers than a rule. It

175

might seem simplistic to note that this aria speaks of love and hate, and that Callas makes one aware of hate here and love there. But the majority of singers do not give one an awareness of such distinctions, and those who do rarely sharpen them or carry them to the heights reached by Callas.

For example, in the cavatina's coda the sentiment "d'affanno morirò" is set by Beethoven with rests between "d'affanno," and "morirò" against a light pizzicato in the orchestra. Callas makes an impulse of each vowel which carries over in one's mind from word to word, as though the quarter rests were as much sung as the notes themselves. The image of a single and quite singular phrase is created, one which carries within it a sense of ebbing life, of a fainting heart. It was always there, implanted by Beethoven; Callas uncovered it.

The final section brings a return to fury, with Callas giving the impression that Beethoven's *ignota* is not upbraiding the lover who has abandoned her, but lashing out at her own weakness. A *più lento* and later an *adagio* arioso interrupt this flood of recrimination, and how lovingly Callas molds two-note phrases on "non son degna di pietà" ("Don't I deserve pity?"). Then, at full sail, she leaps into the final allegros with firm, steady top notes, bringing the scene to a driving reverberant end.

The first Donna Anna aria, "Or sai chi l'onore," from *Don Giovanni* was unfortunately recorded without its recitative, a section Callas would surely have illuminated. The aria begins abruptly, although it is paced as an *andante* rather than the rushed *allegro* often heard. This is also an aria of fury, but of a different sort from "Ah! perfido," for Callas' Anna seems more certain of gaining the upper hand. There is not always ease to Callas' singing here, but there is great strength of purpose, and her top continues to be on target, though it sounds threadbare when supported by less than the full orchestral sound. "Porgi, amor" is, for Callas at least, sketchy. But then she never established a close identity with a character who, when wronged, moons rather than gives vent to her rage. It could well be that Callas sensed the contradiction here between the gentle nature of the music and the Countess' loss. One other technical problem rankles; it is Callas' and not Mozart's, for she chooses not to add an *appoggiatura* on "tesoro" at the end of the aria; this contributes to the lifelessness of the whole.

Rezia's "Ocean" aria, on the other hand, is anything but lifeless; it fairly bursts with vitality and heroism. Although not as
impetuous and ringing as in the London concert of the previous
year, the aria is still performed by Callas in a declamatory style
of the mightiest order. There is great glory in her singing from
the open deep-seated statement of "Ocean" through the majesty
with which her voice rings out over the orchestra's description
of a storm. The triumph of her cries of "Huon" are intensified
by a marvelous *ritardando* made on the name just before the
coda. She is caught short only by the top C and the descent from
it; but by this time her performance has reached so far that a
pair of sour notes could not topple it. Her English is not of the
clearest; her pronunciation of the vowel *a*, in particular, is more
open than the covered sound one would expect. But though every
word is not clean, every meaning is, and diction is no deterrent
in this performance.

Callas' association with Anna's "Non mi dir" dates back over
a decade at least; unfortunately, this recording comes a bit too
late for comfort. It often sounds labored, there are single notes
within passages which do not sound, the same dynamic level is
maintained almost throughout, and the final flourishes do not
fuse together. Yet within these thorny problems is nestled a
remarkable moment: an air of suspension is lent the music when
Callas phrases into the return of the principal theme without a
breath. More sympathetic to her is Elvira's "Mi tradì," and its
running notes make less demands upon her voice than did the
sustained lines of Anna's "Non mi dir." Her response to Elvira's
music is doubly remarkable considering the aria was not planned
for this disc; Callas' performance amounts to an improvisatory
reading. Rescigno remembers that five minutes of music were
needed to complete the record, and as the parts of "Mi tradì"
were on hand, Callas decided to sight-read the aria on the spot.
Obviously she was aided by having just dispatched the mirror
image "Ah! perfido!" As in the Beethoven, Callas plunges headlong into Elvira's recitative, with all her instincts brilliantly
attuned to its needs. As the tessitura for Elvira is higher than
that of "Ah! perfido!" and the orchestration not quite as full,
Callas is consequently more exposed. But her intention is compelling, and she carries the scene through more convincingly than
in either of Anna's arias.

**VERDI:** *Otello:* "Salce, salce . . . Ave Maria"; *Aroldo:* "Ah! degli scanni," "Salvami, salvami, tu gran Dio!"; *Don Carlo:* "Non pianger, mia compagna," "O don fatale!" With the Orchestre de la Société des Concerts du Conservatoire, Nicola Rescigno conducting. [Recorded in Paris 17–27 December 1963 and 20–21 February 1964, for EMI, reissued as 47943.]

Where the first Verdi recital by Callas was made almost entirely from repertory she had performed on stage, this second volume consists, with one exception, of music not included in her stage repertory. It opens with the full scene which begins the final act of *Otello,* minus the response of Emilia. Ever the mistress of mood, Callas' recounting of the tale of the maid Barbara is gentle but tinged with fright. The calls of "Salce," such a feature of this aria, are sung progressively void of tone until the last of the three is but a hollow echo. "Ave Maria," on the other hand, is sustained quietude, with its final A-flat spun out in the best tradition of the aria. The *Aroldo* "Salvami" is well sung but the less involving of the two excerpts included from this early work. It is comparatively brief, with an agitated beginning followed by a short arioso. The better of the two, and the best performance on the disc, is the scene beginning "O cielo! dove son io?" which progresses to the aria "Ah! degli scanni." This prayer is not only rare Verdi but rare Callas. The accompaniment for the cavatina is delicately orchestrated, much in the manner of Amelia's aria in *Simon Boccanegra.* Callas darkens her voice for the cavatina, and she makes this supplication a moment of doubt and unrest. The exchange between Mina and Godvino which follows is omitted, as is the second verse of the cabaletta. In the remaining verse, Callas makes vivid use of words for punctuation and stress. The section beginning "Ah! fuggite" is especially gripping in its resolve, with her voice digging in deeply on the word "maledetto."

Callas' commercial "O don fatale!" (one of two takes with Rescigno; the other remains unpublished) begins with all the fire heard in Hamburg but proceeds to a more darkly shaded, longer-lined "O mia regina." The C-flat and the B-flats are under control but thinner than her top elsewhere. The disc also contains a further souvenir of her Elisabetta in *Don Carlo,* the brief romanza "Non pianger." While there is an abundance of expression from Callas in this short aria, the rising line to B-flat which occurs in both strophes is uncertain and each time the A in the phrase goes off, as does the final A of the aria. The chorus part during the second verse is omitted.

# *1964* ∾

PUCCINI: *Tosca*. With Renato Cioni (Mario), Tito Gobbi (Scarpia), Victor Godfrey (Angelotti), Eric Garrett (Sacristan), Robert Bowman (Spoletta), Dennis Wicks (Sciarrone), Edgar Boniface (Jailer), David Sellar (Shepherd). Carlo Felice Cillario conducting. Performances of 21 January (Acts I and III only), 24, 30, January; 9 February (Act II only) 1964, Royal Opera House, Covent Garden, London. [24 January on Melodram 26011; 9 February on EMI 91283 (laserdisc).]

These *Tosca*s marked Callas' return to the operatic stage after a hiatus of nearly two years. Ironically, considering her lack of enthusiasm for the role of Tosca, it was to be the principal vehicle of her last two years in opera houses in London, Paris, and New York, and her last complete operatic recording for EMI. Though only two of the nonbroadcast performances have surfaced, there is every reason to believe that the remaining three *Tosca*s in the series were taped as well (the performance of 9 February of Act II was for television). The production was a new one directed by Franco Zeffirelli, and his vivid view of the work elicted fresh responses from Callas and Gobbi, in their first complete *Tosca*s on stage together. They dominate the performance not only through their own strength but also through the weakness of Cioni. Callas' voice is warm and lovely throughout, though the final phrases of "Vissi d'arte" are a trial in each performance. Interestingly enough, the high Cs in Act II work better for her, being less exposed than the B-flat in the aria. Also, as they arise out of the dramatic conflict of the action, the force of the music carries her along on its crest. The C in the last act is varied in quality, although the descent from it is always an exciting lunge to full chest voice. As is inevitable in a performance of *Tosca*, the second act is of crucial importance, and many galvanizing moments are heard there in these London *Toscas*. A particularly tense segment comes following the torture scene. To understand why Callas suddenly whispers "Voglio vederlo" ("I want to see him"), it is necessary to retrace the stage action at this moment. When she hurled "Assassino" just before at Scarpia, Gobbi wheeled about sharply, and Callas seemed for a second to be crushed by the fury of his look. Realizing she might further endanger Mario, her voice was reduced to barely audible fright at "Voglio vederlo," as though afraid to ask for even so small a favor. Later, when Tosca demands "un salvacondotto onde fuggire dallo stato con lui" ("a safe-conduct so that I can flee the country with him"), Callas' voice is all bitterness until the final "con lui," which is given a magical caress, through a sudden infusion of ardor in her voice. Though her speaking of "E avanti a lui tremava tutta Roma!" ("Before him trembled all of Rome") would be too melodramatic in a Verdian context, in Puccini it easily passes muster. Another stirring moment comes with Tosca's discovery of Mario's death, especially in the 24 January broadcast. Callas' suddenly wrenching screams followed by sobbing cries of Mario's name take one beyond the theater into reality. You have to pause and remember this is only pretense.

The 9 February telecast of Act II is the principal existing sound-visual document of Callas in actual performance. While this gives the film immense importance, it must be noted that the camera work is quite ordinary. It tends to stay on whoever is singing at a given moment, while often Callas was at her most exciting and involving when silently reacting to another on stage. This was, of course, particularly true of her dramatic episodes with Gobbi. On this film, you only sense the mighty interplay that existed between this pair in the theater.

ROSSINI: *La cenerentola:* "Nacqui all'affanno"; *Guglielmo Tell:* "Selva opaca"; *Semiramide:* "Bel raggio." DONIZETTI: *La figlia del reggimento:* "Convien partir"; *Lucrezia Borgia:* "Com'è bello"; *L'elisir d'amore:* "Prendi, per me." With the Orchestre de la Société des Concerts du Conservatoire, Nicola Rescigno conducting. [Recorded in Paris 4–23 December 1963 and 13–24 April 1964, for EMI. *Cenerentola, Guglielmo Tell,* and *Semiramide* reissued as 49005; *La figlia del reggimento, Lucrezia Borgia*, and *L'elisir d'amore* reissued as 47283.]

With the London *Toscas* behind her, Callas returned to Paris and EMI's studios. But the results of these sessions were extremely varied. The second Verdi record was finished, a third begun, and one of Donizetti and Rossini was concluded. Material for the third Verdi LP was to wait for eight years to be released, and then only five arias were issued.

The bel-canto disc is largely a remake of music recorded earlier in the Tonini sessions; new are excerpts from *L'elisir* and *Figlia del reggimento*. The performances are both lightly and heavily flawed. The question here is not so much a vocal one (for fewer high notes are involved than in the discs made before London) as one of a lack of spirit and charm to her singing. Oddly, given her abundance of rich expressive gifts, Callas almost consistently lacked great charm, if one measures her singing of the light Rossini against a Supervia. Callas could use her voice trippingly, even beguilingly, but the feminine charm with which Supervia continually disarms one on record is missing. Fortunately, the vast majority of Callas' repertory was such that charm was not an essential ingredient. But it is this lack, more than anything else, that defeats her in the aria from *La cenerentola*. Both it and the *Semiramide* aria are too moody, lacking in scintillation, and phrases do not link together with Callas' accustomed skill (though Rescigno's brisker tempos for *Semiramide* are a help, to be sure).

While frequently lovely in line, the music for Adina and Marie seems rather studied in Callas' much too mature sound, and the *acciaccature* of "Convien partir" are not fully finished. The sort of flow and lightness appropriate for these arias is heard in Mathilde's "Selva opaca," the most successful aria on the disc. Its phrases are elastic, and Callas produces lovely *pianissimi* on the top A-flats. Quite attractive as well are the gentle sprints of sound made on "udirà" at the end of the aria's first verse. The *Lucrezia Borgia* extract is lifeless and minus its cabaletta; also omitted are the brief lines for Gubetta, Rustichello, and the Duke. Elsewhere on the disc the choral parts of the *Figlia, Cenerentola*, and *Semiramide* scenes are missing, and their inclusion might have helped brighten the performances.

**VERDI:** *Attila:* Oh! nel fuggente nuvolo"; *I vespri siciliani:* "Arrigo! ah parli a un core"; *Un ballo in maschera:* "Ma dall'arido stelo," "Morrò, ma prima in grazia"; *Il trovatore:* "Tacea la notte placida," "D'amor sull'ali rosee"; *I Lombardi:* "Se vano è il pregare," "Te vergin santa"; *Aida:* "Ritorna vincitor." With the Orchestra de la Société des Concerts du Conservatoire, Nicola Rescigno conducting. [Recorded in Paris 21 February, and 7–22 April, 1964, for EMI. *Vespri*, "Ma dall'arido stelo," "Se vano è il pregare," and *Aida* reissued as 47730; *Attila*, "Morrò, ma prima in grazia," and "Tacea la notte placida" reissued as 47943; "D'amor sull'ali rosee" issued as EMI 54437; "Te vergin santa" unpublished.]

Because Callas wished to remake this material, she suppressed these particular recordings for eight years. A remake was attempted in 1969 but it was unsuccessful. When she at last agreed to publication of the earlier Verdi sessions, Walter Legge was called in on the project to assist in preparing the tapes. He listened not only to the 1964 tapes but to those from 1969 as well, and parts of the latter were spliced into the earlier material to create the performances finally made public (this editing is most apparent in the phrase of the *Lombardi* aria rising to D-flat).

There is no question that this return to Verdi sparked Callas' imagination and her musical response in a way that the Rossini-Donizetti sessions had not. Her voice, while no more comfortable throughout its range, is at least used with vivid importance. This is evident from the first moment of the *Attila* aria. Also strongly in evidence are the extremes used in miking Callas in Paris; moving from the 1961 *Pirata* scene made in London to the *Attila* aria three years later demonstrates this better than words. Odabella's recitative rings with the old Callas authority, and the aria moves with a complete naturalness and beauty of phrase, notably the rounded line beginning "Sospendi o rivo." The *Vespri* excerpt, part of the *Gran duetto* of the opera's fourth act, is spun out further by Callas than in the Florence performance. What a pleasure it is to linger amid such luxurious lengths of sound. Only the second set of descending chromatics (from a top B) troubles her and is somewhat unclean in pitch. But the final cadenza which dips to low F-sharp is more beautifully molded than in Florence.

The first *Ballo* scene continues to be a masterful study in dramatic tension and relaxation, though Callas' top voice is at its wiriest here and her thin high C is anticlimatic. She is least comfortable in the first *Lombardi* aria, which is also plagued by grave uncertainty above the stave. Only half of this rondo for Giselda was recorded. Of all the performances, the *Aida* is the most successful. The aria rages with all the fire, color, and personality which represent Callas at her most involved. No doubt, this was because her singing of the excerpt was in the nature of a challenge. There had been no plan to record "Ritorna vincitor"; Rescigno remembers that this particular session

> . . . had been rough, with Maria laboring under many adverse circumstances. She was nervous, everybody was nervous; so Glotz called a break to calm us down. During the break, he played a tape of "Ritorna vincitor" which had been recorded for EMI by Régine Crespin. Maria became highly indignant. "This is not Verdi or *Aida*," she said. "I remember when I prepared this with Maestro Serafin he wanted such agitation that I could hardly get the words in; this is like a funeral march." Turning to Glotz she said: "Are the parts still here?" He answered "Yes," and she said, "Come on, Nicola, let's sing it!" And we went out and did it, just like that, in a single take.
>
> [To this story, Rescigno also added an interesting comment on recording with Callas.] I have seen her listen to a playback lasting four or five minutes with only her score, taking no notes. Then, she would immediately go into the studio and re-do the aria with all the needed changes exactly as they should be—this more *forte*, that more *piano*, this more open, that more covered. I never ceased to be astonished by the immediate way she could make this adjustment so precisely after only one hearing.

As for the *Ballo* and *Trovatore* arias first published in 1978, they render Callas more a disservice than not by compounding the problems encountered in other Verdi material of this period and because they contain few new insights as compensation. The same is true of "D'amor sull'ali rosee," which was finally published as part of the 1992 EMI CD "Maria Callas Rarities." But though these are problem discs, they play their part as well in the Callas legacy and should be listened to in the spirit of discovering varying aspects of her art and experiencing it in its totality. The second *Lombardi* aria remains unpublished (see page 165).

**BELLINI:** *Norma:* "Casta diva" (recitative only). Georges Prêtre conducting. Rehearsal excerpt from May 1964, Théâtre Nationale de l'Opéra, Paris. [LP only.]

These brief few minutes are the sound track of a newsreel film made at a rehearsal just before the premiere of the new Zeffirelli production of *Norma* for Callas at the Paris Opéra. This was, by union regulations, all that RTF was allowed to film.

**VERDI:** *Aida:* "Pur ti riveggo." With Franco Corelli. L'orchestra du Théâtre de l'Opéra, Georges Prêtre conducting. [Recorded in Paris, June 1964, for EMI, reissued as 54437.]

This recording of the Nile Duet from *Aida* is all that survives from a session set up for a duet album by Callas and Franco Corelli following their appearances in *Norma* at the Paris Opéra. Though Callas would later say that she was unhappy singing with Corelli, it is clear from this recording that whatever misgivings she had concerning his musical instincts, she was the one in dire straits, and the reason why the disc was never completed.

Her performance is riddled with the same sort of fissures and uncertainties that were characteristic of the Paris *Normas*, but here there are no redeeming insights to compensate a listener. But then Aida is a franker, less dimensional character, and little can substitute for a lack of sufficient voice in this role. Not that Callas is as devastated vocally as in the unpublished Philips recording of the same scene with di Stefano (that recording, after all, was still eight years in the future).

But neither does her voice contain the suppleness and allure needed for this scene. Callas is best in the more stentorian sections of the duet, where she matches the heat of Corelli's voice decibel for decibel. But when she takes the pressure off her voice, her support goes as well. While the interest in this sole commercial duet by Callas and Corelli is obvious, making it public (as EMI did in the summer of 1990) was a questionable act.

BIZET: *Carmen:* With Nicolai Gedda (Don José), Andréa Guiot (Micaëla), Robert Massard (Escamillo), Nadine Sautereau (Frasquita), Jane Berbié (Mercédès), Jean-Paul Vauquelin (Dancaíro), Jacques Prevost and Maurice Maievski (Remendado), Claude Cales (Moralès), Jacques Mars (Zuniga). With the Choeurs René Duclos and the Orchestra du Théâtre de l'Opéra, Georges Prêtre conducting. [Recorded in Paris, 6–20 July 1964, for EMI, reissued as 54368.]

Following the Verdi sessions, Callas undertook eight performances of *Norma* at the Paris Opéra, her first complete stage role in that city. The first two performances were recorded privately by Glotz, and this may have been true of one or more of the later ones that spring, as well; no copies of these, however, have as yet come forth. In July, Callas arrived at a project which had long been urged upon her, the performing of Bizet's elusive gypsy. Carmen is Callas' only complete role in French, and the standard version with recitatives by Ernest Guiraud was used.

In her voice, Carmen is a bright, defiant, healthy creature; her singing is very French in attitude and in its fastidiousness and wealth of detail. The "Habanera" is sung lightly and quickly, almost as a throwaway, clothed in a silky vocal line. She makes magical use of the aria's first and subsequent eighth-notes to propel the music's lines along, highlighting key words as she goes— *bien, loin, jamais*—to add texture to phrases. Hearing the recitative before the aria and the chorus within it contributes needed contrasts which further highlight her singing. The only bit of dialogue included in the set comes just after the "Habanera"; "Eh! compère, que fais-tu là?" It is enunciated with the same sort of sarcasm heard later in Callas' voice when it defies Zuniga with a barrage of "Tra-la-las." Nearly all of these taunting phrases are begun with a glottal stop, and they are sung in time without exaggeration. Again, Callas makes special use of eighth-notes to keep the line lively. In her recitatives before the

"Séguedille," her singing is simply, quietly confident that José will be Carmen's. This aria, like the "Habanera," is now begun softly and shaped on a more intimate scale. Even the important line "Qui m'aime, et qu'à mon tour," after the aria proper, is hushed but sensual. Carmen's words to José in the final scene of the act are almost whispered, and Callas sings the reprise of the "Habanera" strictly in tempo, reflecting this Carmen's sureness of herself.

Callas' first full singing comes at the beginning of Act II where Carmen is on home ground, so to speak, and more outgoing. Though Prêtre begins the "Chanson bohémienne" a good deal faster than Bizet's *andantino,* and thus the first two verses are too similar in tempo, the aria nonetheless builds in tension and grows to a whirlwind by its conclusion. Callas' use of words here to bring the line into relief is impressive, particularly her rolling of the *r* in "refrain" and the bounce of "Tra-la-la" in the second part of each verse. The quintet is crisp, without exaggeration, and flies like an arrow to Carmen's important lines, "je suis amoureuse" and "Amoureuse à perdre l'esprit!" With the entrance of José, Callas' voice preens under his attentions, yet she cannot resist teasing him with a half laugh on "jaloux." Callas sings Carmen's vocalise, which accompanies her dance, in a rich variety of colors and insinuations. Her voice is fuller and edged with impatience after José's interruption and the mounting sound of the trumpet call. With "J'étais vraiment trop bête," the cat-like quality which has characterized her exchanges with José turns tigerish. Yet what at first seems outrage in Callas' singing is not; there is a sardonic tone which suggests that this is all a game, all a question of vanity, a test to see if she can bend José to her will. Callas' most expressive singing comes with "Là-bas, là-bas dans les montagnes," as she vocally paints a picture of their life together away from Seville. The words roll gently out, full of promise and mystery; the highpoint of the section, "Et surtout la chose enivrante," is delivered ardently. The first real rage comes with "Eh! bien pars," when it appears José has slipped from Carmen's hook. This is a Carmen who cannot stand losing; with Zuniga's entrance she sees a chance to recoup the momentary loss suffered by José's defiance. In the fight which follows between José and Zuniga, Carmen emerges the victor, and her playful singing of "Bel officier" celebrates a double triumph over the officer who would have sent her to prison and the soldier who would have left her to return to duty.

The curtness in Callas' voice at the outset of Act III leaves no doubt that this Carmen has lost any interest she had in José, and that his desertion for her sake is now a meaningless gesture. The Card Scene is superbly sung as a brooding stream of music, minus the distortions of rhythm which frequently mar this scene. With "Va t'en, va t'en" at the end of the act, all pretense of love is gone as she defies José openly. The last glimmer of ardor in Callas' voice on this recording comes during the duet with Escamillo, "Si tu m'aimes" in the final act. This soon recedes into impatience as Frasquita and Mercédès warn her José is nearby.

Callas deals with him at first in short, hard sounds void of affection and biting in pride. This stance is shortly exchanged for one of indifference, a posture reinforced by Carmen's referring to herself in the third person. But José's pleading causes this Carmen's anger to flare anew, and Callas lashes out as though certain she still retains an upper hand in the situation. Though Callas makes no sound on these records when stabbed by José, one is certain his attack comes as a total surprise in the face of her final lashing "Cette bague autre fois, tu me l'avais donnée— Tiens!"

Of course, the singing of Carmen on records is a different matter from acting and singing the role on stage. In a very real sense performing Carmen in a studio is avoiding the ultimate challenge of the part. Yet despite the shortcomings of this set— the edition, the conducting of Prêtre as opposed to the more subtle performance by Sir Thomas Beecham with de los Angeles (also for EMI), and not the strongest supporting cast—Callas' Carmen stands as a compelling achievement without being fleshed out in the theater.

PUCCINI: *Tosca.* With Carlo Bergonzi (Mario), Tito Gobbi (Scarpia), Leonardo Monreale (Angelotti and Jailer), Giorgio Tadeo (Sacristan), Renato Ercolani (Spoletta), Ugo Trama (Sciarrone), David Sellar (Shepherd). With the chorus of the Théâtre National de l'Opéra and the Orchestre de la Société des Concerts du Conservatoire, Georges Prêtre conducting. [Recorded in Paris 3–14 December 1964, for EMI, reissued as 69974.]

The re-recording of *Tosca* in stereo was undertaken as a sound track for a movie of the opera planned by Zeffirelli with Callas. The idea of capturing her on film dates back to 1958 when Zeffirelli designed and produced a most personal *Traviata* for Callas and the Dallas Civic Opera. It was cinematic in concept, staged entirely as a flashback from Violetta's deathbed. From that time onward, Zeffirelli tried to persuade Callas to make a film with him, but she hesitated to enter so foreign an expressive medium. Finally, in 1964 after the successful *Tosca*s at Covent Garden, she agreed to film the Puccini work. EMI made the sound track, and Callas began to prepare herself for this new artistic adventure. Unfortunately the project floundered because the film rights to *Tosca* had been sold by Puccini's publisher, Ricordi, to a German firm.

Callas' second commercial *Tosca* will not bear as close scrutiny as the first, largely because Prêtre's conducting lacks the subtleties and theatrical thrust of de Sabata's. For Callas herself, this *Tosca* tends to be a throwback to the exaggerations of earlier days, particularly in her encounters with Gobbi, which lack the naturalness and spontaneity of their London performances. Bergonzi, however, is a gain after the whining sounds of Cioni.

# *1965* ❧

PUCCINI: *Tosca.* With Renato Cioni (Mario), Tito Gobbi (Scarpia), Robert Geay and Jean-Pierre Hurteau (Angelotti), Jean-Christoph Benoît (Sacristan), Louis Rialland (Spoletta), Roger Soyer (Sciarrone), Pierre Thau and Georges Daum (Jailer), Jacqueline Broudeur and Janine Collard (Shepherd). With Georges Prêtre (February) and Nicola Rescigno (March) conducting. Performances of 22 February; 1, 3, 13 March, Théâtre National de l'Opéra, Paris. [3 March on Melodram 26033.]

These Paris *Tosca*s were part of an exchange which brought the London production across the Channel and was to have sent the Paris *Norma* with Callas to England. However, the exchange proved to be one-way, for Callas' career was about to be suspended for nearly nine years. The four Paris *Tosca*s preserved through transistor recordings are uneven in sound quality, yet good enough to tell one that these performances were not nearly as polished and convincing as their English counterparts the year before. Indeed, there are stretches where the frenzy of performance outdoes that of the second EMI recording. However, it must be said that Callas' voice sounds impressively secure.

PUCCINI: *Tosca.* With Franco Corelli (19 March) and Richard Tucker (25 March) (Mario), Tito Gobbi (Scarpia), Clifford Harvuot (Angelotti), Lawrence Davidson (Sacristan), Andrea Velis (Spoletta), Russell Christopher (Sciarrone), Robert Goodloe (Jailer), Stuart Fischer (Shepherd). Fausto Cleva conducting. Performances of 19, 25 March 1965, Metropolitan Opera, New York. [19 March on Melodram 26030; 25 March on Melodram 26035.]

During the Paris *Norma*s of 1964, Callas and Bing made up their differences, and the soprano agreed to return to the Metropolitan after a seven-year absence (her last appearance at the house had been as Tosca, the role with which she would now make her rentrée). Because she sang so comparatively little by 1960, there was always an unusual amount of extramusical fuss connected with her appearances. On the occasion of her return to America, the fuss verged on hysteria. The atmosphere of these two *Tosca*s is electric from the first note of music. Her entrance is met by a roar that suspends the performance for minutes. When she is finally allowed to sing, her voice is compact but used rather sparingly at first; one can imagine the tenseness and pressure of the occasion for her. In the second act, her voice is in less dependable shape than in the London or Paris *Tosca*s. She produces some gritty high Cs and a squall at the end of "Vissi d'arte" that served as a B-flat; nor was the high C of the last act a thing of beauty. Yet, however limited the means, her voice still conveys the theater of Puccini as few others have done.

MASSENET: *Manon:* "Adieu, notre petite table." BELLINI: *La sonnambula:* "Ah! non credea." PUCCINI: *Gianni Schicchi:* "O mio babbino caro." With the Orchestra National de la Radio-Télévision Française, Georges Prêtre conducting. Television concert of 18 May 1965, Paris. [Melodram 36513.]

The interest in this TV concert, apart from a return to the music of Amina, lies more in what was not heard, for Callas also taped for the program Duparc's "L'invitation au voyage"; it was excluded for reasons of timing. The *Manon* aria is exquisite in Callas' slim-lined tracing, and the *Sonnambula* excerpt is heightened by the understatement of her singing and the inclusion of the full recitative that precedes it (the cabaletta is omitted). "O mio babbino caro" is sung in the nature of an encore and is quite charming and direct in its expression. (A kinescope of the concert has been preserved.)

BELLINI: *Norma.* With Gianfranco Cecchele (Pollione), Giulietta Simionato (14, 17 May) and Fiorenza Cossotto (21, 29 May)

(Adalgisa), Ivo Vinco (Oroveso), Marie-Luce Bellary (Clotilde), Claude Cales (Flavio). Georges Prêtre conducting. Performances of 14 and 17 (Act II only); 21, 29 May, Théâtre National de l'Opéra, Paris. [29 May excerpts on Melodram 16038.]

Though the sound of these *Norma* tapes is superior to the transistor recordings made earlier in the year of the Paris *Toscas*, no one performance was captured complete. From the first two, we have only the second act (with Simionato's last Adalgisas, sung a month before her retirement from the stage). In the 21 May performance the tape ran out in the middle of the last-act finale, and the final scene of the 29 May performance was canceled when Callas collapsed on stage in a state of exhaustion. Yet what remains is extraordinarily revealing, pro and con, of Callas' state of mind and voice in this period. Where she could wing her way through Tosca on sheer will and the momentum of the drama, Norma and its many high Cs are now a frightening obstacle in her mind; she exchanges the first of them for the written B-flat at the end of the cabaletta of "Casta diva," and another for an A (the mezzo trick) in "Ah! si fa core" of the second act. Yet when one least expects it, out pops the note, full and confident, as in the last act. Middle-voice passages are more meaningfully drawn than ever, and a string of perfect, expressive tones forming a single poignant line cannot be spoiled by a final off-center high note. Though she is comfortable in only some seventy percent of the role, so noble and rapt is her singing at its best that we would have been the poorer without these performances.

PUCCINI: *Tosca*. With Renato Cioni (Mario), Tito Gobbi (Scarpia), Victor Godfrey (Angelotti), Eric Garrett (Sacristan), John Dobson (Spoletta), Dennis Wicks (Sciarrone), David Sellar (Shepherd). With Georges Prêtre conducting. Performance of 5 July 1965, Royal Opera House, Covent Garden, London. [LP only.]

Four performances were announced for Callas' second round of *Toscas* in London, but she continued to be plagued by the low blood pressure which had caused her to faint before the final scene of the 29 May *Norma* in Paris. On her doctor's advice, she canceled the Covent Garden *Tosca*s, except one, a gala before the royal family. Her voice is not used with the same fullness as a year before, and she treads her way through the performance with care. Yet the limits imposed by her physical condition produced one of her most evocative performances of "Vissi d'arte"; it is restrained, small-scale, and truly a prayer. But the familiar fire of her Tosca burns slowly during the rest of the second act. Callas obviously did not think of this *Tosca* as her last operatic appearance, for still on the horizon were the *Norma*s planned for London and talks were under way for a *Traviata* and *Medea* at the Paris Opéra. *Norma,* however, was canceled, the Paris projects evaporated, and Callas as an artist receded into the background.

# *1969* ⌒⟿

VERDI: *I vespri siciliani* "Arrigo! ah parli a un cor"; *Il corsaro:* "Vola talor dal carcere," "Romanza di Medora"; *I Lombardi:* "Te vergine santa"; *Attila:* "Oh! nel fuggente nuvolo." With the Orchestre de la Société des Concerts du Conservatoire, Nicola Rescigno conducting. [Recorded in Paris, February 1969, for EMI. All but *Corsaro* arias reissued as 49428; *Corsaro* arias reissued as 47943.]

By 1968, after three years of inactivity, Callas was restless to return to her career. She had begun work anew on her voice with de Hidalgo and seemed once more to need the identity her life in the theater had offered. By summer, this need became pressing as her nine-year liaison with Aristotle Onassis drew to a close. *Traviata* was the center of her talk; she had rethought the score and was anxious to put her ideas to the test. EMI set up sessions to record the work with Callas in the fall of 1968, but a fall during the summer which damaged her ribs caused the session to be canceled.

However, she did return to the recording studio in 1969 to remake a third volume of Verdi arias begun in 1964. To excerpts from *Attila, Lombardi,* and *Vespri* she added two arias from *Corsaro* and planned to include "Quante volte" from *La battaglia di Legnano* as well. In several of the arias, a number of high notes were omitted to be added later, and the orchestra's playing is riddled with mistakes. Yet the miking is more becoming, and Callas' study with de Hidalgo has realigned her upper register and ironed out a number of its problems. Her voice will still not take great pressure, but she has developed a new use of *pianissimi* above the staff which is very lovely and expressive. In particular, the *Vespri* excerpt is superior to the one finally issued from 1964.

194

But these sessions nonetheless were difficult for all concerned, and numerous takes were needed to produce a single aria. Still, a year after her death, EMI was able to put together enough of the two *Corsaro* arias to make them public (the cabaletta to "Vola talor" had to be suppressed, however, as several crucial high notes had been only lightly sketched by Callas). The balance of Callas' final EMI sessions was made public for the first time in 1987 as part of a commemorative CD marking the tenth anniversary of her death.

Rescigno recalls that Callas moved "inch-by-inch" in the sessions to produce what exists today. They were for him a "nerve-wracking" experience because of Callas' vocal tenuousness and the absence of her old self-confidence and musical security. The *Corsaro* excerpts, however, are the only evidence we have of what Callas sought and attempted to convey from this early Verdi score. How much this justifies their being published is a question each individual must decide.

It could be that the inconclusive results of these sessions led Callas away from a return to the stage and into a film venture with Italian director Pier Paolo Pasolini—a nonsinging enactment of the story of Medea, filmed later that spring and summer on location in Turkey and Italy.

# *1971* ⮌

Master classes in "The Lyric Tradition" at the Juilliard School of
Music, New York, 11 October–19 November 1971, and 7 February–16 March 1972. [Excerpts from ten classes issued as EMI
49600.]

In 1971, Peter Mennin, director of the Juilliard School of
Music, persuaded Callas to undertake a series of master classes,
which were so absorbing they led me to create a book devoted
entirely to them (*Callas at Juilliard: The Master Classes*, Alfred
A. Knopf, New York, 1986). In the spring of 1971 Callas heard
some 300 young professional singers and narrowed their number
to 25 for her classes. She approached her role as a teacher more
as a friend or colleague who was anxious to help her students
over the pitfalls they were certain to encounter. In her wide-
ranging comments, she was soft-spoken, frank, and chary with
praise. She placed great stress on fidelity to the printed page
and, within these confines, to the creation of a living musical
statement.

After a student had performed an aria or a scene, Callas then
retraced the music phrase-by-phrase, and even note-by-note,
often singing entire sections to illustrate her points. These provided stimulating flashes, however uneven, of the Callas vocal
mystique and included moments from *Norma* and *Lucia* as well
as Eboli's "Canzone del velo" from *Don Carlo* and even Rigoletto's "Cortigiani, vil razza dannata."

Of greatest importance, the Juilliard tapes provide the only
glimpse of Callas' voice in Leonore's music from *Fidelio*, during
a lengthy class session on the aria "Abscheulicher." They also
suggest, and often in an exciting way, what she might have
accomplished in the mezzo-soprano repertory, particularly Am-

neris in *Aida,* a role which attracted other famous Aidas such as Astrid Varnay and Regina Resnik. Equally fascinating at the other end of the scale is Callas in music for Micaëla, the Queen of the Night, Fiordiligi, and Norina.

Behind this concentrated giving of herself, it seemed that the Juilliard classes were serving another purpose, the rebuilding of Callas' confidence before an audience. Here she could and did sing out without carrying the responsibility of performance. Behind the scenes, Callas worked daily, almost as a student herself, with the Met coach Alberta Masiello, covering a vast range of repertory. She went through all of *Lucia, Macbeth,* and *Forza,* to name but three of the scores on which she and Masiello concentrated. It was this intensive private schedule, coupled with the public Juilliard sessions, which contributed to the courage she needed to return to the recording studio once again.

# *1972* ~

VERDI: *La forza del destino:* "Ah! per sempre"; *I vespri sicili-*
*iani:* "Quale o prode"; *Don Carlo:* "Io vengo a domandar";
*Aida:* "Pur ti riveggo"; *Otello:* "Già nella notte densa." With
Giuseppe di Stefano. The London Symphony Orchestra, Antonio
de Almeida conducting. [Recorded in London, 30 November–20
December 1972, for Philips. Unpublished.]

In late 1972, Callas returned for the final time to the recording
studio to begin work on an LP of duets with Giuseppe di Stefano, not for her long-time affiliate EMI, but for the Dutch firm
of Philips. The sessions included five Verdi duets (which were
finished enough to be edited into reasonably coherent performances) and "Una parola, o Adina" from Donizetti's *L'elisir*
*d'amore,* which remains incomplete. The record was never finished or approved by Callas.

The Philips material is of special interest for it contains Callas'
only performance of the *Otello* first-act duet and her only version
of the *Don Carlo* duet with orchestra recorded under professional
conditions. Even so, hearing a tape of these sessions provokes
more pain than pleasure. In the *Forza* duet, Callas' voice is hollow, unsteady and lacking in support. Her breathing is also
erratic, and notes above the staff are usually reduced to frantic
lunges. But most dismaying of all, there is a paucity of musical
detail and a number of incorrect pitches, as if she had neither
carefully prepared the music nor thought about it; a far cry from
the Callas of even eight years earlier.

Compounding these problems here and throughout is di Stefano's brutal singing and the tremendous ensemble problems created by his cavalier way with pitches and rhythm. Yet, ironically,

his voice per se is treated kinder by Philips' microphone and enhanced more electronically than is Callas'.

Probably the best of the five scenes here is the one drawn from the first act of *Vespri.* Callas sounds decidedly fresher (although, this is an entirely relative matter), and a ray of the old magic and presence shines through at "Tu dall'eccelse," where she caresses and gives a lift to the phrase that occurs in no other place in these duets. Also the two descending chromatic scales from top B-flat are surprisingly and expressively handled. The double cadenza at the conclusion, however, is a shambles.

In *Don Carlo,* Callas is forced to chop up phrases into small expressive units in order to breathe and survive. The performance here is more or less lifeless until the phrase "Compi l'opra," where Callas' voice suddenly opens up, bringing heat and purpose to the phrase. Also, the final "Ah! Iddio su noi vegliò" is likewise impressive. In the end, however, the rough patches far outweigh this brief surge of expression.

Without question the worst moment is the *Aida* duet. It is little more than desperate, and even "Là tra foreste vergini" no longer works for Callas; it is vocally dried-up and beyond her ability to sustain it or shape the music into anything comprehensive. But saddest of all is the heartrending sound of Callas attempting to cope with the rising phrase in the *stretta* "su noi gli astri brilleranno." It would make a stone weep.

In comparison to the *Aida* duet, the *Otello* is at least plausible, though often unnerving in Callas' inability to keep to pitch or endow a phrase with life and buoyancy. Here, too, di Stefano's blatant scooping and I-don't-give-a-damn sliding is more maddening than elsewhere. Frankly, I cannot imagine that any part of this material could be published, but then to my surprise EMI saw fit to issue the two *Corsaro* arias of 1969, so supposedly anything is possible. But how unfeeling and ghoulish such an issuance would be.

# *1973–1977* ∾

DONIZETTI: *L'elisir d'amore:* "Una parola, o Adina." GOU-NOD: *Faust:* "Laissez-moi contempler ton visage." BIZET: *Carmen:* "C'est toi . . . C'est moi." MASCAGNI: *Cavalleria rusticana:* "Tu qui Santuzza." VERDI: *I vespri siciliani:* "Quale, o prode"; *Don Carlo:* "Io vengo a domandar"; *La forza del destino:* "Ah! per sempre." With Giuseppe di Stefano. PON-CHIELLI: *La Gioconda:* "Suicidio." PUCCINI: *Gianni Schicchi:* "O mio babbino caro." MASCAGNI: *Cavalleria rusticana:* "Voi lo sapete." MASSENET: *Manon:* "Adieu, notre petite table"; *Werther:* "Air des lettres." Ivor Newton and Robert Sutherland, pianists. [Hamburg, excerpts, 25 October, 1973, Eklipse 33; Amsterdam, 11 December, 1973, Eklipse P-3; 9 April, 1974, Brookville, New York, on Legato Classics LCD-137-1.]

The announcement in June 1973 that Callas would embark on a world tour with the tenor Giuseppe di Stefano came as a total surprise. Even more startling was the fact she would choose a recital format with which to pick up the broken thread of her career, and would appear with piano instead of orchestral support. The tour began in Hamburg, Germany, in October. The program in each city visited listed the seven duets above, plus eleven arias for Callas—"Pleurez, mes yeux" from *Le Cid*, "Habanera" from *Carmen*, "Suicidio" from *La Gioconda*, "L'altra notte in fondo al mare" from *Mefistofele*, "Non pianger" and "Tu che le vanità" from *Don Carlo*, "Bolero" from *I vespri siciliani*, "O mio babbino caro" from *Gianni Schicchi*, "Quando m'en vo" from *La bohème*, "In quelle trine morbide" and "Sola, perduta, abbandonata" from *Manon Lescaut*. She performed only half of them but later added "Voi lo sapete" from *Cavalleria rusticana*, "Vissi d'arte" from *Tosca*, the Letter Scene from *Werther* and "Adieu, notre petite table" from *Manon*. Eight arias and four songs were listed for di Stefano.

From this music was chosen the bill for each concert, so that it varied in content from city to city. Less than an hour's worth of music was performed in each, though stretched to fill nearly two hours; programs were without organization or point of view. The performances were as disturbing, especially Callas' part in them. From di Stefano one expected little. He had never withdrawn from his career as had Callas, but his star had waned long before because of his routine singing and the abuse that his voice had suffered. Throughout the tour, he performed with slack rhythm and off-pitch indifference, and either roared or crooned in falsetto. The truth is, di Stefano risked nothing with this tour while Callas risked everything. At the time of her return, Callas' name had never been brighter or more synonymous with music. While the artistry of her greatest years could never be diminished by this tour, it was tarnished.

No one hoped that Callas' voice would be what it had been even in 1965. A singer—like a dancer or an athlete—must continually use his muscles in order to keep on form. Also, the sort of public contact from which Callas had shut herself off is essential in retaining control of these muscles "under fire." Still, it was hoped that her way of looking at and dealing with music would remain unimpaired. But it quickly became evident that her grave vocal uncertainties exerted a tremendous toll on her ability to shape music in the old meaningful way. Gone was the ability to sustain long phrases, and recitatives and flourishes were now weak and often imprecise. Her mind seemed to be more on vocal survival than anything else.

Callas did not help herself by choosing a repertoire that placed too great a demand on her limited powers; "Suicidio," for example, had to be transposed downward for her. Only in the *Carmen* and *Don Carlo* scenes were there momentary flashes of her former commitment and telling use of words, and only in her middle and lower registers were there glimpses of that unique, dark timbre once so poignant and potent. It may have been either a desperate need to be active once again at all costs, or a lack of critical self-awareness, that led to the unmusical and unrealistic program she performed. Had she recognized her severe limitations, she could easily have circumvented them in many instances. What wonders she might have accomplished with the song repertoire, where keys could have been carefully chosen and her mind could have been freed to deal with and color words—songs of Bellini, Verdi, Fauré, or Duparc.

Of the tour repertoire, the main interest lies in scenes from *L'elisir* and *Faust,* music not previously sung in public by Callas. But neither expands one's knowledge of her special way of dealing with music. Both London recitals by the couple (the first at the Festival Hall, the second at the Albert Hall) were recorded by EMI, but so poor was the quality of the singing that not enough material could be salvaged to make up a single disc. Both the London concert of 26 November 1973 and the Tokyo concert of 27 October 1974 are preserved on videotape.

It has long been known that there was recorded material from Callas in the period after her last public concert, including practice tapes made at home of arias and even lieder. Several of the scraps from this residue have been included on potpourri discs. One of the most interesting was a work session on Beethoven's "Ah! perfido" with pianist-conductor Jeffrey Tate on March 3, 1976. It was sung late at night in the Théâtre du Champs-Elysées in Paris; either Callas had the tape made for the purposes of study, or it was made clandestinely by someone in the theater.

Only the recitative and cavatina of the aria were issued (Eklipse Records 14); whether more exists or not is unknown. This inconclusive bit of tape, however, shows Callas in a far better and steadier light than almost any aria or duet recorded during her concert tour with di Stefano. But here her mind was not divided by the demands of public performance. She was alone, with all her energy and thought going into her singing.

The other sound bite to be issued (Eklipse 33) is little more than a snippet from *La forza del destino*, part of "Madre, pietosa Vergine." It was recorded during August, 1977, a few weeks before Callas died. Vasso Devetzi is at the piano. Together they work and then rework the phrase "Deh, non m'abbandonar," with Callas in very solid, easy voice. For a moment, at least, she was able to hold her demons securely at bay.

# Epilogue ❧

Eugenio Gara once, in writing of Callas, invoked this apt Chinese proverb: "Who rides atop the tiger can never get off." When one considers the recorded evidence of Callas' career, and charts the splendors, triumphs, audacity, and dangers of her ride, a compelling conclusion emerges: with so wide a repertoire and so intense an involvement with her roles, there is no doubt that Callas demanded more from her voice than it could comfortably deliver. Yet a parallel conclusion is equally clear: had she put herself in less peril, had she taken fewer chances or remained within safer limits, she would never have been Callas. You cannot achieve as she achieved by halfway measures.

The experience of Callas was not unlike the sensation of watching an aerial act at the circus. The tension and excitement produced was great because of the risks involved. In the circus, however, there is a net below, waiting to correct any error in judgment. The trapeze artist knows it is there; the public knows it as well. Though control and skill are still essential ingredients for success, the act above and the reaction below amount to good-natured pretense on both sides. A totally different atmosphere is created, however, on those rare occasions when the act is performed without a net. The very being of each spectator seems to be bound up in each step taken on high, for there is no longer any semblance of pretense. In a very real sense it can be said that Callas was one of the very few performers in opera to work without a net. Is it any wonder that so strong a bond was forged between her and her public, and that Callas' fascination has persisted—long after her performances ended.

There were times when she fell. But she always survived to

203

return and to dare. This daring was the consequence not only of an overextension of her gifts, but of the flawed nature of her voice itself. Even in its palmy days—the Mexico City period, for example—Callas' voice divided into three distinct registers: a bottled, covered low voice; a reedy middle; and a top that was brilliant at times to the point of stridency and that would, without warning, threaten to wobble out of control.

Yet she conquered, and as much by her "faults," if you accept them as such, as by her virtues. Such a phenomenon is actually not at all new in singing. In 1824, a hundred years before Callas was born, Stendhal wrote these words about Giuditta Pasta, which can apply as fully to Callas:

> She possesses the rare ability to be able to sing contralto as easily as she can sing soprano. I would suggest . . . that the true designation of her voice is mezzo-soprano, and any composer who writes for her should use the mezzo-soprano range . . . while still exploiting, as it were incidentally and from time to time, notes which lie within the more peripheral areas of this remarkably rich voice. Many notes of this last category are not only extremely fine in themselves, but have the ability to produce a kind of resonance and magnetic vibration, which, through some still unexplained combination of physical phenomena, exercises an instantaneous and hypnotic effect upon the soul of the spectator.
>
> [Stendhal goes on to point out, as I would with Callas, that Pasta's voice was] not all molded from the same *metallo,* as they would say in Italy; and this fundamental variety of tone produced by a single voice affords one of the richest veins of musical expression which the artistry of a great *cantatrice* is able to exploit. . . . A large number of other outstanding singers of the old school long ago demonstrated how easily an apparent defect might be transformed into a source of infinite beauty, and how it might be used to bring about a most fascinating touch of originality. In fact, the history of the art might tend to suggest that it is *not* the perfectly pure, silvery voice, impeccably accurate in tone throughout every note of its compass, which lends itself to the greatest achievements of impassioned singing. No voice whose timbre is completely incapable of variation can ever produce that kind of opaque, or as it were, suffocated tone, which is at once so moving and so natural in the portrayal of certain instants of violent emotion or passionate anguish.

It has been suggested, and not without reason, that Callas' "voice had less going for it than any other voice that has achieved international celebrity via the phonograph—a medium that necessarily puts a premium on timbral endowment, since it cannot directly transmit physical and dramatic qualities." Yet it was a voice that was better than beautiful, for it was a voice that once heard could not be easily forgotten. It haunted and disturbed as many as it thrilled and inspired, and it was the very personal colors of her voice, combined with its deficiencies, that made her sound so strikingly individual.

Her manner of singing was equally arresting. Callas had a stern bel-canto upbringing from her teacher Elvira de Hidalgo, a musical outlook later reinforced by her mentor Tullio Serafin. This sort of vocal straightjacketing was ideally suited to Callas' nature. She was a committed traditionalist, a musical puritan, who eagerly sought stylistic boundaries and flourished within them. The greater the confines, the greater was the challenge and, ultimately, the freedom. A score set forth the limitations of a given problem for her. The mastering of a problem was the incentive that spurred Callas on to conquer, and to set and meet new demands on her voice and her abilities. This, in turn, led to a prodigious grasp of such challenges as the trill, the *acciaccatura,* scales, *gruppetti,* and other *abbellimenti.* These, combined with her open throat, an inborn sense of legato, and diction rooted in vowels, all predestined her for prominence in the bel-canto repertory, though her voice was basically that of a dramatic soprano.

In the long run, however, Callas' distinct sound and her technical achievements would have been less influential if she had not employed both to shape music to creative and expressive ends. All the resources open to a singer—breath, tempo, dynamic and agogic accents, embellishments, rubato, even silences—were used to their fullest to communicate impressions and moods. Indeed, Callas seemed incapable of being inexpressive; even a simple scale sung by her implied a dramatic attitude or feeling. This capacity to communicate was something she was born with. It was her capacity for hard work and her equally great curiosity which led her to question relentlessly what a score demanded of her, and what she in turn demanded of herself. Little by little she mastered the art of filling a phrase to exactly the right level of expression and producing unerringly the right stress to underline or high-light a thought. At her finest, Callas' voice became a mirror held up to human emotion. At her best, tone and intent were wondrously interlocked. She never offered a string of high points in performance mixed in with indifferent or unfinished patches, as so many do. With Callas, a recitative was as integrated and thoughtful as an aria. Perhaps you could not agree with this or that aspect of her singing, and you might feel that she was as wrong for this role as she was right for that one, but Callas was usually able to force one to accept or reject her concept as a whole, so clear-eyed and consistent was her approach to a part. This was her ultimate justification as an artist.

For one full decade, the 1950's, her voice and her expressive powers were in their finest balance. Her apprentice years and an understandable amount of rough and even wild singing were behind her, and the eventual decay of her voice was yet to come. It is on the eve of this remarkable and seminal period of music-making that this book begins. Threading its way persistently throughout this study is the role that Callas made most com-pletely her own—Norma. We encounter it first in complete form in Mexico in 1950 and last in Paris in 1965, the year of Callas' final operatic appearances. Perhaps more than any other part, it serves to demonstrate the questioning, the refinements, and the shifts in attitude that Callas' art underwent during the span of this book.

The Mexico Norma came nearly two years after her first appearance in the role in Florence, in November 1948, and it demonstrates that the part did not spring fully formed from her throat and mind. Rather, it announces the beginning of her search for the role's truths. From our vantage point today, we now know how arduous this search would be, how probing and exhausting a journey Callas undertook between Mexico City and Paris, what an enormous price she paid mentally and vocally in coming to grips with this multifaceted role. Though this first documented Norma is superior to any performance preserved in sound up until then, it was, in terms of what the part would become, embryonic, for the emphasis was centered more on exte-rior vocalism than on interior drama. Two years later, at Covent Garden, Callas' voice continues as impressive, but here we sense that lines, sentiments, and thoughts are becoming more contained, and that a conscious effort is under way to scale the role down to dramatic and musical essentials, though the scales are still weighted more toward the public than the private aspects of the character.

However, Callas seemed closer to *her* dramatic truth in London than when she came to record the role in 1954. This EMI set hit with enormous impact when it was first issued; yet how time has altered our perspective, and how differently one listens to the set today after Callas' second recorded version and her performances in Paris. Callas forced us to demand more from the role in the decade following the first *Norma* recording, by implanting in our ears a greater dramatic range, subtlety of color and depth of response. In comparison to what she later wrenched from the music after years of questioning and trial, this first EMI set seems more a performance-in-the-making. The *Norma* heard a year later in concert form on Radio Italiana is closer to London than to EMI. Though Callas' format remains a grand one, there is perceptible scaling down of the heroics heard on the EMI set, and the woman is brought forward to a greater degree.

From the same year, 1955, comes a La Scala *Norma* which builds on the RAI performance. Callas puts herself deeper within phrases rather than heroically riding their surface, and she is making increasing and more exacting differences between Norma's public words and her private thoughts. The dividends realized from her continual searching for dramatic veracity in the part can be heard with greatest immediacy in the second EMI recording, which followed in 1960. Though some have heard vocal deterioration rather than artistic growth from Callas in this set, this would seem yet another restatement of an argument as old as opera itself, and one which whirled about Callas from the outset of her career—the tug-of-war between beauty of sound and an expressive use of sound. Certainly, Callas' upper voice is much less secure here than in the first EMI set, and it would be blind not to acknowledge that she was, in part, turned towards this deeper interpretation by the severe contraction of her vocal resources which began in the late 1950's. Yet there are countless examples of singers, who, when their voice began to give, did not use this change to their own and music's benefit as did Callas.

It would be equally blind and patently unfair not to admit also that her musical curiosity and imagination played an equal role in her search for the fullest meaning of Norma's drama. This 1960 recording stands as the ultimate statement of what Callas sought and found in Bellini's score, for while greater expressive dividends are paid during the 1965 Paris *Norma*s, there are also greater losses. Her voice is sorely reduced in volume and range, and with these constricted means, Callas is forced to compete with the ever-growing spectre of her own reputation. "Casta diva" and much of Act II fall prey to nerves, yet elsewhere in these valedictory performances she sublimely captures the afterglow of Bellini's music. Neither "Teneri, teneri figli" nor "Ah! perchè, perchè" have been as hauntingly traced by another. Even when a note or a phrase emerges doubtful, there is rarely a doubt about either Callas' intent or the meaning of Bellini's music and theater.

Apart from a single performance as Tosca a month later, Callas remained silent until 1973. In the light of the moving accomplishments of heart and mind from Callas through 1965, how can the ill-advised return to her career be explained? There are those who view her attempt to reconquer with a voice broken and largely unresponsive to the music's needs as the inevitable final act of a Greek tragedy. While this is obviously a romantic oversimplification, I think it probable that Callas' re-entry into the public arena was motivated by a deep personal need. Perhaps it was a question of recapturing the identity she abandoned eight years earlier; or perhaps her reasons were more elemental.

Following Callas' appearance in Boston, Richard Dyer, in *The Nation,* came to this conclusion: "Though the evening brought musical illuminations we had demanded but dared not expect, it moved me mostly because it was such a human triumph, the triumph of an artistic personality, the triumph of a will, still daring and risking much when it sets out to dominate ever more refractory means. . . . Callas has long commanded our attention, our gratitude, our awe. Now in her struggle and in her exhaustion she asks and earns, at cost to herself and to us, what she has never before seemed to need, our love."

An explanation of what drove Maria Callas came in 1978, a year after her death in Paris of a heart attack on 16 September 1977. Acting as narrator for a filmed documentary on Callas

created by PBS, her friend and artistic collaborator Franco Zeffirelli remarked:

> There has perhaps been only one faithful companion to Maria
> throughout her life—her loneliness—the price sometimes one has
> to pay for his glory and success.
> Such is the price too of being God's instrument. It really seemed
> to me that God used Maria's talent to communicate to us His
> planet of beauty, to enrich our souls and make us better men.

In a fast-moving world where new faces and new voices crop
up each season, it is all too easy to forget those who are no
longer active combatants in the music arena. But Maria Callas
refuses to be forgotten.

If anything, her influence and the high standards she set for
herself as a singer cast an even longer shadow over the music
world today than when she was alive. Four documentary films
have been made of her tempestuous life, countless magazine articles and at least thirty-two books have tried to explain her magic
and magnetism, and her recordings—studio and live—are reissued
on compact discs. Why?

Why this obsession with an artist who was criticized throughout
her life as a flawed singer with an odd sound, a soprano whose
career ended in an ill-advised concert tour undertaken with a broken
voice, a woman who turned her back on hard-won, extraordinary
artistic achievements for a nine-year liaison with one of the world's
wealthiest men, Aristotle Onassis, only to wind up as "the other
woman" when he married Jacqueline Kennedy?

The answer is not as difficult as you might think. It is to be
found in Callas' ability to excite the imagination. Hers may not
have been an easy voice to listen to, but it was an impossible
one to forget. In its dark, hollow recesses, it held the essence of
theater, just as her haunting, slow-movement gestures onstage
were a mirror that reflected drama and music.

Ironically, offstage she was as ordinary a person as one could
be and still be Callas. By this I mean she was a non-intellectual,
someone who rarely read a book but loved TV cartoons, a
woman who was often petty and frequently bored. But the
moment music was involved, she was transformed into a radiant,

creative creature seemingly in possession of profound wisdom and deep insights denied the rest of us.

Even the flaws in her voice—that bottled low register, a reedy middle range, and a wavering top—were turned into virtues by her use of them to convey a broad panorama of feelings. She was consistently a giver, never just a taker like so many singers currently before the public. Callas was incapable of indifference and was willing to take enormous risks to conquer on stage.

But what of the many who don't know or who care little about opera, but who know Callas' name and are intrigued by her fame? Again, the answer is not that hard. We are all fascinated by storm-tossed, excessive lives, and Callas' life was the stuff from which soap opera is made. To the general public she was the quintessential prima donna—fiery, willful, always in some sort of scrap or difficulty, always the center of attention. There was also the fascination of an ungainly, overweight woman who through a willpower vouchsafed few of us managed to turn herself into a slim, chic member of the jet set.

And there was Onassis. Their affair made news around the world. When he jilted Callas, she received the sort of press coverage usually reserved for movie stars. Finally, there was that sad comeback in 1973 after an eight-year exile from the stage. Here was not simply an aging singer desperate to recapture an audience and what she had been, but an authentic heroine, anxious to show her former lover that the world still wanted her even if he didn't. How could one not respond to this sort of audacity?

As the Earl of Harewood, a longtime Callas admirer, has written: "Every period of history has certain personalities which dominate certain areas: Churchill and Roosevelt, Chaplin and Garbo, Toscanini and Furtwängler. . . . It is not difficult to find them in opera as well . . . Patti and de Reszke, Melba and Caruso . . . and after 1945, Maria Callas."

At the time of her death, Tito Gobbi—one of the few singers in a class with Callas—observed: "We must not forget that her beginning was hard and difficult, and only with tremendous will and supreme dedication did she become the legend. . . .

"She was unique. She was different. She was like a vivid flame attracting the attention of the whole world. I always thought she was immortal—and she is!"

# Recorded Interviews ∾

**1952**

Mexico City, 3 June. Backstage at the Palacio de las Bellas Artes after the first *Traviata* of Callas' last Mexico City season; a brief reaction to the public's reception, talk of forthcoming plans (in Spanish and Italian). [Rodolphe 32431.]

**1954**

Milan, 7 December. Interview between acts of *Vestale* (in Italian).

**1956**

New York, 8 December. With Rudolf Bing and colleagues of *Lucia di Lammermoor* broadcast; a greeting to the Metropolitan Opera radio audience (in English).

**1957**

Milan, September. A lengthy interview taped for radio broadcast in Philadelphia; covers the Edinburgh "scandal," Callas' views on her voice, repertory, colleagues, reactions to her first season at the Met, future repertory (in English).

Chicago, 17 November. Television interview with Norman Ross; a discussion of early years in New York and Greece, her relationship with her mother, her loss of weight, Callas versus Tebaldi, repertory (in English) (LP only).

Milan, 7 December. Backstage during the opening night performance of *Un ballo in maschera*; thanks and greetings to the public, and mention of future engagements (in Italian).

211

### 1958

New York, 24 January. "Person to Person," CBS Television interview with Edward R. Murrow; short exchange about school days in New York, popular music, Callas' temperament, languages, her voice and use of it, the Rome incident, critics, her marriage (in English). [Ornamenti 109.]

New York, 26 February. With Hy Gardner and George Callas; discussion of the Rome *Norma*, Callas' husband and marriage, life in Greece, her mother (in English).

New York, 13 and 27 March. Lengthy radio interviews with Harry Fleetwood during Callas' second Metropolitan Opera season; discussion of records, her voice and repertory, work with de Hidalgo, study and life in Greece, auditions in San Francisco and New York just after World War II, early years in Italy, background to the Met appearances, state of opera, life away from stage, musical comedy, the possibility of a film, temperament (in English).

London, 23 September. With David Holmes, BBC, following a television concert; feelings about the English public and audiences in general, relaxation away from the stage, *Traviata* and switching her voice from heavy to light roles, the future of opera, desire to curtail her career (in English).

Dallas, 7 November. CBS News at time of firing from Metropolitan Opera (in English).

Paris, December. Short interview at the time of her Paris debut dealing primarily with herself as a woman (in French).

### 1959

Milan, 4 and 11 January. "Small World," television interview in two parts with Callas (Milan), Edward R. Murrow (New York), Sir Thomas Beecham (Nice), Victor Borge (Connecticut); detailed discussion of the relationship between performance and audiences—applause, claques—little-known, old, and new music versus the basic repertoire, Callas on Barber's *Vanessa*, life in the concert hall, recordings versus live performance, the responsibility of performance, what is serious music (in English) (LP only).

**1963**

Berlin, 16 May. Short greeting to the German public recalling previous appearances in Berlin (in German and English).

Paris, 25 May. Discussion of Callas' upcoming concert in Paris, plans for her first Norma at the Opéra, preferences in repertory, the quality of Bellini's music, how a character is created, reactions of the press, her voice in general (in French).

**1964**

Paris, spring. Short interview dealing with Callas' attitudes to life and the differences between the artist and the woman (in French).

**1965**

Paris, 8 February. "Trois jours avec Maria Callas," RTF program; a fairly detailed biographical tracing of her career, de Hidalgo and study with her, the challenge of singing, music versus words, the responsibilities of an artist, her "capriciousness," Callas as a person (in French).

Paris, April. With William Weaver for the Metropolitan Opera broadcast intermission of April 10; Callas' reactions to her return to the Met a month before, a discussion of her early years, the preparation of roles, her Greek heritage and its influence on her acting; the quality of improvisation in performance, the character of Tosca, future plans (in English).

Paris, 18 May. Interview during intermission of RTF studio concert; Callas speaks of herself as a woman, her life and its influences on her work, a singer and the conductor, preparation of a role, Norma versus Isolde, her preference for bel-canto music, her feelings about verismo composers (in French). [Melodram 36513.]

**1967**

London, January. A short comment for BBC on Visconti and their Scala *Traviata*s (in English).

New York, December. A two-part interview with Edward Downes for the Metropolitan Opera broadcast intermissions of 30 December (1967) and January 13 (1968); an hour's discussion of the Callas "spell," press agents and managers, beginnings in Greece and Italy, bel-canto schooling with de Hidalgo and Serafin, the singing of Kundry and Isolde,

Callas as an actress, the science of music, repertory, translating a score into a performance, loss of weight, self-criticism, Callas' dislike of Tosca, early audition at the Met, use of ornaments for expression, stage directors, changes in roles over the years (in English) (LP only).

### 1968

Paris, April. With George, Lord Harewood, for BBC television; two detailed programs covering the duties and training of a singer and Callas in particular, work with de Hidalgo, the meaning of bel canto, early performances in Greece and Italy, collaborations with Serafin, Callas' first *Puritani*, Wagner versus Bellini, preparation of a role, background to portrayals of Anna Bolena and Medea, costuming, modern music, opera as an art form, the cutting of scores, a discussion of her best-known roles—Violetta, Norma, Tosca (in English).

London, 25 June. Discussion with Anthony Hopkins for BBC radio (in English).

Dallas, 13 September. "Collector's Corner" with John Ardoin; an hour's discussion of the facets of a singer's art—technique, recitative, cadenzas, tempos, the cutting of scores—and the application of these to a single work, the Sleepwalking Scene from *Macbeth*, dissected by Callas phrase-by-phrase [Eklipse 33.] Also an additional hour of talk not for broadcast on her "scandals" and herself as a woman (in English).

Paris, 30 September. With Jacques Bourgeois; a short exchange about Callas and bel canto, how a role is prepared, the part of Medea, the nature of opera (in French).

### 1969

Paris, 20 April. "Invitée au dimanche." Television interview with Callas, de Hidalgo, Visconti, and others, plus excerpts from Paris concert of December 1958 (in French).

Turkey, May. BBC television documentary on filming of *Medea*, with outtakes of the film (in English).

Rome, July. NBC television interview with Callas and Pasolini on the making of *Medea* (in English).

**1970**

Paris, January. "Journal inattendu," television program, with Pasolini; a discussion of Callas' life and career and the filming of *Medea* (in French).

Paris, 24 February. With Roger Régent; Callas' views on films and film-making, film offers prior to *Medea*, comparison of the operatic and the film Medea as a character, the role music plays in a film, possibility of future films (in French).

London, 11 October. With David Holmes for BBC; Callas speaks of the English singer, opera in the original language versus translation, singing in English (in English).

New York, 10 December. Television interview with David Frost; ninety minutes covering early days in New York and Greece, her retirement and possible return, the role of a singer, Norma and Violetta, Callas the woman, influences in her life, newspapers, her complexes, Serafin, loss of weight, her private life and personal attachments, her friendship with Onassis, "scandals" and problems during her career (in English). [Verona 27058.]

**1973**

Turin, 31 March. Television interview for CBS on staging of *Vespri siciliani* (in English).

Hamburg, October. Interviews on her return to the stage (in German and English).

London, November. Television interview with David Holmes after Festival Hall concert on Callas' return to the stage, her voice, and her crises (in English).

**1974**

Paris, 3 February. "Sixty Minutes." Television interview with Mike Wallace about her voice, her return, and Aristotle Onassis (in English).

New York, 15 April. "Today." Television interview with Barbara Walters on her return and her future, her childhood, her relationship with Aristotle Onassis, her feelings on marriage (in English).

**1988**

February. "Callas in Her Own Words." A four-hour documentary for National Public Radio by John Ardoin and Stephen Paley, using interviews with Callas and live performance material. Also included are interviews with Nicola Rescigno, Tito Gobbi, Jon Vickers, Walter Legge, Giuseppe di Stefano, Renata Tebaldi, Franco Zeffirelli, John Ardoin, Jackie Callas, George Callas, Rudolf Bing, Carlo Maria Giulini, Gian Carlo Menotti, et al. [Pale Moon Music cassettes PM001-1-4.]

# Filmed Performances ⌒

**1955**

Chicago, 9 November. Excerpts Act I *Madama Butterfly* with Giuseppe di Stefano, from dress rehearsal, Lyric Opera (silent).

**1956**

New York City, 25 November. Excerpts Act II *Tosca* with George London, "Ed Sullivan Show."

**1958**

Paris, 19 December. Concert at L'Opéra. Arias from *Norma, Barbiere di Siviglia, Trovatore*, plus *Tosca* Act II, with Albert Lance and Tito Gobbi. [EMI 91258 (laserdisc).]

**1959**

Hamburg, 15 May. Concert at Musikhalle. Arias from *Vestale, Macbeth, Barbiere, Don Carlo, Pirata*. [Pioneer PA-85-150 (laserdisc).]

**1961**

Milan, December. Excerpts from *Medea* with Jon Vickers and Nicolai Ghiaurov, La Scala (silent).

**1962**

Hamburg, 16 March. Concert at Musikhalle. Arias from *Don Carlo, Le Cid, Cenerentola, Carmen, Ernani*. [Pioneer PA-85-150 (laserdisc).]

London, 4 November. Concert at Covent Garden. Arias from *Carmen* and *Don Carlo*. [EMI 91283 (laserdisc).]

## Filmed Performances

### 1964

London, 9 February. *Tosca* Act II, with Renato Cioni and Tito Gobbi, Covent Garden. [EMI 91283 (laserdisc).]

Paris, May. *Norma:* "Casta diva" (recitative only), L'Opéra.

### 1965

New York, March. Excerpts from *Tosca* made from the wings during performance, Metropolitan Opera (silent).

Paris, 18 May. Concert RTF Studios. Arias from *Manon, Sonnambula, Gianni Schicchi.*

### 1969

Italy and Turkey, spring. *Medea.* Film written and directed by Pier Paolo Pasolini; produced by Franco Rossellini. [VAI 17 (videotape).]

### 1973

London, 26 November. Concert at Festival Hall. Arias and duets from *Don Carlo, Gioconda, Carmen, Vespri siciliani, Cavalleria rusticana, Gianni Schicchi.*

### 1974

Tokyo, 27 October. Concert in the Bunka Kaikan. Arias and duets from *Carmen, Cavalleria rusticana, L'elisir d'amore, Gianni Schicchi.*

### 1978

New York, 2 December. *Callas,* a documentary film, produced by WNET-TV. Written by John Ardoin, produced by Peter Weinberg, narrated by Franco Zeffirelli. Uses performance film from Chicago, 1955; Paris, 1958 and 1965; Milan, 1961; London, 1964 and 1973, and interviews with Gian Carlo Menotti, Rudolf Bing, Carlo Maria Giulini, Renata Scotto, Renata Tebaldi, Montserrat Caballé, Tito Gobbi, Nicola Rescigno, Sander Gorlinsky.

### 1979

Paris. *Maria Callas: Vissi d'arte,* a documentary film by Brigette Corea and Alain Ferrari, produced by Radio-Télévision Française. Uses performance film (Paris, 1958) and interviews with Francesco Siciliani, Jacques Bourgeois, Cathy Berberian, Margherita Wallmann, Luchino Visconti, Franco Zeffirelli, Carlo Maria Guilini, Gianandrea Gavazzeni, Nicola Benois, Jon Vickers, Rudolf Bing, Fedora Barbieri and Tito Gobbi.

### 1987

London. *Callas,* a documentary film, produced for the "South Bank Show," directed by Tony Palmer. Uses performance film from Paris 1958 and 1965, Hamburg 1959 and 1962, London 1962 and 1973, and interviews with John Ardoin, Giuseppe di Stefano, Graziella Sciutti, Nicola Rossi-Lemeni, John Tooley, John Copley, Nicola Rescigno, Carlo Maria Giulini, Franco Zeffirelli, Polyvios Marchand, Arda Mandikian, Lord Harewood, Nadia Stancioff, Michel Glotz, Jacques Bourgeois, Tito Gobbi, et al. [Pioneer PA-91-340 (laserdisc).]

London. *Callas: Life and Art,* a documentary film, produced by Picture Music International, directed by Jo Lustig. Uses performance footage from London 1962 and 1964 and Japan 1965 and interviews with Robert Sutherland, Giuseppe di Stefano, Franco Zeffirelli, Carlo Maria Giulini, Lord Harewood, et al. [EMI 91151 (laserdisc).]

# Bibliography

This is a selective listing of books and articles on or by Callas. Articles that are solely reviews of single performances or recordings have been excluded. Primary consideration has been given to material published in English.

BOOKS

Ardoin, John: *The Callas Legacy* (Duckworth and Co., London, 1976; Charles Scribner's Sons, New York, 1977; Noack-Huebner Verlag, Munich, 1979; Charles Scribner's Sons, New York, revised edition 1982; Duckworth and Co., London, revised edition 1982; Charles Scribner's Sons, New York, Compact Disc edition 1991)

—— (with Gerald Fitzgerald): *Callas* (Holt, Rinehart and Winston, New York, 1974; Thames and Hudson, London, 1974; Editorial Pomaire, Spain, 1979)

——: *Callas at Juilliard: The Master Classes* (Alfred A. Knopf, New York, 1987; Longanesi & C., Milan, 1988; Ongaku-no-tomo-sha Ltd., Tokyo, 1989; Fayard/Van de Velde, Paris, 1991)

Bing, Sir Rudolf: *5000 Nights at the Opera* (Doubleday, New York, 1972)

Bragaglia, Leonardo: *L'arte dello stupore* (Bulzoni, Rome, 1977)

Brix, Michael: *Maria Callas* (Schirmer/Mosel, Munich, Paris, London, 1994)

Callas, Evangelia (with Lawrence G. Blochman): *My Daughter Maria Callas* (Fleet, New York, 1960)

Callas, Jackie: *Sisters* (Macmillan, London, 1989; St. Martin's Press, New York, 1990)

Cederna, Camilla: *Chi è Maria Callas?* (Longanesi, Milan, 1968)

Chiarelli, Christina Gastel: *Maria Callas—Vita, immagini, parole musica* (Marsilio Editori, Venice, 1981)

Csampai, Attila: *Callas, Gesichter eines Mediums* (Schirmer/Mosel, Munich, Paris, London, 1993)

Dellinger, Ray: *Maria Callas, The Compact Discs and Videos* (The Maria Callas International Club, Surrey, 1992)

220

Galatopoulos, Stelios: *Callas, La Divina* (Dent, London, 1963)

———: *Callas, Prima Donna Assoluta* (Allen, London, 1976)

Gambetti, Giacomo (ed.): *Medea, un film di Pier Paolo Pasolini* (Garzanti Editore, Milan, 1970)

Gara, Eugenio: *Die grossen Interpreten: Maria Callas* (Kister, Geneva, 1957)

Gavoty, Bernard: *Vingt grands interprètes* (Editions Rencontre, Lausanne, 1960)

Goise, Denis: *Callas la diva* (Editions Guy Authier, Paris, 1978)

Guandalini, Gina: *Callas: L'ultima diva* (Edizione Eda, Torino, 1987)

Herzfeld, Friedrich: *La Callas* (Rembrandt Verlag, Berlin, 1959)

Jellinek, George: *Callas, Portrait of a Prima Donna* (Ziff-Davis, New York, 1960; reissued by Dover, New York, 1986)

Kesting, Jürgen: *Maria Callas* (Quartet Books, London, 1992)

La Rochelle, Réal: *Callas: La diva et le vinyle* (Editions Triptyque, Montreal, 1988)

Linakis, Stephen: *Diva: Life and Death of Maria Callas* (Prentice-Hall, New York, 1980)

Lise, Giorgio: *Maria Callas: Prime e Personaggi/Maria Callas: Parts and Performances* (BE-MA Editrice, Milan, 1987). Bilingual edition.

Lorcey, Jacques: *Maria Callas* (Editions PAC, Collections Têtes d'Affiche, Paris, 1978)

Lowe, David A. (ed.): *Callas As They Saw Her* (Ungar Publishing Company, New York, 1986)

Meneghini, Giovanni Battista: *Mia moglie Maria Callas* (Rusconi Editori, Milan, 1981); *My Wife Maria Callas* (Farrar, Straus & Giroux, New York, 1982)

Merlin, Olivier: *Le Bel Canto* (René Julliard, Paris, 1961)

Monestier, Martin: *Callas: Le livre du souvenir* (Editions Sand, Paris, 1985)

Pasi, Mario: *Maria Callas, La donna, la voce, la diva* (International Music of Italy, Milan, 1981)

Pichetti, Maria Teresa, and Marta Teglia: *El arte de Maria Callas* (Bocarte, Buenos Aires, 1969)

Remy, Jean Pierre: *Callas une vie* (Editions Ramsey, Paris, 1978); *A Tribute* (Macdonald and Jane's, London, 1978)

Riemens, Leo: *Maria Callas* (Brunn & Zoon, Utrecht, 1960)

Rosenthal, Harold: *Great Singers of Today* (Calder & Boyars, London, 1966)

Schonberg, Harold: *The Glorious Ones* (Times Books, New York, 1985)

Scott, Michael: *Maria Meneghini Callas* (Simon & Schuster, London, New York, 1991)

Segalini, Sergio: *Callas, Les images d'un voix* (Editions Francis van der

*Bibliography*

Veldes, Paris, 1980); *Callas—Portrait of a Diva* (Hutchinson, London, 1981)

Stancioff, Nadia: *Maria Callas Remembered* (E. P. Dutton, New York, 1987)

Stassinopoulos, Arianna: *Maria Callas: The Woman Behind the Legend* (Weidenfeld and Nicolson, London; Simon and Schuster, New York, 1981)

Tortora, Giovanna, and Paolo Barbieri: *Per Maria Callas* (Edizioni Recitar Cantando, Bologna, 1978)

Tosi, Bruno: *Casta Diva – L'incomparabile Callas* (Azzali Editoriale, Parma, 1993)

Verga, Carla: *Maria Callas, Mito e malinconia* (Bretta, Rome, 1980)

Wisneski, Henry: *Maria Callas: The Art Behind the Legend* (Doubleday, New York, 1975)


ARTICLES

Ardoin, John: "Callas Today," *Musical America*, December 1964

——: "The Callas Legacy Updated," *Opera News*, August 1978

——: "The Enduring Art of Callas," *New York Times*, 26 November 1978

——: "In Search of Callas," *Vision*, December 1978

——: "Maria Callas," *Fugue*, December 1978

——: "Maria Callas: The Early Years," *Opera Quarterly*, Vol. 3, No. 2

Barnes, Clive: "Callas the Unique," *Music and Musicians*, January 1964

Blivin, Naomi: "Vissi d'arte," *The New Yorker*, 27 April 1981

Buckley, Jack: "An Ancient Woman" (*Medea* film), *Opera News*, 13 December 1969

Callas, Maria: "I am not guilty of all those Callas scandals," *Life*, 20 April 1960

—— (with Anita Pensotti): "Memories," *Oggi*, January and February 1957

—— (with Peter Dragadze): "My Lonely World," *Life*, 30 October 1964

Cassidy, Claudia: "Splendor in the Night," *Opera News*, November 1977

——: "Maria Callas—Dazzling and Doomed," *Chicago*, May 1981

Celli, Teodoro: "A Song from Another Century" (translated by Herbert Weinstock), *Saturday Review*, 31 January 1959

Chusid, H.: "Echoes of a Golden Age," *Opera Canada*, No. 3, 1971

Christiansen, Rupert: "Callas: A Polemic," *Opera*, June 1987

Clark, Robert S.: "Learning From Callas," *Stereo Review*, March 1972

Conrad, Peter: "L'Affaire Callas," *Times Literary Supplement*, 20 December 1974

Du-Pond, Carlos Diaz: "Callas in Mexico," *Opera*, April 1973

Eckert, Thor, Jr.: "Callas," *High Fidelity*, February 1989

Galatopoulos, Stelios: "The Divine Callas," *Records and Recordings*, 1972

Gelatt, Esther: "Maria Callas: Notes on a New Recording of *Carmen*," *High Fidelity*, February 1965

*Gramophone*: "Callas Remembered: Friends, Colleagues and Admirers Pay Tribute," September 1987

Greenfield, Edward: "Art of Maria Callas," *High Fidelity*, March 1964

Grenier, Richard: "Maria Callas Must Do Something Right," *Cosmopolitan*, December 1970

Gualerzi, Giorgio: "Anno 25 Dopo C. (allas)," *Discoteca*, September and October 1973

Gunter, Freeman: "A Callas Primer," *After Dark*, February 1974

Hamilton, David: "The Recordings of Maria Callas," *High Fidelity*, March 1974

Heinitz, Thomas: "Callas at 40," *Records and Recordings*, July 1964

Henahan, Donal: "Maria Callas—Her Decline and Fall," *New York Times*, 1 March 1981

Jacobson, Robert: "Callas: The Tiger Tamed?" *After Dark*, October 1969

Kelly, Lawrence V.: "Callas," *Gentry*, Spring 1957

Kerman, Joseph: "Vissi d'arte," *New York Review of Books*, 2 April 1981

Koestenbaum, Wayne: "Callas and Her Fans," *Yale Review*, Vol. 79, No. 1

Kolodin, Irving: "What Makes Maria Sing?" *Saturday Review/World*, 2 February 1974

Legge, Walter: "La Divina," *Opera News*, November 1977

Leibowitz, René: "Le secret de la Callas," *Les Temps Modernes*, July 1959

Lewin, Lisette: "Maria Callas—the Unhappy One," *Elseview* (Holland), 29 August 1987

Luten, C. J.: "Callas on Compact Disc," *Opera News*, August 1988

McLellan, Joseph: "They Only Love Me When I Sing," *Book World*, 22 February 1981

Maguire, Jan: "Callas, Serafin and the Art of Bel Canto," *Saturday Review*, 30 March 1966

Neville, Robert: "Voice of an Angel," *Life*, 31 October 1955

*Newsweek*: "At La Scala, Triumph of U.S.-Born Maria Callas," 10 January 1954

Osborne, Conrad: "The Callas Master Classes," *Musical America*, June 1972

*Radiocorriere TV*: "Processo alla Callas," 30 November 1969 (reprinted in English as "The Callas Debate," *Opera*, September and October

*Bibliography*

1970, and in *Callas As They Saw Her*, Ungar, New York, 1986)

Rizzo, Francis: "The Callas Class," *Opera News*, 15 April 1972

Schickel, Richard: "Sacred Soprano," *Look*, 17 February 1959

Schonberg, Harold: "Callas at the Met," *Show*, May 1965

Schwartz, Lloyd: "The True Biography of Maria Callas," *Atlantic Monthly*, August 1981

Sievewright, Alan: "Conversations with Maria Callas," *Opera*, November 1977

Soria, Dorle: "The Callas Classes," *World*, 4 July 1972

——: "Artist Life" (Callas as stage director), *Musical America*, August 1973

——: "Greek Sorceress," *Opera News*, November 1977

Steane, John B.: "Maria Callas," *Gramophone*, November 1977 (reprinted in *Gramophone*, September 1987)

Sutherland, Robert: "Callas, Diary of a World Tour," *The Sunday Telegraph* (London), 31 August and 7 September 1980

*Time* (cover story): "The Prima Donna," 29 October 1956

Weinstock, Herbert: "Woman of the Week," *Opera News*, 20 March 1965

Winterhoff, Hans-Jurgen: "Maria Callas, die wichtigsten Einspielungen," *Fono Forum*, January-February-March 1979

# Index of Names ✑

(Note: Names of opera houses and concert halls are listed under the city in which they are located.)

# INDEX OF NAMES

# Index of Recorded Performances

233